D0843130

FIESTA!

OTHER BOOKS BY JANE BUTEL

Favorite Mexican Foods

Jane Butel's Freezer Cookbook

Jane Butel's Tex-Mex Cookbook

Chili Madness

Finger Lickin' Rib Stickin' Great Tastin' Hot & Spicy Barbecue

Tacos, Tortillas & Tostados

Woman's Day Book of New Mexican Cooking

The Best of Mexican Cooking

FIESTA!

SOUTHWEST ENTERTAINING WITH JANE BUTEL

by Jane Butel

TURNER
PUBLISHING COMPANY

Turner Publishing Company
Nashville, Tennessee
New York, New York

www.turnerpublishing.com

Jane Butel's Fiesta!

Cover design: Maddie Cothren
Book design: Mallory Perkins

Library of Congress Cataloging-in-Publication Data

Names: Butel, Jane, author.
Title: Jane Butel's Fiesta! / Jane Butel.
Other titles: Fiesta!
Description: New York, New York : Turner Publishing Company, [2018] | Revised
  edition of: Fiesta! New York : Harper & Row, c1987. | Includes index. |
  Identifiers: LCCN 2018004187 (print) | LCCN 2018006218 (ebook) | ISBN
  9781681624723 (e-book) | ISBN 9781681624709 (pbk. : alk. paper)
Subjects: LCSH: Cooking, American--Southwestern style. | Entertaining. |
  LCGFT: Cookbooks.
Classification: LCC TX715.2.S69 (ebook) | LCC TX715.2.S69 .B8768 2018 (print)
  | DDC 641.5979--dc23
LC record available at https://lccn.loc.gov/2018004187

9781681624709 Paperback
9781681624716 Hardcover
9781681624723 eBook

Printed in the United States of America
17 18 19 20 10 9 8 7 6 5 4 3 2 1

To my nearest and dearest,
who were always an inspiration and terrific help:
Amy, my daughter;
Brennan, my husband;
and my mother, Dorothy Franz

CONTENTS

INTRODUCTION

What makes fiestas such memorable occasions in the Southwest? With their origins in the Spanish feasts held in honor of the saints, they have evolved into happy celebrations with their own very special ambience. Despite the formality of customs and traditions in much of their culture, the Spanish have always seemed to love the informality the fiesta allows—from the brightness to the spiciness to the loudness. A number of forces and factors have combined to make the fiesta what it is today: the excitement of traveling great distances to get together to celebrate, the sun-drenched climate, the legacy of Spanish customs and spirit, and the bounty of the Southwest itself.

A guest at a contemporary fiesta will be struck first by its rainbow colors—the brighter the better. Red, green, and white party dishes (the menu traditionally includes the colors of the Mexican flag as much as possible) featuring a range of chile and corn creations are dressed up with brilliantly hued vegetables against a background of pure primary colors in the table decor—purples, magentas, yellows, oranges, blues, and the like. The party spirit is further heightened by the presence of merry mariachis, whose staccato trumpet and romantic guitars and violins set everyone's foot to keeping time with the music, if not dancing for hours on end. And indeed, because many of the guests would have journeyed for days or even weeks to visit friends and relatives they had not seen for a good while, fiestas have customarily been known for their duration, often lasting at least twenty-four hours.

I grew up on a farm in the Southwest where western hospitality was taken very seriously and food was the focus of most all social gatherings. We processed all our own meats, produce, and dairy products, and even ground our own grain. My mother, who was raised in Texas near the Mexican border, learned a great deal from Mexican cooks. Dad, on the other hand, developed his skills on his father's Kansas farm, which was probably the only chile-growing enterprise for miles around. Uncle Harry, who married and lived in Mexico, taught us all how to prepare a wide range of native dishes. Aunt Virginia, an accomplished bourgeois Spanish cook, shared her subtly flavored and beautifully prepared European-inspired dishes.

My real education in Southwestern cooking came when I moved to New Mexico right out of college. Armed with a degree in home economics and journalism, I was excited to have the opportunity to work as a home economist for the Public Service Company of New Mexico. I traveled the state teaching cooking, equipment, and lighting courses. The most successful programs we developed were a series on Southwestern cuisine. As I taught these classes, I found that I was as much a student as my own pupils, who brought their knowledge of the region's food to my classes.

In this book I've tried to share many of the terrific tastes of the area, reflecting a balance between decades-old recipes from the frontier to innovations I have created especially for these recipes. The foods for fiestas adapted to a home setting are easily planned, as noted in the suggested menus in this book. Many Southwestern foods can be prepared ahead for last-minute heating and serving. Dishes featuring crispy crunches of tortilla, topped with spicy sauces and complemented by delightful fillings, stay worthy of serving for hours. The suggested occasions are as various as the number of guests they accommodate, from a Scintillating Supper to be shared with only one or two additional people to a Texas Barbecue for 50 to a fiesta for an even larger crowd. The planning section for each menu allows for fine scheduling to prevent any last-minute rushing.

INGREDIENTS, TIPS, AND BASICS

SAUCES AND SALSAS 11

INGREDIENTS

The ingredients used in Mexican-Southwestern cooking are simple and easily obtainable. In fact, there are probably fewer basic ingredients involved in preparing these dishes than in those of almost any other ethnic cuisine. Interestingly, this cuisine grew sophisticated in relative isolation and borrowed heavily from Mexican and New Mexican Indian sources, each of which used readily available ingredients, many of them indigenous to the area.

The most popular regional dishes have as their basis either chile or corn, which are both native products. Chiles are the major ingredients of the famous stew best known as plain chili or chili con carne. They are often used to flavor and thicken sauces and fillings, which, when combined with a corn or wheat tortilla, are the basis for hundreds of specialties such as enchiladas, tacos, chimichangos, burritos, and flautas.

The most popular flavorings in the Southwest are onion, garlic, tomato, Mexican oregano, cumin, and cilantro or coriander (the seeds of cilantro). Seeds and nuts are frequently used for flavor as well as thickening. Chocolate is also popular, though more often as an ingredient in drinks and main dish sauces than in desserts.

Beef, pork, and chicken are the standard meats—with game added when available. Fish and shellfish, now found in many dishes, were once seldom encountered in the Southwest, although in Mexico they were abundant.

The breads of the region are quite simple but flavorful, and though time consuming to make, they well reward the effort. The two most popular varieties are the range-top-baked corn or wheat tortillas, and the deep-fried sopaipillas, or Indian fry bread. Another favorite is a hearth bread, which is generally formed into the shape of a bear claw. Sweet rolls, such as moyettes or pan dulce, are also uncomplicated and feature a basic butter and sugar topping, which sometimes includes cinnamon.

Desserts have always been straightforward and are often custard-based dishes, such as natillas or flan. These are sometimes complemented by fresh fruit or rich cookies or pastries. The more elaborate exceptions include *dulce* (sweet) tamales and sweet, nut-laden candies such as pralines.

CHILES

Chiles (the pods, as opposed to *chili*, the dish) provide the personality for the cuisine in the area both north and south of the Mexican border. Their wonderful qualities were first discovered by the Indians, who later shared their knowledge with the Spanish. Christopher Columbus, searching as he was for a new route to the East for the spice trade, thought he had found in the chile a valuable substitute for black peppercorns, and chiles have confusingly been called peppers ever since. They are in fact the same vegetable family as potatoes, tomatoes, and eggplant.

There are only four basic types of fresh chiles I use for New Mex/Tex-Mex cooking. Each is sold in both green and red forms; red chiles are sun-ripened green chiles. Green chiles are tarter and sometimes hotter than the red chiles, which contain natural sugar. Red chiles are usually sold dried, either as whole pods or in pure ground form. Do *not* buy commercial chile powder, which contains as much as 40 percent salt and 20 percent additives, and confuses the rich, natural flavor of the chile.

The domestic New Mexican chile, which is medium hot, is the most commonly used, either fresh or dried. The hotter varieties in the north are quite different in both shape and color from the more abundant southern New Mexico chiles. These are a brilliant, deep red and are generally sold as caribe or ristra chiles. They are considered the finest in New Mexico for red chile sauces, such as those used for making enchiladas.

The California, or Anaheim, chile is about half as hot as the New Mexico types. This milder chile is terrific for creating a bright-red, flavorful base, as it has the greatest thickening power. Then hotter types of chiles can be added for piquancy in as punishing a quantity as you desire.

Jalapeños are most often available pickled in oil and vinegar. If you can find them, however, the fresh green ones are best. Two of my favorite recipes are homemade pickled jalapeños (Jalapeños en Escabeche, page 17) and my much-requested Jalapeño Jelly (page 110).

The fourth chile I use is one that gives a real punch, the pequin quebrado. It is about the hottest of the chiles that still have the characteristic Southwestern or Mexican chile flavor. It was this little guy, which measures only about the size of a little fingernail, that Columbus obtained from the Indians— and the rest is history.

CORN

For centuries corn has held its position on the highest gustatory pedestal. The ancient Indians worshiped the goddess of corn and believed that man was created from corn dough, or *masa*. With this favored status, corn received much special care. Lacking modern refrigeration, the Aztecs learned that, once dried, corn could be stored without spoiling almost indefinitely if generously sprinkled with ground lime. Their corn was not only cured with lime, it was also often stored in the web of limestone caves and caverns honeycombing the Isthmus and mountains of Mexico. The taste, so ubiquitous in multitudes of Mexican corn dishes, originated in this method of preservation.

Dried corn is traditionally white. Blue corn is popular in New Mexico, however, and has quite a different, richer flavor as a result of its curing. (Also, blue corn has 100 percent nutrition, allowing the Ancients to survive.) After it is smoked in adobe ovens with piñon, it is lava-wheel ground to a fine powder or flour, which is used in favorite dishes like blue cornbread, rellenos batter, tamales, and tortillas. Yellow corn, the most popular color used in the United States, is more Texan than Mexican.

From posole (the mother process for all Mexican-based corn dishes made from lime-treated whole kernels of white corn), the soul food that is served at all fiestas, rites, and Indian celebrations, to masa products (which are similarly treated), corn is served at most every Southwestern meal. Fresh corn appears in summertime delights like green corn tamales, corn custards, and vegetable medleys.

CHEESES

In Tex-Mex cooking throughout the Southwest, Monterey Jack, or Jack blended equally with yellow full-cream Cheddar, is the most often used cheese. Monterey Jack cheese was developed in Monterey, California, where the best Jack is still produced. Top-quality Jack is made of whole milk mozzarella blended with approximately 40 percent Cheddar and is formed into giant wheels that are generously coated with paraffin. Wisconsin Jack and most other commercial Jack cheeses are much firmer textured and less creamy and flavorful. They do grate better, but the trade off is generally not worth it if the Monterey is available.

Queso fresco is the traditional Mexican cheese. It is white, somewhat dry, and salty—a bit reminiscent of feta, which can be used as a substitute.

BEANS

The true Southwestern bean is the pinto—a brown-speckled, grayish legume, which happens to be the healthiest of all beans and cooks up to a firm, flavorful, almost nutlike taste. Cooked and mashed, pintos become refritos.

SHORTENING

Lard is the mainstay of Southwestern cooking and is the healthiest of all solid shortenings. Bacon drippings are occasionally used. Substituting butter or solid vegetable shortening will not yield the traditional flavors and texture of the final dish. Vegetable oils work fine for deep frying.

AVOCADOS

The very finest are the Haas, or old-fashioned Mexican alligator pears, which are pear-shaped and have a black, textured skin. They have the richest, most buttery texture and flavor, and are the best base for guacamole and garnishes. The second best is the freckled, dark-green, pear-shaped Fuertes, which has a smaller neck than the Haas. The ones to avoid are the shiny green, smooth-skinned, round varieties, which are too sweet and watery.

When planning to use avocados, purchase them hard about five days ahead to allow them to ripen slowly. The best place for ripening is above your refrigerator (if not built-in), providing it is not in bright sunlight (which will "sunburn" an avocado, forming a dark-brown spot where it is exposed). Another favorite method involves wrapping avocados in a brown paper bag and burying them in the flour bin. In fact, any dark, rather warm place is ideal. Avocados are ripe when their flesh yields to a firm press with your thumb; at this point they can be kept in the refrigerator for several days.

The easiest way to peel an avocado is not to peel it! For making guacamole, just cut the fruit in half, remove the pit, and scoop out the flesh. For salads and garnishes, score the peel vertically with a very sharp knife in about six places; then, using the back of a spoon or the knife, take a section of the skin at a time and curl it back until it comes off.

ONIONS

The preferred onions for almost all cooking purposes are the large, round Spanish onions. White or yellow work the best, with the sweet or purple a second choice. An exception would be for use in a salad, where a milder flavor is sometimes preferable.

GARLIC

Try to find the large, purplish cloves of Mexican garlic for the most pungent and full flavor. If you use other types of fresh garlic with smaller cloves, you should probably double the quantity called for in the recipes in this book. Figure that each clove should fill a generous 1/2 teaspoon or more.

HONEY

In the Southwest, honey has always been a very popular cooking ingredient, perhaps because some of the most aromatic of all blossom honeys are harvested from the local cacti—specifically the Palo Verde, Saguaro, and Prickly Pear. Each has a different potency—the Saguaro being the mildest and the Prickly Pear the strongest. Other favorite blossom honeys in the area include the clovers and fruit trees. Try to select a good-quality aromatic honey for the recipes in this book, as its flavor will often determine the success of the completed dish.

CILANTRO

Cilantro, a close relative of the parsley family (it can often be bought in greenmarkets as Chinese parsley), possesses a special clean, clear, almost stringent flavor that either makes close friends or adamant enemies. For those who appreciate its taste, the leaves of this aggressive herb are an invaluable addition to soups, salads, and relishes. Many like the seed (known as coriander in English) for flavoring sauces, salads, cakes, and baked goods. (Note: In Mexico, *culantro* or *cilantro* is used to refer to both the seed and the green leaves. Be certain when shopping for cilantro to buy the correct form of the ingredient. In many Puerto Rican markets it is known as cilantrillo.) When preparing cilantro for cooking, only very coarsely chop it at the last moment.

STANDARD PREPARATIONS

——— GREEN CHILE PARCHING ———

Green chiles freshly parched, or parched and frozen, are far superior to their canned equivalents. Canning always seems to impart a metallic taste and reduces the texture and flavor. Although freezing does soften the crisp texture, it does not impair the taste. Due to seasonality and perishability of chiles, freezing is often the only alternative. Green chiles are generally available from late June, when the first of the crop comes in, to late September, when they ripen and become red, signaling the end of the season.

Parching is necessary to remove the very leathery peel of fresh or green chiles. The process is easy, but be sure to wear rubber gloves or generously butter your hands to prevent a burn from the chile's irritating oils. Intense direct heat is needed to parch the peel, but take care to leave the flesh itself uncooked. Immediate chilling of the parched chile halts the cooking process and causes the skin to blister away from the flesh. If freezing, freeze on sheet pans with the peel on for greatest flexibility of use. Once parched they can be placed in freezer-weight plastic bags. Parched green chiles freeze well for one year.

With a double oven range, you can parch a bushel of chiles in 1 1/2 to 2 hours. Outdoor grills work very well for parching chiles too.

Wash the chiles, removing all sand and dirt. Leave the stem on, then pierce each once with a sharp knife, about 1 inch down from the stem.

For large quantities, cover the entire top rack of an electric oven with heavy foil; if using gas, cover the broiler rack. For smaller quantities, cover a cookie sheet. If grilling, place directly on the grate. Then place the rack under an electric broiler 4 inches from the broiler unit; if using gas, place the rack on the top shelf.

Preheat the broiler, then place a single layer of chiles on the foil. Allow each side to blister before rotating. Uniformly blister each chile for easy removal of the peel. As soon as each chile is parched, remove to the sink or a large bowl or tub of ice water. Immerse each and allow to cool, then either peel or flash freeze as above, then package in airtight, vapor-proof plastic bags.

To peel, always start at the stem end and pull off strips of the peel. Blot dry between layers of paper towels before using. For rellenos, keep the stem on, and do not blot before stuffing. For other uses, remove the stem. For a milder taste, strip out the seeds and veins with the back side of a knife.

Note: If parching only a few chiles, place each directly on a medium-hot electric surface unit, or hold it with tongs or a meat fork over a gas burner.

If parching outdoors on a charcoal, gas, or electric grill, place the rack about 4 inches above the heat source. Watch carefully as the chiles parch quickly.

BOWL OF RED

This recipe has been in our family for three generations, ever since my Swedish maternal grandfather who worked as a railroad executive got several recipes from trail cooks who served chili all the way from deep in Texas, to the cowboys who worked herds of cattle, to where the railroad ended in Dodge City, Kansas. It's great used as the chile in Frito Pie (page 36), and it is also the very best chili con carne to serve as is with "fixin's 'n mixin's" of coarsely shredded mixed cheeses—Monterey Jack and Cheddar—sour cream with fresh lime wedges, pequin quebrado, jalapeño nacho slices, and chopped Spanish onions.

Makes 6 to 8 servings.

2 Tablespoons lard
1 cup chopped Spanish onion (1 large)
3 pounds lean beef (chuck) cut in 1/2-inch squares
1/4 cup mild, ground California chile
1/4 cup hot, southern New Mexico ground chile
3 garlic cloves, minced
2 teaspoons or more freshly ground cumin, divided
1 quart water
1 1/2 teaspoons salt

Melt the lard in a 5-quart heavy pan, such as a Dutch oven, using medium heat. Add the onion. In a bowl combine the beef with the chiles, garlic, and half of the cumin. As soon as the onion becomes clear, not browned, remove from heat and add the beef mixture.

Stir in the water, return to a medium heat, and bring to a boil, uncovered, and stew for an hour or so until the liquid begins to cook down and the meat is getting done. Taste the stock and add salt to taste, starting with the 1 1/2 teaspoons. Stew for about 3 hours or until bright red, thick, and flavorful. Add the rest of the cumin just before serving.

Note: Will freeze for 1 year.

TOSTADA FRYING

Recipes and tips for making both corn and wheat tortillas, tacos, and tostadas are on pages 162–163. Here is a recipe for frying tostadas—quartered, crisply fried corn chips. (Tostadas have the feminine "a" ending to indicate that they are made from a portion of the tortilla, while the "o" ending of tostado indicates that a whole tortilla was used.) The rewards of preparing tostadas yourself are great! Almost all packaged varieties are filled with extra calories since most commercial manufacturers shortcut the frying process and leave in enormous amounts of retained fat.

Makes 4 dozen.

2 quarts corn or vegetable oil
1 dozen corn tortillas (any color)
Salt

Use an electric deep-fat fryer, if available, and heat the oil to 375°F (190°C). If fryer is available, use a large 5- to 8-quart cooking pot over medium-high heat, using a candy thermometer to measure the temperature of the oil. The fat must be maintained at 375°F (190°C) for crisp, dry, nonfatty tostadas.

With a very sharp large knife make 4 cuts at right angles to each other through the stack of tortillas, cutting almost but not completely through the center. This method saves the trouble of frying four separate pieces and fishing out each individual tostada. It also guarantees more uniform frying.

Fry a few tortillas at a time, taking care to let the oil return to 375°F (190°C) before frying the next batch. Fry until the bubbling stops and each tortilla has become crisp. Drain on several layers of paper towels on a cooling rack. While still somewhat warm, tap each in the center and the four pieces will separate, then place in a paper bag and sprinkle with some salt and shake. Serve warm for best flavor with freshly prepared salsas.

CARNE DESHEBRADA
(SHREDDED BEEF OR PORK)

The traditional Mexican filling for tacos, enchiladas, flautas, and the like is shredded meat rather than a chilied sauce laced with cooked ground meat, as is standard for Tex-Mex dishes. Try occasionally substituting this simple preparation in the menus in this book. (A recipe for shredded chicken can be found on page 93; the preparation of the chicken for serving is the same as below.)

Makes 12 servings.

3 pounds beef chuck or pork shoulder or butt
2 teaspoons salt
6 peppercorns
2 bay leaves
1 medium Spanish onion, quartered
2 garlic cloves, coarsely chopped
4 cups beef stock or water flavored with bouillon

Using a Dutch oven or large heavy cooking pot, brown the meat until the outside edges are dark brown over medium-high heat. Add the salt, peppercorns, bay leaves, onion, garlic, and beef stock and simmer over low heat, covered, for 2 hours, or until fork-tender. Cover and let remain in juices until cool. Then using two forks or your fingers, shred the meat, discarding the bones and any excess fat.

DESHEBRADA FRY MIXTURE

1/2 cup lard or bacon drippings
4 garlic cloves, minced
2 medium Spanish onions, finely chopped
Shredded pork or beef filling (recipe above or chicken filling on page 93)
2 to 3 jalapeños, minced, optional

Melt the lard in a large heavy skillet over medium heat. Add the garlic and onion, and as soon as they start to become golden, add the shredded meat and stir fry until it becomes browned on the edges, about 15 minutes, adding jalapeños toward the end of cooking, if using. If the meat should start to become too dry, add some broth from roasting to moisten.

SAUCES AND SALSAS

——————— RED CHILE SAUCE ———————

This sauce—sometimes called enchilada sauce—is probably the most frequently served sauce in the Southwest. Although it is sold canned, which is always dreadful, and frozen, which is barely acceptable, you can easily whip up a homemade version in five minutes, with another five minutes or more of simmering. The critical ingredient is ground, pure red New Mexico or California chile. The best color and texture come from blending the two. The milder chiles, sometimes called Anaheims or Southern New Mexico chiles, have a higher starch level, which acts as a thickener, and are a deeper, almost bluish-red color, which blends beautifully with the orange-red New Mexico chile, which supplies the heat.

You can easily adjust the piquancy to taste—even at the meal itself—by making a mild sauce and providing a bowl of the ground, pure, hot New Mexico chile at the table. Don't ever make this sauce with commercial chile powder as it will be briny, dark, and stale-tasting due to the salt and chemicals that have been added.

You'll find this sauce terrific over enchiladas, burritos, chimichangos, eggs, hamburgers, pork chops, and rellenos. For convenience, freeze in 1- to 2-cup portions, which keep well for up to 8 months.

Makes 3 pints.

1/4 cup lard
1/4 cup all-purpose flour
1/4 cup ground pure mild chile powder
1/4 cup ground pure hot chile powder
1/4 teaspoon ground cumin
1 quart well-flavored beef stock
1 teaspoon salt or to taste
2 garlic cloves, minced

Melt the lard in a heavy saucepan over low heat, then stir in the flour. When it is lightly browned, remove from the heat. When the pan has cooled slightly, thoroughly stir in the mild and hot chile powders.

Add the cumin, then stir in about 1 cup of the beef stock; when well blended, return to the heat and cook and stir, adding a little stock at a time until all has been added. Season to taste with the salt and garlic and simmer for at least 5 minutes—up to 15 minutes—over low heat until the sauce thickens and the flavors blend. Use as desired or freeze.

Variation: For beef enchiladas, brown 2 pounds of hamburger first over medium heat in a skillet, omitting the lard. Then add the flour and proceed with the recipe.

HOT GREEN CHILE SAUCE

Hot green chile sauce is popular in both New Mexico and California, where so many green chiles are grown. At its best when made with freshly parched green chiles, it is a great sauce with pork, chicken, or seafood, and with traditional dishes like enchiladas, chimichangos, burritos, or eggs. Canned green chiles can be substituted, but the effect will be less pronounced.

Makes 3 pints.

1/4 cup lard
1/2 cup finely chopped Spanish onion
1/2 cup all-purpose flour
1 quart rich chicken broth
2 cups chopped green chiles that have been parched, peeled, and deseeded (page 7)
2 garlic cloves, minced
Pinch of ground cumin
1 1/2 teaspoons salt

Melt the lard in a heavy saucepan. Stir in the onion and cook until it becomes clear. Stir in the flour. When the mixture becomes lightly golden, gradually add the broth, cooking and stirring until the sauce slightly thickens. Add the green chiles, garlic, cumin, and salt and simmer over low heat for about 5 to 10 minutes, until the flavors blend and the sauce is thickened. Taste and adjust flavor. Add the cooked meat just before layering for enchiladas.

FRESH GARDEN SALSA

Fresh as a garden bouquet! When you have a bit of extra time, the sophistication of the flavors and the versatility of this salsa are well worth the effort. This is one of my very favorites, which I first developed for a chain of restaurants and then set about perfecting for my own pleasure.

Makes 28 ounces (enough for 24 tacos or servings).

2 cups canned whole, good-quality tomatoes, drained and coarsely chopped
1/3 cup finely diced whole fresh red ripe tomato, unpeeled
2 Tablespoons red wine vinegar
1 Tablespoon finely diced Spanish onion
2 Tablespoons freshly squeezed lime juice
2 teaspoons minced flat-leaf parsley
1 1/4 teaspoons sea or kosher salt
1 garlic clove, minced
1/4 cup water
1 Tablespoon pickled jalapeño juice
2 Tablespoons minced fresh chives
1 small jalapeño, minced (either fresh or canned)
2 fresh green chiles, parched, peeled, and diced (page 7), or use 2 canned green chiles
1/3 cup chopped green bell pepper
1/4 teaspoon sugar
1/4 teaspoon ground Mexican oregano
1/4 teaspoon ground cumin

In a glazed pottery or glass bowl add canned and fresh tomatoes, vinegar, onions, lime juice, parsley, salt, garlic, water, jalapeño juice, chives, jalapeño, green chiles, green pepper, sugar, oregano, and cumin and gently toss and stir to blend evenly together. Cover and refrigerate overnight, if possible, or at least 4 hours. Serve as a table sauce, taco sauce, or over any grilled meat.

If any is left over after 3 days, it can be added to 2 Tablespoons melted unsalted butter in a medium-hot sauté pan and cooked and stirred to create a ranchero sauce for serving over eggs to make huevos rancheros, or it can be frozen for later use for up to 3 months.

COLD SALSA VERDE

Here is a very traditional green sauce that is excellent over chicken, seafood, or pork dishes, and is also frequently served as a table relish. Tomatillos (Mexican green tomatoes) are called for here to give the sauce its traditional flavor; they are increasingly available at gourmet and department stores and Mexican specialty shops.

Makes 1 pint.

1 pound fresh tomatillos, or 1 (10-ounce) can undrained tomatillos
1/2 cup coarsely chopped Spanish onion
2 Tablespoons fresh cilantro leaves and stems
1 fresh jalapeño or to taste
1/2 teaspoon salt

If using fresh tomatillos, peel and quarter them, then simmer over medium heat in water to cover for about 6 to 8 minutes or until fork-tender. Reserve the cooking liquid.

Using a slotted spoon, place the cooked tomatillos (reserving the juice) along with onion, cilantro, jalapeño, and salt in a blender or food processor. Purée them, adding the tomatillo cooking liquid to create the desired consistency, which should be like a thick gravy, then adjust seasonings and piquancy. This sauce is predictably mild.

CREAMY SALSA VERDE

Amy, my daughter, has probably been my greatest and most enduring fan of this salsa. Its spicy, rich flavor, cooled by a creamy base, makes it perfect as a topper for tacos or as a dip for vegetables and snacks.

Makes 1 1/4 cups.

1/2 cup sour cream
1/2 cup mayonnaise
1/3 cup Cold Salsa Verde (recipe above or substitute any other favorite green salsa)
1 Tablespoon freshly squeezed lime juice
Sprinkle of caribe or other crushed dried red chile for serving, optional

In a small bowl combine the sour cream, mayonnaise, salsa verde, and lime juice and allow to blend together in the refrigerator for at least 1 hour. Sprinkle with caribe, if desired, before serving.

SANTA FE SALSA

This is the salsa that made a Mexican restaurant in Santa Fe famous, but beware: it is the hottest of all. The sharp, tangy flavor is often a favorite of those who like their salsas hot, like myself. Serve with warm tostadas to take you back to the capital city of the Land of Enchantment.

Makes 1 pint.

2 cups canned whole tomatoes, undrained and coarsely crushed with a fork
4 teaspoons freshly squeezed lime juice
4 teaspoons cider vinegar
4 garlic cloves, minced
1/2 teaspoon Mexican oregano
1/2 teaspoon cumin
1 teaspoon crushed cilantro (coriander) seeds
1 teaspoon salt
1 Tablespoon or more crushed pequin quebrado

Combine the tomatoes, lime juice, vinegar, garlic, oregano, cumin, cilantro, salt, and pequin quebrado in a pottery or glass bowl, adding the pequin 1 teaspoon at a time to make certain that you will not get the salsa too hot. Taste and adjust seasonings. Let stand 30 minutes at room temperature and serve. Can be stored for several days in the refrigerator. Do not freeze.

SALSA FRESCA

The basis of all fresh table sauces, salsa fresca, literally translated, means "fresh sauce." Although there are many, many more sophisticated versions of this salsa, I still like it best at its simplest, as either a dipping sauce for warm tostadas or over hamburgers on tarragon-basil buttered buns. Make it just an hour or less before serving, as it is at its best very fresh.

Makes 3 cups.

1 cup finely diced red, ripe tomato, excess juice and seeds removed
1 cup finely diced Spanish onion, preferably red and white mixed
1 cup finely diced green chiles, preferably New Mexico type, that have been parched, peeled, and deseeded (page 7)
2 garlic cloves, finely minced
3/4 teaspoon salt

Combine the tomatoes, onion, chiles, garlic, and salt in an earthenware or porcelain bowl. Stir gently and set aside for at least 30 minutes before serving.

CHILE CON QUESO

Fast-food operations have popularized hot nacho cheese sauce, which is not nearly as flavorful or colorful as this dish, on which it is based. Traditionally, chile con queso has been served warm as a dunk for tostadas, but it's also very good over hamburgers, eggs, chimichangos, and other Southwestern specialty dishes, including fajitas.

Makes 1 quart.

2/3 cup soy-based vegetable oil
1 cup finely chopped onion
2 cloves garlic, minced
2 Tablespoons all-purpose flour
1 1/2 cups evaporated milk
2 fresh medium-size tomatoes, chopped
2 pounds processed American cheese, cubed
1/2 cup shredded full-cream yellow Cheddar cheese
1/2 cup shredded Monterey Jack cheese
1/3 cup finely minced jalapeño, stems and seeds removed

Heat the oil over medium-low heat in a heavy saucepan. Add the onion and garlic and cook until the onion becomes clear. Stir in the flour, mixing well. Gradually add the evaporated milk and cook until the mixture thickens. Add the tomatoes, American cheese, Cheddar, Monterey Jack, and jalapeños and cook over very low heat until the cheeses have all melted and the mixture is thick and smooth.

Serve with warm tostadas or as a sauce. The sauce can be frozen for up to 4 months. For this, you may wish to package in 1-cup containers.

JALAPEÑOS EN ESCABECHE

This recipe, from a dear friend in Albuquerque, is one of the best I know. It is especially suited to small-batch preparation, but you can certainly "batch it up" if you wish. The only tedious part is the preparation of the chiles, but the light sautéing in sesame oil adds excellent flavor and serves to tame them a bit. You can use these as a relish or as an ingredient in sauces, salsas, and guacamole.

Makes 3 to 4 pints.

3 medium-size carrots, peeled and sliced 1/4 inch thick
1 cup cider vinegar, 5 percent acidity
1 cup water
2 medium Spanish white onions, very thinly sliced and separated into rings
6 garlic cloves
1 teaspoon salt
2 teaspoons Mexican oregano
3 large, whole bay leaves, preferably fresh
2 pounds small to medium-size firm-fleshed, blemish-free jalapeños, halved, seeded, washed, and blotted dry
1/2 cup sesame oil

Cook the carrots in a saucepan in a small amount of salted water until slightly tender. Drain and cool and set aside. In a saucepan combine the vinegar, water, onions, garlic, and salt. Cook until onions are slightly tender. Add oregano and bay leaves. Bring just to a boil.

In a skillet sauté the jalapeños in the sesame oil until the skins blister. Peel the jalapeños and add with the carrots to the vinegar mixture. Cool and refrigerate for 24 hours before serving.

Note: When preparing the chiles, always be very careful to either wear rubber gloves or very generously butter your fingertips and palms to prevent a chile burn, which lasts up to 24 hours. A melon-ball scoop or a grapefruit knife helps to scrape out the seeds and veins easily.

BRUNCHES

SUNDAY SUMMER BRUNCH

Bloody Marias

Fruit Tostados Compuestos

Chile-Corn Custard Cazuelas

*Navajo Fry Bread with Homemade Apricot Jam and Sweet
Butter topped with Freshly Grated Nutmeg*

Mexican Cinnamon Coffee

This colorful menu for twelve, a typical New Mexican or Arizonan brunch, is intended for a lazy summer weekend when you'll have the time to enjoy preparing these foods. If you make the tostado shells and the jam a day or so ahead, you can easily create the rest of the foods within two hours.

The eye-openers were developed through the years as an adaptation of the familiar Bloody Marys and are especially attractive with the curled cucumber garnish. For another departure from the traditional, I place fresh, brilliantly colored, perfectly ripe fruits cut in various shapes in tostado baskets, which are guaranteed to bring compliments from your guests. The Chile-Corn Custard Cazuelas were developed from the favorite local products, and are a pleasure both to serve and eat. The Navajo Fry Bread, a delicious Southwestern classic, can, if you prefer, be used as the basis for Navajo Tacos: just place taco fillings on top of the freshly fried disks of bread.

I recommend serving this meal on a patio, terrace, or deck, or in any outdoor setting. Decorate the table and dining area with large, old-fashioned bouquets of field or garden flowers, such as daisies, zinnias, gladioli, dahlias, and the like.

MENU PLAN

Day before:
Fry the tostado baskets.
Make the jam.

Two hours before:
Prepare the Bloody Marias and cucumber garnish. Salt the rims of the glasses and place in the freezer.
Place the butter in a crockery bowl and smooth off the top. Grate nutmeg over the top and chill.
Prepare the fruits for the tostados, gently stir in the dressing, and chill.
Combine the ingredients for the Navajo Fry Bread and knead; set the dough aside. Heat the oil.
Prepare the Chile-Corn Custard Cazuelas and bake; keep warm in a 150°F (65°C) oven.
Set out the coffeepot.

At serving time:
Garnish the Bloody Marias and serve.
Warm the tostados, fill with fruit, and serve immediately.
Serve the Chile-Corn Custard Cazuelas.
Fry the Navajo Fry Bread. Serve with the jam, butter, and freshly grated nutmeg.
Brew the coffee and serve.

BLOODY MARIAS

I first started serving these years ago as an Albuquerque adaptation of the favorite brunch drink and have discovered that most of my guests prefer them to the classic Bloody Mary. Serve Bloody Marias in large, heavy Mexican glass goblets or tumblers, or other large tall glasses. An hour or so ahead, frost the glasses in the freezer, adding a salty rim as you would for margaritas. Do include a generous garnish—I prefer the curled cucumber stick, as described.

Makes 12 drinks.

2 (46-ounce) cans good-quality tomato juice
1/4 cup Worcestershire sauce
2 Tablespoons jalapeño juice or more to taste
1/4 cup hot salsa, optional
1 large dark green cucumber, unpeeled
2 large or 3 small limes, cut into 12 wedges
About 1 teaspoon caribe or other crushed dried red chile
1 fifth good-quality natural blue agave tequila, 80 proof or better

Salt the rims of the glasses as directed on page 82 in the margaritas recipe and freeze. Combine the tomato juice, Worcestershire, jalapeño juice, and salsa, if using, in a large pitcher. This can be done hours ahead if desired.

Prepare the garnish. Using a very sharp knife, slice the cucumber lengthwise, then cut lengthwise again into quarters, then cut each quarter into thirds to gain 12 long wedges. Using the point of your knife, carefully pull back the peel about halfway up the length of the cucumber wedge. Soak in ice water, if time permits. This should help the cucumber peeling to curl. Just before preparing the drinks, cut one lime in half or use the cut lime you used for juicing the rims of the glasses to salt them. Squeeze a dribble of the juice down the top of each wedge of cucumber and lightly dust with caribe. To do this, place the caribe on a piece of wax paper and press the top of the cucumber wedges into it. This makes a very pretty effect—sometimes I've added a sprinkle of kosher salt.

To serve, place three or four ice cubes in each glass, then add 2 ounces of tequila to each and about 1 cup of the spicy tomato juice mixture. Stir each and serve, garnished with a wedge of fresh lime (squeeze it just before adding) to float on the surface. Attach the cucumber wedge over the rim of each glass before serving. The curled peel will hang over the edge, with the chilied side facing into the glass.

— FRUIT TOSTADOS COMPUESTOS —

A beautiful and innovative way to serve fresh summer fruits, these tostado baskets are always a big hit. The crisp bites of tostado are an ideal complement to the meltingly soft summer fruits.

Makes 12 servings.

2 quarts vegetable oil
12 (10-inch) wheat tortillas
12 cups fresh summer fruits—use a variety of colors, shapes, and sizes such as melon balls,
   strawberries, blueberries, and pineapple wedges or banana rounds
1/4 cup cactus honey or strong-flavored blossom honey
1/4 cup freshly squeezed lime juice

Heat the oil to 375°F (190°C) in an electric deep-fat fryer or in a deep heavy pot, using a thermometer to maintain the correct temperature. Fry the tortillas using the compuesta technique on page 162. Drain the fried tostado shells on layers of paper towels.

Prepare the fruit and place all together in a large bowl. In a small bowl combine the honey and lime juice. Pour over the fruit and carefully stir to coat the fruit; do not bruise it. Chill until just ready to serve. You can let it marinate up to 2 hours, but not more than that as the fruits will start to weep.

Warm the tostado baskets in a 250°F (130°C) oven for 10 to 15 minutes, or until warm and crisp if fried ahead. To serve, place the marinated fruits in the tostado baskets. Try to spoon the fruits in carefully, and artistically arrange the top of each basket. Evenly distribute the juice. Serve immediately.

CHILE-CORN CUSTARD CAZUELAS

The green chiles in this recipe form a lovely and unusual crust for the golden custard. For greatest flair, prepare and serve in earthenware bowls (*cazuelas*).

Makes 12 servings.

2 dozen large, fresh New Mexican green chiles, parched (page 7)
6 large eggs, beaten
4 (15-ounce) cans yellow cream-style corn
1 1/2 cups yellow cornmeal (if desired, crumbled tostado or taco shells may be substituted)
1 1/2 teaspoons salt (reduce amount if using salted tostados)
2 garlic cloves, minced
1 teaspoon baking powder
12 Tablespoons unsalted butter, melted
2 cups shredded sharp Cheddar cheese (not necessary to shred if using a food processor or blender)

Butter 12 ovenproof earthenware bowls or individual casseroles. Then peel the chiles and rinse out the seeds. Remove the stems, leaving the chiles whole. Place two chiles in each casserole, big or stem end up, slightly above the rim of each bowl. As uniformly as possible, stretch the two chiles to cover the bottom and sides of each.

Using a food processor or blender, place the eggs, corn, cornmeal, salt, garlic, baking powder, butter, and cheese in the jar and process until well blended. Pour into the individual, chile-lined casseroles, dividing the mixture evenly. Bake 30 minutes at 375°F (190°C), then reduce the temperature to 325°F (170°C) for another 10 minutes or until an inserted knife comes out clean. These keep amazingly well. I've kept them in a 150°F (65°C) oven for 3 or 4 hours while awaiting serving time and they really do not suffer. Serve in the dishes.

NAVAJO FRY BREAD

This historic bread is always a treat and can be served in many different ways. For this menu I recommend serving it freshly fried. In fact, you can even get your friends involved. I've often found that many Southwestern food appreciators—or just those with a curiosity and a healthy appetite—enjoy learning the special processes involved in making this bread, as they do sopaipillas.

Navajo Fry Bread is an adaptation of sopaipillas, for while their frying techniques are different, the doughs themselves are nearly the same. Sopaipillas are squares of deep-fried dough that puff and become hollow whereas this bread is fried in large disks. To keep it from becoming one huge puff, holes are poked into the dough after it has been rolled. Traditionally it is cooked on the end of a green piñon twig by Navajo women at fairs, festivals, rodeos, horse shows, and many local events in the New Mexico/Arizona area, where they are always a major attraction. With gorgeous turquoise dripping about their wrists and necks, the Navajos fry the breads in a big cast iron pot of lard, heated over a piñon open fire. Just the memory makes me yearn for some!

Makes 24 medium disks.

2 quarts or more vegetable oil (or lard if you want to be traditional)
4 cups all-purpose flour
1 Tablespoon plus 2 teaspoons baking powder
1 teaspoon salt
1 Tablespoon lard
1 1/3 cups warm water, approximately
Additional flour or cornmeal and/or herbs, optional

Heat the oil to 375°F (190°C) in an electric deep-fat fryer or deep cooking pot. Use a deep-fat thermometer to maintain the proper temperature if you do not have the fryer.

In a large bowl mix the flour with the baking powder and salt. Work in the lard with a pastry blender or a fork. Add about 1/2 cup of the water. Mix and stir, then add water until a very stiff but cohesive dough results. The consistency should be like bread dough. When punched, it should be very firm. Knead it generously to gain a very smooth dough.

Let it rest about 10 minutes, covered. Then pull off small balls of dough, about 2 to 3 inches in diameter. Form into a circle by overlapping the edges as you would to seal a double-crust pie pastry. Then roll and turn with a small rolling pin (in New Mexico a *bolillo*, usually 8 inches long and 2 inches in diameter) to create even pressure as you roll. Sprinkle additional flour, adding cornmeal, crushed herbs, even juniper berries for a traditional, novel, yet interesting taste and texture. Using a large meat fork, pierce 4 to 6 holes, with a predominant one in the center of the disk.

Fry one at a time, watching carefully. If they start to puff, immediately pierce deeper holes. Use tongs to turn as soon as each side becomes golden. Drain each on paper towels. Keep warm in a low oven while you fry the remaining disks. Serve warm with cinnamon-sugar, honey, or preserves.

HOMEMADE APRICOT JAM

Apricot trees grow easily and bear abundantly in Albuquerque and throughout New Mexico all along the river valleys. We had a favorite tree in our backyard, which brings back memories of the wondrous, perfumy flavor of freshly made jam.

The jam was a perfect way of using the windfalls—being certain to use mostly under-ripe fruit, with some overripe to create the best texture and flavor. If you prefer jam that retains the shape of the fruit, allow the sugared fruit to stand overnight, or at least for a few hours. If your preference is for a puréed consistency, then begin the jam immediately after preparing the fruit, mashing it as it cooks.

Makes 6 jars.

2 1/2 cups sugar
3 cups apricots, halved, pits removed

Mix the sugar very well with the apricots in a large heavy saucepan. Depending on the preferred consistency, let it set with the sugar or proceed immediately. Place over medium-high heat and bring to a boil, then reduce the heat somewhat to maintain a boil, yet not scorch. Cook and stir frequently until it reaches 7 degrees above the boiling point at whatever altitude you are, 219 at sea level. Or test by holding the spoon up at a right angle, 3 to 4 inches above the surface of the jam. The drops will fall into a sheet when the jam is ready.

Meanwhile, scrub and clean the jelly jars and place them in a large shallow pan. Add an inch of water and boil for 5 minutes to sterilize the jars.

Once the jam is done, set aside on the counter to cool slightly. Skim the surface and top sides of the pan of the foamy mixture. Then place the still warm jam in the sterilized jars. Seal and cool away from drafts, or seal with melted paraffin after the jam has cooled.

MEXICAN CINNAMON COFFEE

Mexican coffee has many interpretations. Restaurants often serve it with liqueurs and multicolored whipped cream. Following a rather heavy meal, I prefer the simplicity of a good, dark roast Mexican abaka coffee, carefully brewed. You can use any favorite dark roasted coffee. For greatest flavor, freshly grind your coffee and brew it with a hint of cinnamon. For 12 cups or more, the quantity for this brunch, use about 1 1/2 teaspoons cinnamon sprinkled over the grounds.

Later in the day you can also serve Kahlúa or brandy on the side.

Makes 12 cups.

3/4 to 1 cup freshly ground dark roast Mexican abaka coffee or enough to brew 12 cups of
    strong, full-flavored coffee in your pot
1 1/2 teaspoons ground cinnamon
1 cup heavy cream
1/2 teaspoon Mexican vanilla, if available, or 1 teaspoon pure vanilla extract
1/4 cup sugar
12 cinnamon sticks, each 4 inches long
Piloncillo or raw natural sugar crystals

Place the ground coffee in the drip basket or wherever grounds are held in your pot. Add the ground cinnamon. Brew the coffee. Meanwhile, in the bowl of an electric mixer, whip the cream, adding the vanilla and sugar as it whips. Whip to a firm consistency with stiff peaks. Serve the coffee in mugs—heavy Mexican pottery would be perfect. Add a cinnamon stick to each and serve with the whipped cream and the piloncillo.

WINTER BRUNCH

Chorizo Chalupitas
Rolled Ham 'n Chile Omelet Pinwheel with Mushroom Ratatouille
Tropical Fruit-Stuffed Pineapple
Champagne
Coffee

This is a perfect brunch to serve by the fireside in a cozy country cabin. I first served it as a toast to the New Year, and it was a winner. The foods are not complicated to cook, and you only need to pay special attention to the omelet instructions. Ready the base for the Chalupitas the day before, and the rest of the preparations will require only about an hour.

Select a colorful old quilt for the tablecloth and place it over a large, low coffee table in front of your couch before the fireplace. Or set the quilt on your dining room table with a complement of bright print napkins folded into fans and stuffed in large wine goblets. Complete the table with a winter bouquet of multicolored mums or other favorite flowers.

Menu Plan

Day before:
Fry the chalupitas.
Chill the champagne.

One hour before:
Prepare the pineapple and fruits.
Prepare the ratatouille.
Cook the chorizo and warm the tortilla flutes 30 minutes before serving. Assemble the chalupitas and garnish the platter.
Prepare the pan and ingredients for the Omelet Pinwheel.
Set out the coffeepot.

At serving time:
Bake the Omelet Pinwheel while serving the Chorizo Chalupitas with the champagne.
Roll and serve the Omelet Pinwheel with the ratatouille and more champagne.
Arrange the Tropical Fruit-Stuffed Pineapple and serve with the coffee.

CHORIZO CHALUPITAS

Chalupas are perhaps one of the most liberally interpreted dishes in Mexican fast-food operations. You'll find everything from an open-face salad in its own edible bowl (which should be called a tostado compuesto) to a simple, fried whole flat corn or wheat tortilla layered with taco types of fillings. Traditionally, Mexican chalupas were shaped like boats (from which they take their name) and were made in the Mexico City area as a treat for the children while their mothers cooked—an origin somewhat similar to that of tacos farther north.

I developed these as an innovative twist to the traditional. Chorizo is a wonderful breakfast meat, yet it can be far too spicy for some unless it is combined with other ingredients—hence, this tasty little appetizer. Instead of the traditional masa "canoe" shape for the chalupas, I recommend using small corn tortillas—half size, if available, which are 3 inches in diameter. Otherwise, use the 6-inch size. You can make these the day or evening before and reheat to serve.

Makes 12 appetizers.

2 quarts cooking oil
12 (3-inch) corn tortillas or 6 (6-inch) ones
3/4 pound (12 ounces) chorizo sausage, preferably the New Mexican or Mexican-American type
1 cup sour cream
1 1/2 cups thinly shredded iceberg lettuce
1/2 cup halved black olives
2 Tablespoons finely chopped fresh cilantro, optional

Heat the oil in an electric deep-fat fryer to 375°F (190°C) or in a 5-quart heavy Dutch oven using a deep-fat frying thermometer to maintain the proper temperature. Meanwhile, if using the 3-inch tortillas, find a 6-ounce juice can, and using a beverage opener, cut three holes evenly spaced around the top and three more alternating between the top ones on the vertical side adjacent to the top holes. This will create a frying form. If using the 6-inch tortillas, cut each in half and roll around your finger to create a flute shape; secure with a toothpick.

For the 3-inch size, place one tortilla at a time on top of the fat and immediately plunge it into the fat, using tongs to hold the can down on top of the tortilla. Fry until the bubbles subside and the tortilla is crisp and bubbly. For the 6-inch size, fry the flutes, holding each with tongs to be certain it is completely immersed, until they are crisp. Drain well on a cooling rack covered with paper towels.

About 30 minutes before serving, remove the casings from the chorizos and coarsely chop the meat. Fry over low heat, stirring frequently to be certain it is uniformly fried and crumbled. Drain on paper towels, discarding the fat.

Using warm tortilla flutes—you can reheat them in a 350°F (180°C) oven for 10 minutes—fill each with the crumbled chorizo, top with sour cream, and place on an attractive platter. Garnish each with shredded lettuce, using the balance to garnish the platter. Top each with a few slices of olive and a sprinkle of cilantro, if using.

ROLLED HAM 'N CHILE OMELET PINWHEEL

Gorgeous is the only word to describe this whirl of brilliant color. A pinwheel omelet is one of those dishes that is actually fun to make, and once you've mastered its techniques, there is no limit to the variety of fillings. The major trick is buttering the wax paper or parchment paper generously enough; otherwise, what should be a lovely fluff of baked omelet loses its muscle immediately and becomes very skinny and scruffy looking. Do be certain to make the Ratatouille ahead of time for serving alongside.

Plan carefully so that the omelet, once done, can be served immediately. Have the eggs separated, the pan ready, and the fillings laid out in advance. Then allow 20 to 25 minutes to prepare the omelet and bake, roll, and serve it.

Makes 6 servings.

12 thin slices of cooked ham, approximately 4 inches square (about 1/2 pound)
12 extra-large very fresh eggs, separated
3/4 teaspoon salt
Few grinds of black pepper
6 large New Mexico green chiles (can be frozen), parched, peeled, and coarsely chopped (page 7)
6 large red leaf lettuce leaves, rinsed and drained

Preheat the oven to 350°F (180°C). Prepare a 10 x 14-inch jelly roll pan by generously buttering the pan, then cutting a piece of wax or parchment to cover the bottom of the pan precisely. Generously butter the top of it. Place the ham on a pan in the oven to heat a few minutes while you beat the eggs.

Beat the whites until very stiff and dry using an electric mixer. In a separate bowl add the salt and pepper to the yolks and beat with a whisk until thick and lemon colored. Then fold together, carefully blending the two, and retaining as much air as possible—the mixture should stand in definite peaks. Portion out on top of the pan, dividing the mixture into four piles in the corners of the pan. Working gently with a spatula, smooth off to uniform thickness, making certain that the mixture is smoothed to all sides of the pan. Air pockets will make for a ragged-appearing edge.

Place in the center of the preheated oven. (Also place six serving plates in the oven.) Bake 15 to 20 minutes. When done, the omelet will be dry when pierced with a sharp knife or toothpick. As soon as done, place on a wire cooling rack and cut around the outside edge to free it from the pan. Then add a layer of the ham, spreading out to cover the top of the omelet. Sprinkle the green chile uniformly over the top.

Begin to roll by lifting up the long side next to the edge and rolling like a jelly roll, gently pressing the omelet down and removing the paper as you roll. Sometimes I like to have a nimble-fingered helper assist with this. Continue to roll until you have completely rolled the omelet into one large, long roll. Do be very careful not to rip or tear the omelet as this will destroy the overall appearance. Serve immediately on warmed plates, garnishing each with a lettuce leaf. Add a ribbon of the ratatouille (recipe follows) and serve the extra alongside.

MUSHROOM RATATOUILLE

A lovely, flavorful topping that is really quite simple to make. For generous appetites or dedicated sauce appreciators, you may wish to double this recipe, as it is lovely cold or hot tucked into omelets, as a topping for hamburgers, or even in salads.

Makes 6 servings.

2 Tablespoons unsalted butter
1 pound large button mushrooms, cleaned and thinly sliced into half-moons, leaving the stems on
1/2 cup finely chopped Spanish onion
2 large fresh or canned tomatoes, peeled and chopped
2 teaspoons chopped fresh thyme or 1 teaspoon dried
2 teaspoons chopped fresh Mexican oregano or 1 teaspoon dried
6 leaves fresh purple sage, chopped, or 1 teaspoon dried, crumbled
Few grinds of black pepper
1/2 teaspoon salt

Melt the butter in a large heavy skillet. Add the mushrooms and cook and stir until they have lost their water and started to brown. Add the onion and cook and stir until it becomes clear. Add the tomatoes, thyme, oregano, sage, pepper, and salt and cook and stir until a thick sauce results. This should not take very long—about 10 minutes or so. Taste and adjust seasonings. Serve over and with the omelet.

TROPICAL FRUIT-STUFFED PINEAPPLE

For the prettiest servings, slice the pineapple lengthwise into boats, following my suggested cutting directions. Be certain to select a very juicy, ripe, symmetrically shaped fruit. You can tell if a pineapple is ripe when it has a fragrant aroma, thumps hollowly, and its green top leaves pull out easily. Try to find a fruit with attractive leaves, and do not remove more than one or two to test for ripeness.

Makes 6 servings.

1 very large pineapple
1 mango, peeled and cut into half circles
1 papaya, preferably the watermelon or pink type, cut into squares
1 pint red ripe strawberries, left whole (if not available, substitute red seedless grapes)
12 fresh orange or lemon leaves, optional

To prepare the pineapple, select a large, sharp cutting knife or an electric knife (about the only time I really like to use one). Hold the pineapple upright by the top and slice all the way through the leaves down into the flesh, completely cutting all the way through into two halves. Then cut each half into three equal parts.

Next, starting at the base of each sixth, cut the flesh evenly away from the rind, cutting close enough to the rind to get a nice deep, fleshy portion, but without too many eyes. Cut each in two equal lengthwise parts, then cut into 3/4-inch-wide crosswise slices. Press alternating slices, one to the left, the next to the right, then artistically scatter the tropical fruits and strawberries over the pineapple. Garnish with leaves if available.

LUNCHES AND PICNICS

TEXAS INDEPENDENCE DAY LUNCH

Gazpacho
Frito Pie
Frijoles Slaw
Fireworks Sundaes
Iced Tea

Here is a simple, typical Texas luncheon, its main dish hailing from Dallas, where Texas Fever is about as strong as it ever gets! Big D has always been one of my favorite towns, a place where sophistication beautifully mellows the brash boldness of the Old West.

Texas Independence Day, April 21, commemorates the freedom won from the Mexicans in the Battle of San Jacinto at the Alamo and has been celebrated in a very colorful ten-day fiesta in San Antonio every year since 1836.

This menu is a perfect one for easy entertaining and can be served even for brunch or supper. It's ideal for serving outdoors, as each of the dishes involved is so easily transported.

Traditional decorations are very bright, using hot pinks, reds, purples, yellows, and blues in table coverings as well as in oversized paper flowers. Or try a simpler Texas type of decoration with the Lone Star cut out of white cloth overlaying a bright red or blue cloth.

MENU PLAN

Day before (or early in the day):
Prepare the Frijoles Slaw and refrigerate.
Make the Bowl of Red or whichever chile con carne you will be using in the Frito Pie. Break up the tostados or whichever chips you'll be using. Chop the Spanish onion and grate the cheeses.
Prepare the blueberry compote for the Fireworks Sundaes. Place a layer of ice cream in 8 parfait glasses and freeze.
Prepare the gazpacho.

One hour before:
Place the gazpacho goblets in the freezer.
Assemble the Frito Pie; bake 15 minutes before serving.
Prepare the iced tea, brewing your favorite type.
Slice the strawberries for the sundaes.
Chill the salad plates for the slaw.
Warm the luncheon plates.

At serving time:
Arrange the gazpacho with the lettuce leaves and serve first, followed by the Frito Pie and Frijoles Slaw.
Serve the iced tea.
Assemble the sundaes just before serving and light the sparklers.

GAZPACHO

A perfect opener for a truly Texas luncheon, this particular version of gazpacho is a favorite that I've served on many memorable occasions. Whether at picnics on the green at Central Park in New York City, on boating outings on New Mexico's lakes, or under blazing blue skies on my deck overlooking Santa Fe, I've always found guests and family absolutely love this simple-to-prepare cold soup from Spain.

A large, open-mouthed thermos is perfect for carrying gazpacho to picnics, and depending on the setting, I usually try to bring along both the large, chilled leaves of romaine lettuce and goblets for the prettiest of servings.

As a variation, this gazpacho is also good served following a spicy hot meal.

Makes 8 servings.

2/3 cup tomato juice
1 Tablespoon red wine vinegar
1/4 cup extra-virgin Spanish olive oil
2 garlic cloves, minced
1 cup finely chopped Spanish onion (preferably chopped by hand for the prettiest servings)
4 large red, ripe tomatoes, peeled and diced
2 cups peeled and diced cucumber
1 medium green bell pepper, chopped into 1/4-inch squares
1 fresh jalapeño, finely chopped
2 Tablespoons chopped fresh cilantro
1 head romaine lettuce, well rinsed

Whisk together the tomato juice, vinegar, oil, and garlic in the bottom of a large mixing bowl. Add the onions, tomatoes, cucumber, green pepper, jalapeño, and cilantro and fold together. Taste and add salt if desired. Adjust seasonings. Chill in the refrigerator at least 1 hour, preferably overnight. Serve in frosted goblets, with the tops of the whole lettuce leaves peeking over the top.

FRITO PIE

This luncheon dish has always been a star attraction in Texas and New Mexico for church and other fund-raising organizations. Because I've helped cook and serve thousands of servings of this pie for worthy causes, it's not surprising that I chose it as an ideal Texas Independence Day lunch entrée. This dish is also extremely practical, giving you a way to profit from all those tostado tidbits and broken taco shells you may have been saving. (As an aside, some restaurants and fund-raisers serve the pie inside the smallest bag of Fritos, mashed.)

Makes 8 servings.

2 Tablespoons unsalted butter
5 cups broken tostados or taco shells
2 cups coarsely chopped Spanish onion (a food processor works fine)
4 cups (one recipe) Bowl of Red (page 8) or other favorite chile or even chile pork (in fact more
    than one type can be combined)
1 1/2 cups shredded Monterey Jack cheese
1 1/2 cups full-cream sharp Cheddar cheese

Coat a large 10 x 14-inch baking dish or two 9 x 9-inch or any similar combination of casseroles with the butter. Preheat the oven to 350°F (180°C). Spread half the broken chips in the baking dish. Top with the onion, then add the chile in an even layer. Top with the rest of the corn chips. Mix the cheeses and sprinkle uniformly over the top. Bake 15 minutes or until bubbly.

FRIJOLES SLAW

A very pretty combination of colors and contrasting textures make this slaw quite different from the ordinary. Should any ever be left, it keeps at least a week in the refrigerator. Try it along with chilied beef or pork for wonderful burritos or tacos.

The slaw is best when made with home-cooked frijoles that have been stewed with heavily smoked country ham bones and hocks.

Makes 8 servings.

2 cups well-drained cooked pinto beans
3 1/2 cups shredded white cabbage (about a third of a 5- to 6-inch head)
1 cup long, thin curls of carrot made with a vegetable peeler (about 1 large carrot)
1/2 cup minced Spanish onion
1/2 cup mayonnaise
1/2 cup plain nonfat yogurt
1/4 cup Fresh Garden Salsa (page 13), divided
16 large romaine or leaf lettuce leaves, rinsed, drained, and chilled

At least 2 hours or a day or so before serving, in a large bowl combine the beans, cabbage, carrot, and onion. In a small bowl mix together the mayonnaise, yogurt, and 2 Tablespoons of the salsa. Add the dressing to the vegetables and stir and toss together until the vegetables are well coated. Taste and adjust seasonings. To serve, place two lettuce leaves on each chilled plate. Top with the slaw and a dollop of the salsa centered on each serving.

FIREWORKS SUNDAES

What could be more appropriate for celebrating the anniversary of the "Don't tread on me" state than these? Layers of red, white, and blue, however, will suit red-blooded occasions of any type.

Makes 8 servings.

1 quart rich French vanilla ice cream
1 pint fresh strawberries, rinsed, stemmed, and sliced
Blueberry Compote (page 89) or use prepared blueberry topping
8 sparklers

Place a layer of ice cream in each of 8 parfait glasses. Add a layer of strawberries, then more ice cream, then a layer of the blueberry compote. Top with a final small spoonful of ice cream and push a sparkler into each. Light to serve.

FLYING FANTASY

Mesquite-Grilled Fajitas with Sour Cream and Pico de Gallo
Marinated Avocado Salad
Warm Wheat Tortillas
Medley of Vegetables Vinaigrette
Mango Mélange
Cabernet Sauvignon
Coffee

Inspired by the jet-setters of West Texas—who think nothing of preparing fabulous feasts for the lonesome hours in the sky aboard their private jets as they fly off on a pleasure jaunt like a football game or a skiing trip—the menu works very well for any outing, backyard to back-packed to a sybaritic setting.

This meal is quite easily managed just a few hours in advance of take-off and includes foods that are both complementary and travel well. (Of course, if you are not transporting the foods, just disregard the travel container tips.) As there is little seasonality to any part of this menu, it is good for entertaining at any time of the year.

Keep the decor very simple, especially if you are traveling. Use brightly colored tin or plastic plates and bandanna handkerchief napkins on a gingham cloth. If flowers can be accommodated, use daisies or simple field flowers.

MENU PLAN

Four hours or more before:
Marinate the skirt steaks.
Prepare the pico de gallo.
Prepare the Medley of Vegetables Vinaigrette.
Prepare the Mango Mélange.
Make the Marinated Avocado Salad.
Make the coffee.
Grill the fajitas and pack to keep warm.
Warm the tortillas.
Pack up.

MESQUITE-GRILLED FAJITAS

From their humble beginnings, fajitas have caught on like a prairie fire fanning out from South Texas. Originally the food that farm laborers along the border prepared for themselves from the trimmings their bosses gave them, fajitas are made in the Southwest from relatively inexpensive skirt steak (the belly trimmings). In the North and East, one often has to settle for bottom round, which must be cut very thinly. The authentic smoky flavor comes from marinating the beef in lime juice and garlic and grilling it over mesquite, which for this recipe is optional but preferable. Fajitas are traditionally served on sizzling steak platters on top of warm wheat or flour tortillas, sauced with peppery hot pico de gallo and sour cream.

For this menu, the meat is grilled ahead, placed in a heated earthenware casserole, and sealed in layers of newspaper and foil to keep it warm.

Makes 6 to 8 servings.

3 pounds skirt steak or very lean, scaloppini-cut bottom round steak, fat and sinew removed
2 limes
6 garlic cloves, minced
1 teaspoon salt
Freshly ground black pepper to taste
6 to 8 (12-inch) wheat tortillas
12 to 16 leaves of rinsed, whole romaine lettuce
Pico de gallo (recipe follows)
1 cup sour cream

Pound steaks as thin as possible. Cut into strips 4 to 6 inches long by 2 inches wide.

Squeeze the limes in a bowl and combine the juice with the garlic, salt, and a generous amount of pepper. Place a small amount of the lime mixture in a shallow bowl, then swish the steak pieces in it. Drizzle the top with the rest. Roll and turn to get the maximum amount absorbed into the meat. Let set at room temperature at least 30 minutes, preferably for 2 hours.

Meanwhile, about 45 minutes before serving or before packing, start the fire, using mesquite wood or chips to flavor the charcoal briquets.

Adjust the grill as you would for steak—3 to 4 inches from the bed of coals. Grill the beef strips until charred on each side but still rare in the center. When done, pack for the picnic. If serving immediately, heat foil-wrapped wheat tortillas for 15 minutes in a 350°F (180°C) oven, or heat each tortilla a few seconds directly on the grill.

To serve, place a piece of steak in the center of each tortilla with a piece of romaine on either side. For those who like it hot, spoon some pico de gallo on the inside. Wrap and serve garnished with sour cream with a drizzle of pico de gallo over the top.

PICO DE GALLO

"Cock's comb" is the literal translation of this southeastern Texas border sauce borrowed from northern Mexico. The traditional accompaniment to fajitas, it is also an excellent spicy red table salsa. Chipotle (smoked jalapeños) are preferable, and the powdered is the easiest to use. One half teaspoon equals a pod. Many recipes also call for serrano chiles, which I eliminated from my lexicon of ingredients quite some time ago. To me, their only reason for being is to create undiluted pain without pleasure, and they offer very little flavor in contrast to the jalapeños and other American chiles.

Makes 6 to 8 servings.

1 1/2 teaspoons chipotle chile powder
1 large red, ripe, unpeeled tomato, coarsely chopped (to equal 1/2 cup)
1 medium white Spanish onion, coarsely chopped (to equal 1/2 cup)
2 garlic cloves, minced
1/2 teaspoon salt
3 Tablespoons coarsely chopped fresh cilantro

Combine the chile power, tomato, onion, garlic, salt, and cilantro in a bowl and allow to marinate and develop natural juices for at least 1 hour before serving.

MARINATED AVOCADO SALAD

A perfect complement to almost any Tex-Mex or Southwestern menu, this great picnic salad offers just a bit of a twist to the traditional guacamole.

Makes 6 to 8 servings.

1/4 cup freshly squeezed lime juice
3/4 cup extra-virgin olive oil
2 garlic cloves, minced
1 Tablespoon caribe or other crushed dried red chile
3 ripe Haas or Fuertes avocados
1 head red leaf or Boston lettuce

Combine the lime juice, olive oil, garlic, and caribe in a small bowl. For ease, peel back the tough rind of the avocados using the back side of a spoon. Then cut into 1-inch cubes. Place in a favorite pottery serving bowl or a food storage container and gently toss with the dressing so as not to break up the cubes of avocado.

Rinse and pack the lettuce leaves in a moistened paper towel within a plastic bag. To serve, place a portion of the marinated avocado on two to three lettuce leaves on a chilled plate. For picnicking, use the salad to garnish plates.

Note: The avocado should be well sealed against oxidation either by wrapping tight with plastic wrap, placing it carefully down against the avocados, or by sealing into rigid freezer or food storage containers. It will keep at least a day.

MEDLEY OF VEGETABLES VINAIGRETTE

For picnics and outings, these are a natural. I've suggested here a pretty summer or early fall selection of vegetables, but they can easily be varied depending on the season.

Makes 6 to 8 servings.

1/2 pound tiny green beans
1/2 pound tiny yellow wax beans
2 medium-size carrots
1 large red bell pepper
1 ear of large-kernel white (not shoe-peg) corn
2 cups boiling water
1/2 teaspoon salt
1/2 cup virgin olive oil
3 Tablespoons white wine vinegar

Wash the beans and leave them whole, trimming off just the tips and ends with a sharp knife. Scrape the carrots, then cut into 1/4-inch-thick diagonal cuts, made by holding the knife at about a 45-degree angle. Cut the red pepper into 1-inch squares. Shuck the corn, removing all the silk.

Steam the vegetables in a medium-size heavy saucepan, adding the 2 cups water and salt over medium heat. Steam 5 minutes, or until the color of the vegetables deepens and they are still somewhat crisp—do not overcook!

Drain the cooked vegetables and cut the corn off the cob, holding the ear with a potholder or tongs. Combine the oil and vinegar in a small bowl, return the vegetables to the pan, add the vinaigrette, and cover. Allow to heat together about 5 minutes. Then place the vegetables in a bowl or traveling container and spoon sauce over; stir the vegetables periodically. Let marinate at room temperature at least 2 hours before serving.

MANGO MÉLANGE

This very simple marinated fresh fruit dish can be varied in countless ways. For this menu I prefer mangoes—perhaps simply because I love them, particularly when they are at their juiciest ripeness. Lacking those, any Mexican fruit—thumping ripe pineapple, watermelon, papaya, melon, and even some peeled cucumber cut in chunks—can be used.

Makes 6 to 8 servings.

3 very large or 4 medium mangoes (should yield to thumb pressure but not be squishy)
Juice of 1 lime
2 Tablespoons honey, such as palo verde or prickly pear or any other flavorful honey
1/4 cup triple sec or Cointreau

Do not peel the mangoes. Slice each side lengthwise, cutting as close to the seed as possible, using a very sharp knife. Then slice the rest of the flesh as close as possible to the seed all around. Score each half into 1/2 inch squares, then using your thumbs, force the skin of each up to reveal the scored flesh and cut the squares off. This method is the easiest and best way to get the most fruit.

Place in a bowl, or for traveling, in a sealable container; in a small bowl mix together the lime juice, honey, and triple sec and pour over. (If the honey is thick, warm it slightly. A microwave oven is most convenient—just cover a glass measuring cup with a piece of plastic wrap and warm for 10 to 15 seconds.) Stir and spoon the sauce over the fruit, taking care not to break up the pieces of mango. Serve at room temperature for the greatest flavor.

FOLIAGE OUTING PICNIC

Tex-Mex Torte
New Mexican Marinated London Broil with Green Chile Stew Topping
Warm Wheat Tortillas Rolled with Sweet Butter
Prickly Pear Marmalade
Iced Beer
Freshly Picked Apples
Sharp Cheddar Cheese

Memories of New Mexico's very special fall bounty—golden aspens against purply blue skies . . . crisp, crunchy, just-picked apples . . . and the musky aroma of freshly fallen leaves on rocky trails—were the inspiration for this picnic, which combines many of my favorite flavors from that state. Enjoy these dishes either on a day trip or simply out on the patio—either way, their aromas are made for the out of doors. Simplicity in presentation is the key here: serve on rustic pottery, tinware, or any plain dinnerware.

I've given packing instructions within each recipe to simplify preparation and setup. The only dish that is somewhat cumbersome is the Tex-Mex Torte, but it's a wonderful nibbler while the fire is getting ready and takes only a couple of minutes to assemble at the site.

MENU PLAN

Day before (or several days before):
Make the Prickly Pear Marmalade.
Prepare the Green Chile Stew.

Two hours before:
Marinate the London broil.
Refry the beans, make the guacamole, and prepare the other ingredients for the Tex-Mex Torte.
Bake the wheat tortillas if you prefer to make them, following the recipe on page 163, or heat packaged or previously made ones. About 20 minutes before leaving, heat the wheat tortillas in packets of six. Then brush each with melted butter, roll, and repackage in several layers of foil to insulate. Pack in a cloth-lined basket.
Wash and polish the apples.
Package the chunk of Cheddar on a board with a sharp knife.
Ice the beer and place in a cooler along with the torte ingredients and other perishables.
Pack up all serving items.

At serving time:
Assemble the torte.
Build the fire.
Set up the serving area while guests nibble the torte with tortillas and drink beer.
Grill the steak, reheating the stew and the tortillas if necessary.
Serve the tortillas with the marmalade.
Serve the apples with the Cheddar.

TEX-MEX TORTE

A beautiful and easy-to-create sensation that is truly a Texan's dream, Tex-Mex Torte combines the flavors of guacamole and the border favorite frijoles refritos (refried beans) and tops them with palate-cleansing, lime-scented rich sour cream, artfully garnished with curls of rich yellow Cheddar and squares of tomato and jalapeño. The only catch is that it is best by far if whipped together at the last minute. For traveling, line the casserole with the beans before departing. Pack the guacamole in an airtight container and each of the other ingredients in separate bags. The shredded cheese and tostados will carry best in rigid containers.

Makes 6 to 8 servings.

THE BEANS

2 Tablespoons lard or bacon drippings
1 large garlic clove, minced
2 Tablespoons minced Spanish onion
2 cups cooked or 1 (16-ounce) can pinto beans

THE GUACAMOLE

2 large Haas avocados
1/4 cup chopped ripe tomato
1/4 cup chopped Spanish onion
1 Tablespoon finely chopped jalapeño
2 garlic cloves, minced
1 teaspoon or more freshly squeezed lime juice
3/4 teaspoon salt
2 Tablespoons cilantro, very coarsely chopped, optional

GARNISHES

1 cup sour cream
Juice of 1 lime

1 1/2 cups coarsely shredded full-cream sharp Cheddar cheese
1 medium ripe tomato, coarsely chopped
2 fresh jalapeños, stemmed, seeded, and very finely chopped
12 blue or white corn tortillas or a combination, quartered and crisply fried

Melt the lard in a large heavy skillet over medium-high heat. Add the garlic, and as soon as it starts to turn golden, add the onion. When the onion begins to soften, add the pinto beans. Mash and stir, using a potato masher and a large heavy wooden spoon to completely mash the beans as they fry. When thick, remove from heat.

Halve and scoop out the flesh from the avocados and place in a bowl. Combine with the tomato, onion, jalapeño, garlic, lime juice, and salt. Use a fork and knife to cut the avocados coarsely; do not mash finely or use a food processor or blender. When ingredients are well mixed but not overly mixed, taste and adjust flavors.

Combine the sour cream with the lime juice to taste in a bowl. You may not need all the lime juice.

Using a Mexican or pottery casserole, place the refried beans in the bottom and tightly cover with foil if packing for the picnic. At the picnic site, place the guacamole mixture 1 inch inside the beans so the beans show all the way around. Indenting another inch, place a generous circle of the lime-flavored sour cream.

Top with the cheese, tomato, and jalapeños. Serve with a basket of freshly fried or warmed, fried tortillas.

NEW MEXICAN MARINATED LONDON BROIL
WITH GREEN CHILE STEW TOPPING

This dish is so wonderfully flavorful and so reminiscent of many a trek to the aspen-covered mountains of New Mexico. I have frequently made Green Chile Stew in one form or another for autumn day trips, in part because the green chile harvest coincides beautifully with falling leaves. But even more, everyone to whom I've served this spicy, hearty stew—either as a topping or as a meal unto itself—considered it one of the best dishes they had ever eaten. And it has the virtue of traveling extremely well. I've covered long distances with it either in a knapsack or a backpack, or tied onto a saddle. Atop rare, crisp-edged beef, it's just the thing for fresh air–sparked appetites. Be sure to serve with buttered, rolled tortillas, which are perfect for sopping up the wonderful stew.

Makes 6 to 8 servings.

New Mexican Marinated London Broil

1 cup good-quality dry red wine
1/2 cup olive oil
3 garlic cloves, minced
3 1/2 to 4 pounds 2-inch-thick well-marbled London Broil
Green Chile Stew (recipe follows)

Combine the wine, olive oil, and garlic in a large glass rectangular dish and place the steak in it. Ideally, the steak would come almost to the edges of the dish. Cover and let stand at room temperature at least 2 hours. Turn once or twice and spoon additional marinade over the top every 30 minutes or so.

Broil as soon as the marinating time is up, or drain well and place in a plastic bag and seal well for transporting to the picnic site. The steak is good either way, freshly broiled or broiled in advance.

To broil, place a stack of briquets in your grill and ignite. When the white ash is uniform, raise the grill to a height of about 3 inches above the coals and grill until the meat is crisp and deeply browned on the outside and rare, or to your preferred doneness, on the inside. Allow about 5 minutes on each side. Test with a sharp knife to determine the doneness. Serve with generous spoonfuls of the Green Chile Stew.

Green Chile Stew

2 Tablespoons olive oil
2 1/4 pounds bone-in pork loin, cut into 3/4-inch cubes
3 garlic cloves, finely minced
28 green chiles (fresh, canned, or frozen), parched and peeled (page 7), cut in 1-inch lengths
  (approximately 4 cups)
2 cups chopped Spanish onion
1 (28-ounce) can peeled whole tomatoes

1/2 teaspoon Mexican oregano
1/2 teaspoon cumin
1/4 teaspoon whole coriander, crushed
3 cups water, rinsed in can
1 teaspoon salt

In a large stewing pot, at least 5 quarts, heat the olive oil until it almost begins to smoke. Add the pork cubes and lightly brown. Add the garlic, chiles, onion, tomatoes, oregano, cumin, coriander, water, and salt. Cook for about 1 hour. Taste and adjust seasonings.

Note: At this point, the stew is ready to serve. For an outing, I place it in a thermos with a wide mouth or in any heat-retaining container, preferably one you can serve from. A heavy casserole wrapped in many layers of newspaper works well too. If serving soon, set aside and reheat immediately before serving. In addition to serving over the steak, it is also good served alone or over hamburgers, chicken, or pork.

PRICKLY PEAR MARMALADE

I like to make several recipes of this truly Southwestern specialty every August when the pears are the most bountiful so that I can give gifts from the desert year-round. Use attractive jelly jars or hand-crafted pottery that is glazed inside and can be boiled.

Makes 4 to 6 jars, depending on their size.

2 pounds ripe prickly pears
4 oranges (thin-skinned juice-type oranges are best)
1 lemon
1 box fruit pectin
4 cups sugar

Carefully clean the cactus, washing and quartering each one. Place in a kettle and add water to come not quite to the tops of the fruit. Simmer slowly until the fruit is soft and pulpy.

While the prickly pears are simmering, peel the oranges if they do not have very thin skins, laying out the peel on a board. Cut away any thick white portions of the peel, then cut the peel in fine strips. Thinly slice the flesh of the oranges, removing all seeds and any coarse membrane. Prepare the lemon the same way. The oranges and lemon should yield at least 2 cups.

Simmer the lemon and oranges in a very small quantity of water for 10 to 15 minutes or until the rinds become tender. Then place in a crockery or other heavy bowl and let set overnight, covered with a cloth.

Meanwhile, place the prickly pear juice in a cloth jelly bag that has been moistened with hot water. Hang the bag overnight in an out-of-the-way place over a large bowl to collect the drippings. Please, never squeeze the bag.

Next morning, scrub out 6 jelly jars or crocks and place in a shallow pan to boil. Measure 2 cups of the juice and combine with 2 cups of the citrus pulp and rind in a large, deep stainless steel or porcelain-lined pot. Add water if need be to make 4 cups total. (Any excess juice can be used in drinks or desserts or over pancakes.)

Add the fruit pectin and stir well, then bring to a boil, reduce heat, and cook gently for 1 minute. Immediately add the sugar and stir well. Bring to a full rolling boil and boil hard for 1 minute, stirring constantly. The marmalade should pass a sheet test—when the mixture will fall off in a sheet from a metal spoon held at right angles to the surface of the mixture—or reach 220°F (105°C) on a candy thermometer at sea level. Remove from heat and skim and stir for 7 minutes.

Quickly ladle into glasses. Allow to cool for a few hours, then cover with melted paraffin or seal with the lids. Allow to set up at least overnight for the best serving texture.

SPECIAL DINNERS

CINCO DE MAYO

Quesadillas

Tequila Sours

Roast Loin of Pork en Mole Salsa

Sweet Red Peppered Rice

Oaxacan Fresh Fruit Salad

Rioja Wine

Tia's Monterrey Flan Flambé

Mexican Coffee

The fifth of May, a popular celebration in Mexico commemorating its gaining independence from France, is honored increasingly throughout the United States. Cinco de Mayo gives everyone the opportunity to have a huge fiesta and to enjoy the mariachi music and all the color and trimmings that can be conjured.

The entire menu for this meal is based on traditional dishes—with some innovative touches. The quesadillas, prepared in a trio of flavors, are actually inside-out nachos, whose filling is blanketed with a grilled wheat tortilla. In addition to the traditional cheese and jalapeño filling, I have developed chorizo–sour cream and avocado-chicken versions. All are laced with guacamole and garnished with cilantro. Served with Tequila Sours, which are quite popular in Mexico, they make a super introduction to this celebration dinner.

The mole, a rich brown, highly colored, well-flavored sauce, gently permeates the pork tenderloin. Because of the firmer texture of the pork, as opposed to the more often used turkey or chicken, the flavoring of the meat is quite subtle. For those who wish a stronger flavor, serve additional sauce alongside for spooning over the pork and the rice.

Sweet red peppers and vegetables punctuate the rice accompaniment, adding an explosion of color and a richer flavor that perfectly complements the mole.

The Oaxacan Fresh Fruit Salad was inspired by my visits with my uncle and Mexican aunt, whose favorite city was Oaxaca. It is a beautiful, historic, and picturesque place nestled in the mountains below Mexico City, where its citizens enjoy the bounty of the tropics in a high-altitude climate. The flan, which is my aunt's recipe, is a glorious finale!

Stage this meal with color and verve. Create a definite Mexican atmosphere with lots of brightly colored flowers—either real or paper—in tall urns or baskets. Use red, green, and white with other bright accents in the table linens. Be sure to have mariachi music, even if it's recorded.

Menu Plan

Early in the day (or the day before):
Marinate the pork loin in the mole sauce.
Prepare the flan.
Prepare the salad dressing.

Three hours before:
Cook the pork loin; let stand 30 minutes before carving.
Prepare the salad fruits.
Prepare the vegetables for the rice. Cook the rice just before the guests arrive.
Prepare the quesadillas. Grill them about 30 minutes before the guests arrive.
Warm the dinner plates and chill the salad plates and forks.
Make the guacamole.
Make the Tequila Sours.
Set up the coffeepot.

At serving time:
Cut the quesadillas into sixths and garnish. Serve with the Tequila Sours.
Carve the pork and dress the salad. Serve with the rice.
While the guests are eating, heat the flan and make the coffee.
Serve the flaming flan at the table.
Serve the coffee.

QUESADILLAS

Quesadillas are wheat tortillas folded over an oozing blend of Monterey Jack and Cheddar cheeses spiked with pickled jalapeños and any other filling you wish, then quickly grilled with a light brush of unsalted butter for the flakiest texture. For this celebratory dinner I have chorizo, chicken, avocado, and beans that can be added as fillings in addition to the traditional cheese and chile combination. Slather on freshly made guacamole for perfection.

Makes 6 servings.

About 2 Tablespoons melted unsalted butter or more
6 (10-inch) freshly made wheat tortillas
1 1/4 cups mixed shredded Monterey Jack and Cheddar cheeses
1/4 cup pickled jalapeño slices or to taste
4 chorizo sausages, fried, drained, and crumbled
1 cup chopped, cooked chicken
1/2 cup cooked pinto beans
1/2 ripe avocado, cut in long, thin slivers
1 recipe guacamole (page 96)
Bunch of fresh cilantro, rinsed

Heat a grill or griddle over medium-high heat; when hot, reduce the heat to medium and brush the melted butter sparingly in a half-moon shape the size of a tortilla. Place the tortilla over the butter, making sure the tortilla is centered. Then place a 1/2-inch layer of the cheese, being careful to reserve a 1-inch margin; then sprinkle with the jalapeño slices and other fillings (sausage, chicken, beans, avocado) as you desire. When the cheese starts to melt and the tortilla on the grill is becoming light brown, fold the other side of the tortilla over the first side. Lightly brush the second side of the tortilla with butter before turning it to brown.

To serve, cut each into sixths by first cutting in half and then cutting into equal portions, then place them on a Mexican or earthenware oversized platter. Center a dollop of guacamole on each at the tip ends and nestle a bunch of cilantro around the crust edge.

TEQUILA SOURS

For ages, these have had a following in Mexico as well as along the border, where many bartenders have learned to make very good versions. This variation is easy to prepare for a crowd and is quite good.

Makes 6 drinks.

1 (6-ounce) can frozen lemonade concentrate
1 1/3 cups light tequila
12 ice cubes or more
6 slices orange, rind and all
6 maraschino cherries

Using a blender, place the lemonade, tequila, and 6 ice cubes in the jar and process on high speed until well mixed. Add 6 more cubes and blend until slushy. If not slushy enough, keep adding ice cubes and processing. Serve in goblets, with a slice of orange curled over the rim of the glass and a cherry attached with a toothpick.

ROAST LOIN OF PORK EN MOLE SALSA

Mole is unquestionably the national dish of Mexico, so it is an obvious choice for this celebratory dinner. The only adaptation I've made is to use pork instead of the more traditional turkey or chicken. The ancient origins of mole are lost in the mists of time, but its popularity as a festive dish stems from the seventeenth century, when the nuns of the Santa Rosa convent used it either (historians differ) to celebrate their release from captivity or as thanks to the archbishop for building them a grand convent. Oaxaca is known as a mole capitol.

The variations for the sauce are endless and vary regionally. This is a simplified version of the Mole Poblano, which is a blend of chiles, chocolate, and spices with varying quantities of nuts, tortillas, tomatoes, and other additions. Mole is now available in a powder or concentrate, which I've used in this recipe. I've found that the Dona Maria brand in an 8 1/4-ounce glass jar is quite good. It is regularly imported from Mexico and available in specialty stores.

This dish requires marination for most of a day or overnight.

Makes 6 servings.

3 1/3 pounds pork loin
8 1/4 ounces mole concentrate
1 1/4 cups warm water
2 large garlic cloves, minced

Clean and trim the pork, removing any excess fat, leaving a thin blanket of fat around the exterior. Put in a large shallow glass baking dish.

Place mole paste a small bowl, then stir in warm water and the garlic and mix well. Drizzle over the pork, turning to coat the entire roast evenly. Spoon the sauce over the roast every 15 minutes and rotate frequently. Leave covered at room temperature for at least 2 hours or refrigerate overnight.

Roast in a 325°F (170°C) oven, basting frequently, for 3 hours. Allow to cool at least 30 minutes before carving. Serve with a side dish of the sauce, which is terrific over the rice.

SWEET RED PEPPERED RICE

This pretty, vegetable-flavored rice is an essential accompaniment to the mole, as it allows the rich sauce to be fully savored.

Makes 6 servings.

2 Tablespoons unsalted butter
1 large fresh red sweet pepper, chopped into 1/4-inch pieces
3/4 cup finely chopped carrot
3/4 cup finely chopped celery
3/4 cup finely chopped Spanish onion
1 1/2 cups long-grain rice
3 cups chicken stock
1 teaspoon salt or to taste (depends on seasoning in broth)
3 Tablespoons chopped flat-leaf parsley

Melt the butter in a 3-quart heavy saucepan, then add the red pepper, carrots, celery, onions, and rice and lightly sauté until all are coated with butter. Add the chicken stock and bring to a boil, then reduce the heat to a simmer, cover, and cook for 15 minutes. Do not peek. When the time is up, stir, add salt, and replace the cover, ajar. Serve sprinkled with the parsley.

—— OAXACAN FRESH FRUIT SALAD ——

The influence is clear here—this salad contains the tropical fruits of Mexico and is laced with a favorite dressing I've been making since I was a kid. The colors are festive and follow the Mexican custom of always decorating at least one dish with the national colors: red, white, and green.

Makes 6 servings.

1/2 Mexican pineapple, peeled, cored, and cut into wedges
1 papaya, preferably the watermelon pink, peeled, seeded, and cut into squares
2 cups watermelon balls
Honey Poppy Seed Dressing (recipe follows)
1 head red leaf lettuce, rinsed well and blotted dry
2 Haas avocados, cut into long, thin strips
1 pomegranate, seeded (can be omitted if not in season)

In a bowl combine the pineapple, papaya, and watermelon. Prepare the salad dressing. Add the dressing to the fruit mixture and gently toss. Then arrange the lettuce leaves on chilled salad plates. Spoon the salad onto the lettuce and garnish with the wedges of avocado, spooning remaining dressing left in the salad bowl over the avocado. Sprinkle pomegranate seeds over each salad.

HONEY POPPY SEED DRESSING

Makes 1 1/2 cups.

3/4 cup fragrant blossom honey
1 teaspoon salt
1 teaspoon dry mustard
1/3 cup white wine vinegar
1 1/2 Tablespoons chopped onion
1 1/2 Tablespoons poppy seeds
1 cup vegetable or peanut oil

Place honey, salt, mustard, vinegar, onion, poppy seeds, and oil in a blender jar or food processor and process until well blended. Keep at room temperature until ready to use. Can be successfully stored in the refrigerator for at least 2 weeks.

TIA'S MONTERREY FLAN FLAMBÉ

My Mexican aunt from Monterrey, Mexico, was a fabulous cook, and this was one of her favorite desserts, which she prepared as an excuse for celebrating almost anything! Served flaming, it's most impressive, yet quite easily done.

Makes 6 servings.

3/4 cup sugar, divided
1 Tablespoon unsalted butter
1 1/4 cups coarsely chopped pecans
1 (15-ounce) can sweetened condensed milk
1 (15-ounce) can milk, rinsed in the condensed milk can
6 large eggs
1 teaspoon Mexican vanilla or pure vanilla extract
1 cup 80-proof light rum

Caramelize 1/2 cup of the sugar in a heavy skillet. While it is still hot and syrupy, pour over the bottom of a buttered 1 1/2-quart mold or baking dish. Immediately sprinkle the pecans uniformly over the sugar.

In an electric blender, food processor, or mixer, combine the sweetened condensed milk, milk, eggs, and vanilla and combine well, but do not allow to get foamy. Slowly pour over the caramelized sugar. Bake at 350°F (180°C) for 1 hour or until a knife inserted in the center comes out clean.

Serve warm. If made ahead, reheat at 300°F (150°C) in the mold until a knife inserted allows steam to escape. Unmold on a warm plate, preferably silver. To serve flambé, carefully warm the rum, watching for the very first bubble. Immediately sprinkle the top of the flan with the remaining 1/4 cup sugar, dim the lights, pour the rum over the top, and ignite and present the flan at the table.

EARLY JUNE DINNER

Frozen Lime Daiquiris
Chilled Tomato Cilantro Soup
Soft-Shell Crabs with Jalapeño Salsa
New Mexican Pesto and Capellini
Fresh Strawberries with Cointreau Cream
Pinot Chardonnay
Coffee

When the crickets begin to hum and your heart turns to an early-summer menu to perk up winter-hardened appetites, consider this meal, which is as fresh in its flavors as early June flowers.

Innovation is the keynote to this menu, and the bright, clear, spring-like color and flavor of the daiquiris provide an ideal opener to whet appetites in this pastel setting. The light, subtle tang of the Tomato Cilantro Soup, followed by the delicate soft-shell crabs laced with hot spicy salsa, make for a wonderfully balanced meal. By the way, be sure to select the tiniest, freshest, softest soft-shell crabs you can find. Steer away from those with papery shells and the harder, larger crustier crabs—they are not nearly as fine.

Serve a New Mexican pesto as an accompaniment—its hot green chile adds a welcome piquancy to the fragrant basil. What could be a finer treat for stroking and soothing the palate than a pillow of whipped cream tinged with bitter orange cradling luscious red ripe strawberries?

For perfection, serve this dinner either in your dining room, on a porch or patio, or in the garden. The table will be prettiest if you decorate it in pinks and softest greens. Lacking regular linens in these shades, you can improvise with ginghams or other fabrics from a yard goods store, or look through your scarves, or use bed linens. Even an accent of pink and lime-green satin ribbon on white or natural lace or linen would be nice. Flowers are a must for so special a salute to the beginning of wonderful outdoors times! If you have your own garden favorites, take a few minutes in the afternoon to gather them. Arrange huge garden bouquets for the side tables if serving indoors, and create a smaller, lower level one for the centerpiece.

Menu Plan

Day before (or early in the day):
Prepare the Tomato Cilantro Soup and chill.
Prepare the Jalapeño Salsa and chill.
Prepare the pesto and chill.
Prepare the Cointreau Cream and chill.
Chill a dry white wine such as a Chardonnay, Sauvignon Blanc, or Blanc de Blanc.

Two hours before:
Rinse, hull, and sugar the strawberries.
Set out the pot for the pasta, filling it with salted, oiled water.
Place the soup bowls and the goblets for both the daiquiris and the strawberries in the freezer.
Make the Frozen Lime Daiquiris.

At serving time:
Serve the daiquiris.
Lightly sauté the crabs just before serving the soup and set aside.
Heat the dinner plates.
Boil the water and carefully cook the pasta to the al dente stage while you are serving and clearing
   the soup.
Toss the pasta with the pesto and serve with the crabs.
Arrange the strawberries in the cream in the chilled goblets just before serving.

——— FROZEN LIME DAIQUIRIS ———

These spring-green, refreshing drinks key in perfectly with this dinner. And like all rum drinks, they always seem to promise beaches, seafood, and all the wonderful pleasures of summer.

Makes 6 drinks.

   1 (6-ounce) can frozen limeade
   1 1/3 cups light rum
   12 or more ice cubes
   6 thin rounds of fresh lime
   6 sprigs of fresh mint

   Place the limeade, rum, and about half the ice in a blender jar and process until ice is crushed, then continue adding ice until desired consistency. Serve in chilled tall globe-shaped goblets, garnishing each with a thin slice of lime and a sprig of mint.

CHILLED TOMATO CILANTRO SOUP

Somewhat reminiscent of a puréed gazpacho, this delightfully light, mildly spicy soup features the brisk, clean taste of cilantro. The flavors marry best when prepared a day or at least a few hours in advance.

Makes 6 servings.

2 Tablespoons virgin olive oil
1 large Spanish onion, coarsely chopped in a food processor
1 large carrot, scraped and coarsely chopped in a food processor
1 (28-ounce) can whole tomatoes, coarsely chopped in a food processor
1/2 teaspoon caribe or other crushed dried red chile
1 (4-ounce) can chopped green chiles
1/4 cup fresh cilantro

Place the olive oil in a heavy 2-quart saucepan. Add the onion and carrot and cook about 4 minutes, stirring frequently. Add the tomatoes and caribe and cook for 10 minutes more. Place the mixture in a food processor and process with the green chiles and cilantro until puréed. Chill the soup, then serve in chilled soup bowls.

SOFT-SHELL CRABS WITH JALAPEÑO SALSA

Soft-shell crabs—once nearly impossible to get in New Mexico and throughout most of the Southwest—are now more easily available and are one of my favorite springtime treats. Although I am very fond of them prepared in almost any fashion—including simply sautéed with fresh lemon, butter, and parsley—this recipe is perhaps my favorite. Be very selective when you shop for crabs: check to see that they are alive and that their skins are greenish, very soft, and fresh looking. Papery shells make for less pleasurable eating. I've specified tiny ones for the menu, as I find the larger crabs, along with the pesto, make for too heavy a meal. If only medium-size ones are available, you may wish to serve just one to a diner.

Makes 6 servings.

1/2 cup (1 stick) unsalted butter
12 tiny soft-shell crabs, cleaned*
1/2 cup or more all-purpose flour
Salt to taste
Freshly ground black pepper to taste
1 fresh lime, cut into six long wedges
6 sprigs of cilantro
Jalapeño Salsa, chilled**

Melt the butter in a large skillet. Prepare the crabs as directed. Place the flour in a shallow bowl or plate and mix with the salt and pepper. Lightly dust each prepared crab with the flour. Sauté over medium heat, turning when the first side becomes golden. When done, place on hot plates, pouring the pan juices over them. Garnish with lime, cilantro, and a ribbon of Jalapeño Salsa.

*Prepare live crabs as follows: Cut off the apron or flap that folds under the rear of the body. Turn the crab over and cut off the face at a joint just back of the eyes. Lift each point at the sides with the fingers and clean out the gills. Wash crabs with cold water and pat dry with paper towels.
**Follow the Salsa Fresca recipe on page 15, substituting 4–6 deveined, seeded, and very finely chopped fresh jalapeños for the diced chiles. It's not necessary to parch and peel them.

NEW MEXICAN PESTO AND CAPPELLINI

Create this flavorful pesto whenever you can lay your hands on fresh basil. I make dozens of jars of pesto different ways in late summer in my Woodstock kitchen, then freeze it to enjoy during the winter and spring. The New Mexican touch is the addition of fresh green chiles, which produce just the right pizzazz. If you have a batch of ready-made pesto, you can process it with the proper amount of green chile in the food processor. For another variation, substitute an equal amount of fresh cilantro for the fresh basil.

Makes 6 servings.

2 cups fresh basil leaves, rinsed, torn, and packed together lightly enough so as not to crush the delicate leaves
1/2 cup virgin olive oil
3 Tablespoons piñons (pine nuts)
2 large garlic cloves, minced
1/4 teaspoon salt or to taste
1/2 cup finely chopped New Mexican green chiles, freshly parched and peeled (page 7)
1/2 cup freshly grated Parmesan cheese
3 Tablespoons freshly grated Romano cheese
3 Tablespoons unsalted butter, softened
12 ounces capellini (very fine spaghetti)
1 Tablespoon salt
2 Tablespoons olive oil

Place the basil, oil, piñons, garlic, and salt in a food processor or electric blender. Process only until puréed, being careful not to overprocess. Pour into a 1-quart mixing bowl and add the green chile, Parmesan, and Romano. Stir until evenly mixed together. Stir in the softened butter and combine well.

Prepare the pasta, boiling it in 5 quarts water with salt and olive oil. Add 1 or 2 Tablespoons of the hot water from cooking the pasta to the pesto. Cook only until al dente—about 4 minutes in rapidly boiling water. Rinse with hot water, drain, and toss with the pesto. Serve alongside the crabs with salsa.

— FRESH STRAWBERRIES WITH COINTREAU CREAM —

What single food announces June and the coming summer as satisfyingly as strawberries? I remember so well the painful pleasures of hours and hours of backbreaking work picking berries in the earthy heat of the strawberry beds. Somehow the rewards of popping occasional berries, hot and juicy, into one's mouth and the anticipation of the many tasty treats to be made from the berries always kept us going. Freshly picked vine-ripened berries are always the best and well worth the ride to the fields if you are a city dweller. If you have to buy them from a greengrocer, though, be sure to select very ripe, firm berries for this dish.

Makes 6 servings.

1 quart red ripe strawberries
1 cup powdered sugar, divided
1 cup vanilla ice cream
1 cup heavy whipping cream
1/3 cup Cointreau or other orange-flavored brandy

Carefully rinse the berries and select only the firm ripe ones. Hull and leave whole. Generously sprinkle 1/2 cup powdered sugar over them. Gently toss to coat evenly. Allow to set at room temperature at least 2 hours.

Slightly soften the ice cream so that it can be beaten with a whisk. Whip the cream in a well-chilled bowl using high speed on the mixer. Once the cream begins to foam, add the remaining 1/2 cup sugar and continue beating until very stiff. Fold in the ice cream and Cointreau. Taste and adjust flavoring.

Serve in well-chilled crystal goblets (place in freezer before serving the meal), arranging the strawberries in layers with the whipped cream. Top each with a perfect berry.

HOT SUMMER SPECIAL

Jalapeño Martinis
Posole en Escabeche with Tostados and Hot Salsa
Chicken Avocado Fettuccine
Three Pepper Salad
Marinated Melons with Mint
Minted Iced Tea

Plan this dinner when you really want to relax at your own dinner party. Most everything on the menu is easily prepared, and very little kitchen time over a hot stove is required. The only dish that needs any amount of cooking is the appetizer, which will have the best flavor if prepared before but will be delicious even made only six hours ahead.

The jalapeño-studded martinis will awaken the most seared late-summer appetite. The fettuccine dish is spectacular and versatile—you can easily substitute seafood such as crab or shrimp for the chicken. The tart, tangily dressed, colorful salad, followed by the soothing, minty melon dessert, makes this a real celebration dinner.

I recommend serving this dinner in an air-conditioned dining room or on a cool porch. Complement the pastel colors of the foods with late-summer flowers such as gladioli, dahlias, daisies, or asters. Use a light-green or yellow cloth and napkins.

MENU PLAN

Day before (or early in day):
Cook the posole, cool, and marinate it.
Make the salsa.
Poach the chicken breast for the fettuccine.
Fry the tostadas if making them yourself.

Two hours before serving:
Prepare the melons and marinate.
Prepare the salad ingredients.
Chill the salad and dessert plates and forks.
Prepare the sauce for the fettuccine.
Brew strong dark tea, adding several sprigs of mint. Make the Jalapeño Martinis and freeze.

At serving time:
Heat the pasta plates.
Garnish and set out the Posole en Escabeche. Serve with the Jalapeño Martinis.
Fifteen minutes before serving the main course, boil the water and cook the pasta; reheat the sauce.
Dress the salad and serve with the fettuccine.
Pour the iced tea and garnish each glass with a lemon round and a sprig of mint.
Serve the Marinated Melons.

JALAPEÑO MARTINIS

For this recipe, simply prepare your favorite martini, substituting a round of pickled jalapeño for the lemon twist, olive, or pickled onion. If you don't usually make martinis, then get a shaker or nice glass or silver pitcher and a long-handled spoon. For 6 generous drinks, put several ice cubes in the shaker and add half a fifth of at least 80-proof gin or vodka (measures 24 ounces or 3 liquid measuring cups) and a generous optional splash or Tablespoon of dry vermouth. Some omit the vermouth and add a splash of jalapeño juice from the pickled jalapeños. Be careful if you are inexperienced with this! You may want to sample the proportions ahead of time. Mix vigorously or shake to mix well. Serve garnished with a round of pickled jalapeño. For an added touch, place the glasses in the freezer about 30 minutes before making the drinks.

POSOLE EN ESCABECHE

Here is a very special snack or appetizer, suitable for all sorts of occasions. It is a wonderful switch from the predictable—no one who has ever tasted this mildly spicy, corn-based dish when I've served it has correctly identified its ingredients; most people have guessed it is chicken or seafood. Do try always to use posole, as it produces a far finer flavor than canned hominy, which should only be substituted as a last resort.

Any leftovers can wait it out in the refrigerator for several weeks. They can be served later as a garnish or major ingredient in a salad on a bed of lettuce, or used as a filling for an avocado half. By adding flaked crab, fish, or chicken with a topping of Creamy Salsa Verde or a dollop of sour cream and lime, you can make a light lunch or tasty snack. Posole en Escabeche can also be served as a garnish for egg dishes or for almost any Mexican entrée on a bed of shredded lettuce or in a lettuce leaf cup.

Makes 8 cups.

1 (1-pound) package dry posole
1/4 cup freshly squeezed lime juice
2 teaspoons salt
1/3 cup virgin olive oil
2 garlic cloves, minced
1 1/2 fresh or dried bay leaves
2 leaves purple sage, chopped, or 1/2 teaspoon dried
1/4 teaspoon Mexican oregano, ground or crushed
1 teaspoon ground cumin
1 Tablespoon ground pure mild California red chile
1 large Spanish onion, thinly sliced, separated into rings
1/2 fresh or canned jalapeño, finely chopped
1 cup white vinegar
1/4 cup coarsely chopped fresh cilantro, divided
4 leafy lettuce leaves
6 ounces warm tostados, preferably made from blue corn (to make your own, see page 162)
1/2 cup Creamy Salsa Verde (page 14)

Rinse and sort the posole. Place the good kernels in a heavy 5-quart cooking pot. Add water and nothing else to cover and boil, covered, until tender—about 2 hours. Cool to room temperature. Be sure not to season until kernels have softened!

As soon as the posole becomes tender but not soft, sprinkle with the lime juice and salt. In the meantime, while the posole is cooking, combine the oil, garlic, bay leaves, sage, oregano, cumin, ground chile, onion, jalapeño, and vinegar. Whip until well blended, using a food processor or blender, or chop the seasonings and herbs and whip with a small whisk or fork.

Pour over the drained, cooled, room-temperature posole and stir well, using a gentle folding motion and taking great care to not break the posole kernels. Add 2 Tablespoons of the cilantro and stir again. Allow to marinate, stirring occasionally, at least 4 hours or overnight. Several days ahead is all right.

Place in a shallow Mexican or earthenware bowl—rectangular, if possible—tucking leafy lettuce leaves into each corner. Garnish with the remaining 2 Tablespoons coarsely chopped cilantro. Serve with a small bowl of toothpicks, the warmed tostados, and a dish of salsa.

— CHICKEN AVOCADO FETTUCCINE —

The creamy-smooth texture of the Monterey Jack sauce laced with New Mexico green chiles blends luxuriously here with the subtle flavors of chicken and avocado. Do buy green noodles if possible, as they are the best partner for the flavors of this dish.

Makes 6 servings.

5 Tablespoons unsalted butter, divided
2 cups fresh white button mushrooms, thinly sliced in half-moons, stems attached
1 1/2 cups cubed, poached chicken breast
Salt
Freshly ground black pepper
1 1/2 cups half-and-half, divided
4 ounces Monterey Jack cheese, cut into 1/2-inch cubes
2 whole New Mexico green chiles, parched, peeled, seeded, and chopped (page 7)
Olive oil
12 ounces green (if not available, substitute white) fettuccine noodles
4 ounces thin natural spaghetti
2 Haas avocados, cut into 1-inch cubes
Freshly grated Parmesan and Romano cheese to taste

Melt 3 Tablespoons of the butter in a heavy large skillet over medium heat. Add the mushrooms and brown lightly. Remove to a plate. Melt the remaining 2 Tablespoons butter in the skillet and add the cubed chicken. Brown lightly. Season with salt and freshly ground pepper.

Return the mushrooms to the skillet and add 1 cup half-and-half, the cubed cheese, and the green chiles. Cook only until the sauce thickens, 3 to 5 minutes, over medium-low heat. Remove from heat. Cover and set aside.

About 15 minutes before serving, bring 5 to 6 cups of water, a splash of olive oil, and 1 Tablespoon salt to a boil in a large pot. When it boils, add the noodles, then the spaghetti, and cook about 9 minutes or until al dente. Meanwhile, peel the avocados by first scoring with a sharp knife, then removing the peel.

Reheat the sauce, taking care not to let it bubble up. Add remaining 1/2 cup half-and-half. Cube the avocado. When the pasta is done, drain, rinse with hot water, and return to the pot. Add the sauce and toss. Serve on warm plates with a side dish of freshly grated Parmesan and Romano.

THREE PEPPER SALAD

A beautiful vision of summer! Any time you can get large, waxy, blemish-free red, yellow, and green bell peppers, try this colorful salad, which is especially pretty served on a bed of fluffy, purple-edged leaf lettuce or baby greens.

Makes 6 servings.

2 garlic cloves, minced
1/2 cup virgin olive oil
1 large green bell pepper
1 large red bell pepper
1 large yellow bell pepper
1 large head red leaf lettuce or baby greens
1/4 cup red wine vinegar

At least 1 hour before serving, marinate the garlic in the oil. Then cut the green, red, and yellow peppers into long, thin strips, removing all the ribs and seeds. Rinse, drain, and chill the lettuce. Chill the salad bowls—clear glass ones are best if you have them. Chill the salad forks. In a jar shake the vinegar with the garlic oil until well mixed. To serve, place the lettuce leaves in the bowls. Add the peppers and lace with the vinaigrette. Serve with a pepper grinder.

MARINATED MELONS WITH MINT

To provide a cool, soothing, and perfectly simple ending to a Southwestern meal, I always like to marry the perfume flavor of a ripe, deep-green honeydew with the less predictable Persian or Casaba melon and tingle the edges with fresh lime, spearmint, and a drizzle of honey.

Makes 6 servings.

1/2 large ripe honeydew melon
1/2 to 1/3 Persian or Casaba melon
Juice of 2 limes
1/2 cup fresh mint leaves, macerated, reserving 6 perfect three-leaf sprigs
1/4 cup fragrant blossom honey

Cut the honeydew lengthwise into six portions. Then carefully cut away from the rind and score into bite-size portions, not cutting completely through the flesh. Place on serving plates, preferably clear glass or pastel plates. Cube the Persian melon. Randomly place on the honeydew. In a small bowl combine the lime juice, mint, and honey (warming honey if thick).

Two hours before serving, drizzle the juice mixture over the melon and set aside loosely covered at room temperature. To serve, garnish with the mint sprigs.

QUIET SCINTILLATING SUPPER

Iced Champagne

Poquito Potatoes with American Gold Caviar

Crab Quiche Mexicano

Chicory Salad with Grapefruit

Mexican Pecan Toffee Tartlets in Chocolate Chip Cookie Crust

Consider this sensuous—almost sinfully so—menu when entertaining six of your nearest and dearest. Or if you prefer, choose it to please your very own dearest, either reserving the balance of the quiche and the tartlets in the freezer, or cutting each recipe in thirds. In either case, it is a relatively simple meal to prepare and a delight to savor in a comfortable, pretty setting. Although the soothing foods I have combined here are particularly pleasing late at night after the theater, or an evening outing of most any kind, this menu, inspired by the innovations of nouvelle cuisine, would be equally appropriate as a late Sunday brunch.

Take some extra time to create an especially beautiful setting for this supper. Select a romantic white-on-white color scheme, using laces, linens, crystal, and sterling items for the table. For the flowers, arrange a very special centerpiece of whatever is seasonal—from white poinsettias to lilies, dogwood, mums, or of course, the grandest of all, white long-stemmed roses. Use fern, smilax, rhododendron, or any similar dark-green leaves to offset the striking arrangement. A tall, vertical arrangement in a clear, round vase is striking. Lay a lime- or dark-green table runner down the width of the table, and decorate with additional greens, stringing an occasional white blossom between them.

MENU PLAN

Day before (or early in the day):

Prepare the potato skins and stuffing for Poquito Potatoes; refrigerate both.

Prepare the quiche and bake.

Prepare the Mexican Pecan Toffee Tartlets and freeze.

Rinse greens, prepare grapefruit sections and onion rings, and wrap each separately.

Prepare salad dressing.

Chill the champagne.

One hour or sometime before:

Chill the salad plates and forks.

Warm the dinner plates and saucers for potatoes.

Place potato skins in a 350°F (180°C) oven 15 minutes before serving. Reheat the potato stuffing.

Place the quiche in same oven, checking it as you remove the potato skins. (It should require 10 to 15 minutes more to be heated through. Watch carefully, however: the quiche should be hot, so that an inserted knife comes out clean and steam releases, but not too hot, or it will break down and become watery.)

At serving time:
Stuff the potato skins and serve with champagne.
Arrange the salad on the chilled plates.
Pour dressing over each and serve with the quiche.
Serve the dessert.

———— POQUITO POTATOES ————

WITH AMERICAN GOLD CAVIAR

So wonderful you really should allow three to four per person—unless your guests have very hearty appetites, in which case allow up to six. First popularized in Northern California, these elegant appetizers prove that the whole is often more than the sum of its parts.

Makes 6 servings.

18 to 24 new potatoes, 1 1/2 to 2 inches in diameter
4 Tablespoons unsalted butter, divided
3/4 teaspoon salt
Several grinds of black pepper
1 cup sour cream, divided
2 ounces American gold caviar or other type

Preheat oven to 425°F (220°C). Wash the potatoes and blot dry, then butter the skins, using no more than 2 Tablespoons. Place them on a baking sheet. Bake 30 minutes, then squeeze gently, using a potholder to protect your hands. If they are done, the potatoes will yield to pressure and the skins will be somewhat crisp.

When done, allow to cool slightly, then cut each in half. Using a sharp knife, cut about 1/4 inch in from the skin and scoop out contents of each potato and place in a large bowl of a food processor. Add the remaining 2 Tablespoons butter, salt, pepper, and a scoop of the sour cream and beat until the potatoes are fluffy.

If serving immediately, return the skins to the hot oven and bake about 20 minutes more to really crisp the skins. If preparing the potatoes earlier in the day or even a day or two before, refrigerate, then wait to crisp the skins in a 350°F (180°C) oven just before you are ready to serve.

For refrigerated potatoes and stuffing, heat the skins as above and reheat the mashed potatoes. If using a microwave, cover and heat for a minute, then rotate a quarter turn, continuing until hot. If using a double boiler, place in covered top pan over the boiling water and heat for 10 to 15 minutes or until hot.

To serve, spoon the potato filling back into the shells, dividing it evenly among them. Then top each with the remaining sour cream and garnish with caviar. Serve very warm on warm saucers or if serving informally from a buffet, place them on a heated serving tray and encourage guests to eat them with their hands.

CRAB QUICHE MEXICANO

My guests, and especially my daughter, Amy, have always been so fond of this dish that they never cease to request repeat appearances. Prepare it in advance and reheat, or because it can be held uncooked a few hours, assemble the quiche, go to the theater, and bake just before serving.

Makes 6 servings.

3 wheat tortillas
1/4 cup lard
4 fresh green chiles, parched, peeled, and deseeded (page 7)
3/4 cup shredded Monterey Jack cheese
3/4 cup shredded yellow Cheddar cheese
1 (6 1/2-ounce) can flaked crab or 3/4 cup fresh or frozen
3 chopped green onions (scallions), including some of the tops
1 Tablespoon coarsely chopped cilantro, optional
4 large eggs
1 1/2 cups half-and-half
Few grinds of black pepper
1/2 teaspoon salt
3/4 teaspoon caribe or other crushed dried red chile
2 or more green chiles, parched, peeled, deseeded, and chopped (page 7), optional
1/2 cup sour cream, optional

Select a round cake pan that is the same diameter as the tortilla so that it will just fit. Then cut 2 of the tortillas in half. Melt the lard in a heavy skillet and fry all the tortillas until lightly browned on each side and drain on paper towels.

Arrange the whole fried tortilla in the bottom of the pan, then stand the halves of tortilla around the rim of the baking pan, creating a crust. Place the whole green chiles in a smooth, uniform layer over the fried tortilla on the bottom of the baking pan. Mix the Monterey Jack and Cheddar together, and top tortilla with 1 cup of the shredded cheeses, the crab, onions, and the cilantro.

Meanwhile, beat the eggs with the half-and-half, pepper, and salt. Pour over all, then top with the remaining 1/2 cup of shredded cheese and sprinkle with the caribe. If baking later, cover and refrigerate.

When ready to bake, place in a 375°F (190°C) oven for 30 to 40 minutes, or until puffed and lightly browned. Serve with the chopped green chiles and sour cream if desired. If some in the family like the cilantro and others do not, the cilantro can be served separately.

CHICORY SALAD WITH GRAPEFRUIT

Both tart and light, this salad is an ideal counterpoint to any seafood, chicken, or pork main dish as well as to quiches.

    1 head of curly chicory
    2 large red grapefruit, peeled
    6 thin slices of a large, round red salad onion
    1/2 cup salad oil
    1/4 cup white wine vinegar
    1 Tablespoon honey

Using chilled plates, place the chicory leaves on each, artfully topping each with a pinwheel design created from the grapefruit sections, which have been carefully cut from the membrane. Be careful not to allow any white from the skin to remain. Top each with the separated onion rings. In a small bowl combine the oil, vinegar, and honey and drizzle over each.

MEXICAN PECAN TOFFEE TARTLETS
IN CHOCOLATE CHIP COOKIE CRUST

Who doesn't like chocolate chip cookies? Judging from the thriving cookie establishments and cookie wars announced by the trade, we know they're a hit, and when combined with pecan-studded coffee-toffee ice cream pie filling, the result is a rich blend of flavors that no dessert-lover can resist.

Makes 6 servings.

24 small or 12 medium-size chocolate chip cookies
4 Tablespoons unsalted butter, melted
1 pint coffee ice cream (select a good, rich one)
1 (4-ounce) toffee candy bar
1/2 cup very coarsely chopped pecan halves, divided
1/2 pint heavy whipping cream
3 Tablespoons vanilla-scented sugar (made by storing sugar with a broken piece of vanilla bean)
1/2 cup thick, rich chocolate fudge sauce

Using a food processor, blender, or a rolling pin, crush the cookies until finely crumbed. Butter the insides of 6 small soufflé cups or any other suitable small serving dishes—even coffee cups.

Combine remaining butter with the cookie crumbs in a bowl. Divide the mixture evenly among the 6 cups, then press it firmly into them. Freeze.

Soften the ice cream by scooping it into a mixing bowl and letting it set a few minutes, then process in a food processor or mixer. Crush the toffee bar in the processor or with a rolling pin until it is in chunks about 1/2 inch across, not too fine. Add to the ice cream along with 1/3 cup of the pecans. Process or mix until just combined so as not to overly crush the texture of the candy and the nuts. Divide among the cookie crusts, leaving the surface of each somewhat uneven and interesting looking as you would frosting.

Meanwhile, whip the cream with the vanilla sugar. Divide the chocolate fudge sauce among each of the tarts, drizzling it in a swirl in the center of each, allowing some of the ice cream filling around the edges to show.

Top each with a dollop of the whipped cream. If you have too much, place the extra in dollops on a cookie sheet covered with wax paper and freeze for later garnishing for drinks or desserts. Sprinkle reserved pecan pieces over the top of the cream. Freeze until serving time.

LATE NIGHT'S PLEASURE

Champagne
Avocado Torta Salada
Chimis Maximos
Mint Chocolate Mousse with Chocolate Fudge Sauce

Another menu for late-night dining, this meal was developed for those who agree that living well is the best revenge. There is nothing tired or predictable here: showy, spicy first courses are followed by a refreshing fillip of dark chocolate mousse tinged with mint.

Popping the cork on the champagne just as soon as you've arrived home will keep the guests pleasantly occupied while you quickly make the guacamole and assemble the torta, which doubles as an appetizer and salad. Then warm the chimis and presto—you can be your own party guest.

Serve this dinner informally in a cozy, comfortable area: in the winter, before the fireplace; in warmer months, on the patio or in the living room. Simple table settings are best here. All you need are large napkins wrapped around the silverware.

MENU PLAN

Day before (or several days before):
Prepare the Carne Adobado for the Chimis Maximos and fry or bake them.
Fry or bake the tostados for the torta.
Make the Chocolate Fudge Sauce.

Early in the day:
Chill the champagne.
Fill, roll, and bake the chimis.
Make the mousse, spoon into individual parfait or sherbet glasses, and chill.
Whip the cream and chill.
Prepare the ingredients for the torta.

At serving time:
Serve the champagne while you heat the tostados, make the guacamole, and assemble the torta.
Warm the chimis and serve with the torta.
Warm the Chocolate Fudge Sauce. Top the individual mousses with whipped cream and crème de menthe. Serve with the sauce.

AVOCADO TORTA SALADA

This novel and attractive way to serve guacamole, the all-time favorite Tex-Mex salad or dip, involves forming a "torta" by layering the guacamole with warm tostados and crisp, crunchy vegetables. Though it must be assembled at the very last moment, it can be prepared in minutes if you ready all the ingredients ahead.

Makes 6 servings.

1 quart cooking oil*
12 corn tortillas
3 ripe avocados, preferably Haas
1/2 cup finely chopped red or white Spanish onion
1 medium red ripe tomato, peeled and chopped medium-fine
2 garlic cloves, finely minced
1 jalapeño, very finely minced
1/4 cup cilantro, coarsely chopped
Juice of 1 lime
1 teaspoon salt, divided
12 cherry tomatoes, halved
1 green bell pepper, cut in 1/2-inch-wide strips
1 yellow bell pepper, cut in 1/2-inch-wide strips
1 red bell pepper, cut in 1/2-inch-wide strips

You may bake these at 425°F (220°C) at the same time you are baking the chimis if you choose to bake both and save hundreds of calories. If frying, heat the cooking oil to 375°F (190°C) in an electric fryer or cooking pot.

If baking the tortillas, place 2 on a cookie sheet with a smaller sheet on top. After 5 minutes of baking, remove the top sheet, as it is used to keep the tortillas flat. Bake until crisp—about 3 to 5 more minutes. For the remaining 10, quarter and spread on a sheet pan, turning every 3 to 5 minutes to evenly crisp. Or fry 2 whole tortillas and quarter the remaining 10, using a sharp knife or scissors to make 4 deep cuts almost to the center, dividing each into fourths. Do not cut apart as they will be much easier to fry. When crisply fried, remove and drain. When slightly cooled, tap the center portion and they will quickly fall into fourths (tostados). Lightly salt.

Just before serving, warm the tostados for 15 minutes in a 350°F (180°C) oven while making the guacamole. Cut each avocado in half and scoop the flesh into a bowl. Coarsely chop the avocado using a knife and fork, then add the chopped onion, tomato, garlic, and jalapeño. Add lime juice to taste and 3/4 teaspoon salt.

Arrange the torta by placing one of the flat, crisply fried tortillas on an attractive serving plate. Top with about one-third of the guacamole, then add a few of the cherry tomato halves. Add the other fried tortilla and top with the remaining guacamole. Garnish with the rest of the tomato halves, the tostados, and the strips of pepper to make an artistic arrangement. The remaining tomato, peppers, and tostados should be scattered around the plate to create an attractive presentation. To serve, either allow guests to eat the top layer and break the whole crisp-fried tortilla tostados into pieces or cut into sixths and arrange on 6 individual plates.

CHIMIS MAXIMOS

"Maximo" in the name of this recipe for wonderful-tasting, crisp chimis refers not only to their being about as good as you'll ever eat but also to the fact that they are truly maximally filled—with carne adobado, a personal favorite. If you can't find the twelve-inch tortillas, adjust the amount of each filling accordingly.

Makes 6 servings (double for hearty appetites).

6 cups Carne Adobado (recipe follows)
1 1/2 cups cooked pinto beans
1 1/2 teaspoons lard
1 large garlic clove, finely minced
1 cup finely chopped Spanish onion, divided
6 (12-inch) wheat tortillas or largest available
1 quart cooking oil or 2 pounds lard, if frying
1 cup sour cream
1 cup coarsely shredded Cheddar cheese
1 cup coarsely shredded Monterey Jack cheese
6 lettuce leaves, coarsely torn (use red leaf or a bright-green leafy lettuce, not iceberg)
6 cherry tomatoes, halved

Prepare the carne adobado the night before or up to 3 months ahead and freeze. Refry the pinto beans by placing the lard in a heavy skillet; when melted, add the garlic. When it begins to turn golden, add 1 Tablespoon of the finely chopped onion and cook until it begins to soften; then add the beans and mash and fry until the mixture becomes stiff and almost dry.

Warm the wheat tortillas to room temperature. If not extremely fresh, steam slightly in a steamer or put in the microwave oven for 15 seconds each. Place 1/4 cup warm refried beans on each tortilla, working with one at a time. Add 1 cup carne adobado and 1 Tablespoon chopped onion. Roll each as for a blintz, bringing the bottom over the filling with about one-fourth of a tortilla overlap. Then fold in the tortilla from each side. Fold the top down over the filling and secure with toothpicks. Set aside. These can be filled and rolled up to 12 hours in advance.

Bake in a 425°F (220°C) oven for 12 to 15 minutes on a well-greased baking sheet or deep-fry in 375°F (190°C) oil or lard until each is golden brown. Drain on paper towels. Before serving, warm them in a 350°F (180°C) oven for about 15 to 20 minutes or until thoroughly warmed.

Garnish with sour cream, shredded cheeses, and remaining onion, placing them in a ribbon over the top of each. Then garnish the plates with lettuce and tomato halves.

CARNE ADOBADO

One of the best, if not the very best-tasting pork creations from northern New Mexico. Traceable back to Conquistador days, this dish has somehow never gained the favor it deserves. I always make a full five-pound recipe because I like to have lots available for burritos, tacos, enchiladas, main dish servings, or over rice, beans, or eggs.

Makes 3 1/2 quarts.

4 cups water
1/2 cup caribe or other crushed dried red chile
1/4 cup ground pure California or mild red chile
1/4 cup ground pure southern New Mexico hot chile
3 large garlic cloves, minced
2 Tablespoons freshly ground cumin
2 Tablespoons freshly ground Mexican oregano
2 teaspoons salt 5 1/2 pounds bone-in shoulder or loin pork chops, cut 1/2 inch thick (trimmed so as to keep a narrow layer of fat around the edges)

Place the water in a large blender jar—if using a 1-quart blender jar, add only 2 cups water, then add the caribe, red chile, hot chile, garlic, cumin, oregano, and salt and blend until smooth. If using the smaller blender, stir in 2 more cups water. Using a large 10 x 14-inch lasagna pan or similar baking pan, pour one-half of the chile mixture into pan, then dip each pork chop into the marinade and turn over. Add balance of chile mixture to top of pork chops. Let marinate 2 hours at room temperature, periodically spooning the chile mixture over the top and turning the chops over. Then refrigerate overnight. (The pork can be frozen for up to 3 months at this point.)

In the morning, bake at 325°F (170°C), covered with a lid or foil for the first 45 minutes. After removing the cover, bake another hour or hour and a half, spooning the sauce over the chops every 30 minutes.

Let cool on the counter. Using a sharp knife, remove the bones and pull the meat apart with your fingers to shred the pork into rather coarse 1- to 2-inch pieces. Place the shredded meat back in the baking dish. Return to the oven to allow the sauce to cook in—about 30 minutes. When done, the pork should be a bright rosy-red color and the meat should be very tender.

Note: If the sauce is rather dry and firm, stir in enough water to make the consistency of gravy before adding the meat back into the sauce. If rather dry, heat covered—if the sauce is rather soupy, leave uncovered.

—— MINT CHOCOLATE MOUSSE ——

This is enormously soothing as a finishing touch after foods that are seething hot—which the chimis certainly can be. Make the mousse up to six hours ahead, then serve in parfait glasses with a dollop of whipped cream swished with a drizzle of crème de menthe, and with the Chocolate Fudge Sauce that follows.

Makes 6 servings.

6 squares good-quality semisweet chocolate
3/8 cup water
6 large eggs, separated
3/4 cup plus 2 Tablespoons superfine sugar, divided
1/4 cup heavy cream
2 Tablespoons white or green crème de menthe, plus additional for pouring over the top
Chocolate Fudge Sauce (recipe follows)

Combine the chocolate and water in the top of a double boiler or place over low heat and melt, stirring occasionally, yet watching carefully to prevent burning. When melted, set aside.

Beat the egg whites in a large bowl of an electric mixer until very stiff, making sure that there is no fat of any kind on the beaters or in the whites, as it will prevent stiff whites. Place the yolks in a large bowl, then add 3/4 cup sugar very gradually, continuing to beat until thick and lemon colored. Add the cooled, melted chocolate and beat until well blended.

Stir about 1 cup of the egg whites into the chocolate mixture, then blend well. Add this mixture to the rest of the egg whites, using a rubber scraper to fold the two mixtures together to form a very smooth chocolaty mixture.

Make the whipped cream by beating heavy cream with 2 Tablespoons superfine sugar in electric mixer. Serve with dollops of whipped cream drizzled with a few drops of crème de menthe. Serve a pitcher of crème de menthe on the side, as well as the warm Chocolate Fudge Sauce, for guests to help themselves.

CHOCOLATE FUDGE SAUCE

This creamy, rich sauce is best served slightly warm over the mousse. If there's any left, reheat it carefully and you have a fondue for fresh fruits: strawberries, bananas, and squares of pineapple.

Makes 6 to 8 servings.

6 squares good-quality unsweetened chocolate
1 cup half-and-half
1 1/2 cups sugar
1/2 cup (1 stick) unsalted butter
1/8 teaspoon salt
2 teaspoons pure vanilla extract
1/2 teaspoon ground cinnamon
1 1/2 ounces Kahlúa

Place the chocolate, half-and-half, sugar, butter, salt, vanilla, cinnamon, and Kahlúa in a small heavy saucepan and heat over medium-low heat, stirring frequently. Cook and stir until the chocolate melts, then reduce the heat to low and continue cooking for 5 minutes more. Allow to set at room temperature, then warm over low heat to serve with the mousse.

FESTIVE FORMAL DINNER FOR FOUR

Perfect Margaritas
Marinated Mexican Mushrooms
Creamy Chilled Cucumber Sopa with Cheesed Tortilla Strips
Watermelon Sorbet
Swordfish with Lime Anchovy/Caper Butter Grilled over Mesquite
Pasta Shells with Caribe and Eggplant
Watercress Jícama Salad
Double Blueberry Delight with Crème Fraîche

Whenever you're in the mood for a somewhat extravagant dinner party that is not terribly tough to pull off, consider this one. This menu is really a showcase for the foods of late summer, and from the Perfect Margaritas down to the Double Blueberry Delight, you'll be very pleased with how smoothly the flavors flow.

With some early preparation, you can quite easily add the finishing touches with only minimal kitchen time. I strongly urge you to serve the dinner in seven courses, starting with the Marinated Mexican Mushrooms and margaritas in a social setting, say in the living room or out on the patio. Then proceed to serve each item individually—using your finest china, crystal, and sterling on a snowy white linen tablecloth. White roses would make a lovely centerpiece.

Menu Plan

Day before (or early in the day):
Prepare the Marinated Mexican Mushrooms.
Prepare the Creamy Chilled Cucumber Sopa and Cheesed Tortilla Strips.
Prepare the Watermelon Sorbet.

Two hours before:
Prepare the Lime Anchovy/Caper Butter.
Prepare the sauce for the pasta dish.
Slice the eggplant, salt it, and place between layers of paper towels. Thirty minutes later, dice and fry the eggplant.
Set out the kettle with water for boiling the pasta and all remaining ingredients.
Prepare the jícama, rinse the watercress, and make the salad dressing. Chill separately.
Prepare the Double Blueberry Delight with Crème Fraîche.
Frost the glasses for the margaritas.
Chill the wine, salad plates, soup bowls, and goblets or sherbets for the dessert.
Set out the coffeemaker.
Start the fire to grill the fish.

At serving time:

Add the 1 cup fresh berries to the cooked blueberries.

Make the margaritas just before the guests arrive.

Set out the Marinated Mexican Mushrooms and serve with the margaritas.

About 15 minutes before serving the soup, warm the Cheesed Tortilla Strips and boil the water for the pasta.

Heat the plates for the fish and the pasta.

Boil the pasta while you serve Cucumber Sopa with the Cheesed Tortilla Strips.

Start to grill the fish.

Warm the sauce and eggplant for the pasta dish.

Turn the fish and serve the sorbet.

Serve the fish on heated plates.

Combine the ingredients for the pasta dish and serve on heated plates.

Toss the jícama and watercress with the dressing and serve the salad on chilled plates.

Serve the Blueberry Delight in chilled goblets along with coffee.

PERFECT MARGARITAS

Be prepared! These high-octane margaritas just might sweep some of your guests off their feet. They are wonderfully flavored, made according to the most potent of formulas. For the very best margaritas always squeeze fresh limes, preferably the juicy, thin-skinned, yellowish Mexican variety, which have the traditional pungent flavor. In a pinch the dark green, thicker-skinned Persian limes will work too. Take a shortcut and squeeze the limes whenever you can get them, and keep the juice frozen. Whenever I am near the Mexican border or in the Caribbean, I put away quantities of freshly squeezed lime juice in half-pint freezer containers or jars and bring them home solidly frozen. Be sure to keep the juice frozen until you use it.

For the tequila, always buy at least 80 proof, made from the blue agave plant, sometimes called *mezcal* in Spanish or mescal in English. The very finest tequilas are 92 proof. To be labeled all natural, with the NOM seal, the Mexican tequila distillers' association requires that only 100 percent agave be used. Under Mexican law, however, tequila need only contain as little as 51 percent blue agave in order to be called tequila. The gold tequila is not worth the extra money as these products contain caramel coloring extenders.

Offer only one round—at most two—before serving the delectable dinner. The Marinated Mushrooms are a delicious cocktail nibble alongside the margaritas.

Makes 4 large margaritas.

8 fresh limes, preferably Mexican varieties
Coarse salt
1/2 cup triple sec or to taste
1 1/2 cups 80-proof pure agave silver tequila
1 large egg white
Crushed ice

Squeeze the limes, being certain to get all the flesh plus the juice. Measure, and use only 1/2 cup juice. Reserve the rest.

Prepare the glasses. If salt is desired, rub one of the lime rinds from squeezing around the top rim of the glass. Crunch the glass into the salt. Then place in the freezer—allowing at least 30 minutes to really frost.

Meanwhile, prepare the margaritas by placing the lime juice, triple sec, tequila, and 1 teaspoon beaten egg white in the blender. Add ice so the blender is about half full. Process. If the texture is not slushy enough, add ice to desired texture. Taste and add more triple sec if not sweet enough. Serve immediately in the frosted glasses.

Note: You can freeze leftover margaritas for at least a month.

MARINATED MEXICAN MUSHROOMS

Since I first sampled them in Hermosillo, Mexico, these mushrooms have been a favorite of mine. None ever goes begging, but should any be left, they are delicious as a salad dressing.

Makes 4 servings.

12 ounces (2- to 3-inch) white button mushrooms, wiped clean and stemmed
1/3 cup virgin olive oil
1/3 cup white wine vinegar
2 garlic cloves, minced
1 teaspoon caribe or other crushed dried red chile
1/2 teaspoon Mexican oregano
1/4 teaspoon salt
1 large Spanish onion, thinly sliced and separated into rings

Put the mushrooms in a heatproof bowl. Then combine the oil, vinegar, garlic, caribe, oregano, and salt in a saucepan and bring to a boil, adding the onions once the mixture begins to boil. Cook and stir frequently until the onions just begin to lose their crispness. Pour over the mushrooms, and let them marinate at room temperature for at least 2 hours, stirring frequently.

Chill just before serving. They can be made several days before—they keep very well up to a week. I like to serve these in a shallow rectangular or oval bowl, with the mushrooms surrounding the edges and the onions in the center. Add a sprinkle of the caribe for an added touch. Serve with toothpicks.

CREAMY CHILLED CUCUMBER SOPA

This quickly prepared sopa, or soup, is also good for a light lunch with finger sandwiches or a salad. It will keep up to three days in the refrigerator.

Makes 4 servings.

1 Tablespoon unsalted butter
1 medium cucumber, peeled, seeded, and coarsely chopped
1/4 cup sliced green onions (scallions), very thinly cut, greens and all, discarding the coarse ends, divided
1 1/4 cups skim milk
1 teaspoon chicken bouillon granules (1 packet) or bouillon paste
2 Tablespoons cilantro, coarsely chopped, divided
1/2 cup nonfat plain yogurt
1 Tablespoon ground pure mild red chile

In a small saucepan melt the butter, then add the cucumber and 2 Tablespoons of the onion and cook and stir until the cucumber becomes clear and somewhat soft, about 3 minutes.

Put in a blender or food processor, add the milk, chicken bouillon, and 1 Tablespoon of the cilantro. Process until smooth. Stir in the yogurt. Pour into a small pitcher or bowl and chill. To serve, pour into small bowls, cups, or wineglasses and garnish with the remaining cilantro, then sprinkle with the mild chile.

CHEESED TORTILLA STRIPS

A great topper for soups and salads, Cheesed Tortilla Strips might be considered a kind of Tex-Mex crouton. They are also a great way to use tired corn tortillas. For a variation, you can leave them plain or sprinkle with chile or other spices.

Makes 4 servings.

2 corn tortillas, cut into strips 1/2 inch wide and 3 inches long, discarding the odd-shaped corner pieces
1 quart cooking oil or can be baked
1/4 cup shredded Moneterey Jack cheese
1/4 cup shredded Cheddar cheese

Cut the tortilla strips while the oil is heating to 375°F (190°C). Then fry a batch at a time in a fry basket until the bubbles subside and the strips are crisp and golden. Quickly drain each batch on paper towels, place on a cookie sheet, and sprinkle with the cheese while still hot.

If baking, preheat the oven to 425°F (220°C). Place on a large sheet pan spread out over surface of pan. Bake 5 to 8 minutes or until crisp. When removing from oven, quickly sprinkle with the cheese.

When all are fried or baked, place in a 350°F (180°C) oven for 5 to 10 minutes to melt the cheese. They should be rewarmed if prepared in advance, as they taste best warm.

WATERMELON SORBET

Watermelon has been a special favorite of the Pueblo Indians in New Mexico for centuries. The mountain range sheltering the east side of Albuquerque is named Sandia, which is Pueblo Indian for watermelon—a fruit they stash away in caves between layers of straw. I have even been served watermelon in Pueblo homes in the winter. Although its flesh had almost caramelized into a deep, rosy-tan color, it was wonderfully flavored.

I am quite fond of this simple summery palate cleanser, as either a course after spicy foods or as a dessert. Choose an extra ripe, thumping good watermelon for the best flavor. Sorbet is a wonderful way to preserve summer's bounty, as it will keep its flavor for about six months in the freezer.

Makes 2 quarts.

8 cups cubed, seeded watermelon
Juice of 1 fresh lime, preferably Mexican variety (at least 3 teaspoons)

Process the watermelon and lime juice in a blender or food processor until it is frothy and pulpy. Place in a large bowl, preferably stainless steel as it will freeze best. Place on the bottom of the freezer and stir every 30 minutes until firm. This takes about 3 hours. If making in advance, place in the refrigerator 2 to 3 hours in advance of serving. To serve, make little balls of sorbet using a round teaspoon or melon scoop, and place 3 to 5 in a fluted wineglass.

Note: Other melons or fruits can be substituted.

SWORDFISH

WITH LIME ANCHOVY/CAPER BUTTER GRILLED OVER MESQUITE

Elegant and easy, this grilled dish is distinguished by the special smokiness of mesquite, a flavor many have come to love. Being a westerner, however, and having coped with it for pasturage, I find it difficult to devote a lot of resources—either time or money—hunting for it. Substitute a good hardwood charcoal, if you wish, tossing on some smoky wood chips of hickory, oak, or fruitwood, or use grapevine cuttings.

Shark or other firm-fleshed, substantial fish can be substituted for the swordfish. The lime butter is a delightful, light, and delicious foil for the strength of the anchovies.

Makes 4 servings.

1 large lime
1/2 cup (1 stick) unsalted butter, softened
1 (2-ounce) tin flat anchovy fillets
2 Tablespoons capers
Vegetable oil or spray oil
4 (6- to 8-ounce) swordfish steaks
1 small bunch watercress, rinsed

Build a small fire of mesquite or other hardwood charcoal briquets and let it rest and become white coals. If using charcoal, then toss on soaked wood chips. When it smolders a good bit, you are ready to grill the fish.

Meanwhile, prepare the butter by squeezing the lime and mixing the juice into the butter, adding smashed anchovies and capers. Mix in a mortar or in a small heavy bowl.

Oil the grill with a cloth soaked with vegetable oil or generously spray on oil. Use tongs so you can coat the grill well and prevent burning your fingers. Raise the rack to a height of 6 inches above the coals.

Place the fish on the grill and sear the first side. After about 5 minutes, turn and grill the other side. Five minutes later, check to be sure the flesh is cooked. It should be very moist and dull looking, not shiny like raw fish. When done, arrange on warmed plates and place a large spoonful of the lime/anchovy butter on each serving. Garnish each plate with a handful of watercress.

PASTA SHELLS WITH CARIBE AND EGGPLANT

The hearty flavor of this pasta preparation is a perfect accompaniment to any subtle seafood, veal, or chicken dish.

Makes 4 servings.

2 Tablespoons plus 1/4 cup virgin olive oil, divided
1 (16-ounce) can crushed Italian plum tomatoes
1 Tablespoon minced fresh basil leaves or 1 teaspoon dried
1 1/2 teaspoons finely chopped fresh oregano or 1/2 teaspoon dried
1 eggplant, about 1 pound
1 1/2 teaspoons salt
8 ounces pasta shells
1 Tablespoon salad oil
1/4 cup freshly grated Romano cheese
1 1/2 teaspoons caribe or other crushed dried red chile

Heat 2 Tablespoons olive oil, then add the tomatoes, basil, and oregano. Allow to simmer over very low heat.

Meanwhile, cut the rinsed eggplant into 1/2-inch-thick slices. Generously salt each side of the slices. Place between double sheets of paper towels. Top with another layer, always making sure to place the towels between layers. Allow the eggplant to set for about 30 minutes.

Cut the eggplant into 1/2-inch cubes. Heat the 1/4 cup olive oil in a very large heavy skillet. Add the cubes of eggplant and cook and turn until each square is browned. Set aside.

About 15 minutes before serving, bring 4 quarts of salted water to a boil, adding salad oil. Add the pasta and cook according to the package instructions—6 to 8 minutes—or until it becomes al dente. Taste and adjust seasonings in the sauce.

To serve, place the drained pasta shells in a large heated bowl. Add the sauce and the fried eggplant cubes. Sprinkle with the cheese and the caribe and toss well. Taste and adjust flavors, if desired.

WATERCRESS JÍCAMA SALAD

Light, delicate-looking, and tangily dressed, Watercress Jícama Salad sets the scene ideally for the dessert to follow.

Makes 4 servings.

1 cup peeled jícama cut in long, slender matchsticks
1 fresh lime
1 teaspoon caribe or other crushed dried red chile
1 teaspoon coarse sea salt
1/2 cup walnut oil
3/4 cup raspberry vinegar
1 large garlic clove, minced
1 teaspoon Dijon mustard
1 good-size bunch of watercress, rinsed and stems removed

Cover a shallow pan with wax paper and lay the jícama out in a single layer. Squeeze lime juice over, then sprinkle with the chile and salt. Allow to marinate for 30 minutes. Meanwhile, prepare the salad dressing, combining the oil, vinegar, garlic, and mustard in a small bowl; whisk and set aside. Chill the jícama and watercress until serving time. Combine at the very last moment, lightly tossing with the dressing.

— DOUBLE BLUEBERRY DELIGHT —
WITH CRÈME FRAÎCHE

I discovered this dessert quite by accident one weekend while cooking at our cottage, which has bountiful blueberries, both wild and domestic. With such abundance, I've had great fun experimenting and am quite pleased with the friendly flavors of this particular result, especially when it follows a meal with a complex array of tastes. You can substitute almost any berry here, and even prepare the dish a day or two ahead.

Makes 4 servings.

1 pint ripe blueberries
1/2 cup freshly squeezed orange juice
1/2 cup sugar or more to taste
1 teaspoon freshly grated orange rind
1 teaspoon freshly grated lemon rind
Few grinds of fresh nutmeg (a generous pinch)
1 ounce Grand Marnier or Cointreau
1/2 cup (4 ounces) crème fraîche
8 to 12 finely cut fresh orange curls

Rinse and sort the blueberries, discarding any that are blemished or not good. Reserve 1 cup of fresh berries. Place the balance in a small heavy saucepan. Add the orange juice, sugar, and orange and lemon rinds. Cook over low heat until the berries cook down, about 30 minutes. Then add the nutmeg and liqueur. Taste and adjust the seasoning if desired—the flavor should be somewhat intense. Cool in a medium-size earthenware or stoneware bowl. Before serving the appetizers, add the uncooked blueberries.

To serve, place in goblets and top each with a Tablespoon of crème fraîche and a few fresh, finely grated curls of orange rind.

APRÈS SKI

Hot Buttered Rum
Janet's Chile Meatballs
Enchiladas Suizas
Chablis
Manzanos en Crisp

Following any kind of winter activity, nothing could be more satisfying than spicy, filling Southwestern food. Here is a menu designed for entertaining hungry, cold, weary guests, giving them instant gratification and sparing the cook any frantic last-minute preparation. All the dishes in the meal can be prepared well in advance and easily heated just before serving. While you and your guests are warming up, the foods will be too, ready soon for serving in front of a fire or around a big kitchen or dining room table.

The Chile Meatballs are a delicious appetizer, perfect with hot buttered rum, and are especially memorable grilled in a fireplace over a hibachi. The Enchiladas Suizas recipe has been adapted to use easily available ingredients and suffers not a bit from advance preparation—even freezing. The Manzanos en Crisp also bears up wonderfully well under the same treatment. Served warm with whipped cream or rich vanilla ice cream, it is, to quote my father, "food for the gods."

Keep the decor rustic and minimal. I always like to serve a meal like this on a quilt, either on the floor in front of the fire or simply on the table. Use calico or gingham napkins and tin or pottery plates. Lacking any fresh flowers, create a centerpiece of waxy vegetables or fresh fruits.

MENU PLAN

One day before (or up to three months in advance):
Prepare the batter for the Hot Buttered Rums and refrigerate.
Prepare and bake the Chile Meatballs. Refrigerate or freeze.
Prepare the Enchiladas Suizas and refrigerate or freeze.

Two hours before:
Chill the wine.
Make the Caliente Dip.
Prepare the Manzanos en Crisp.
Place the meatballs out for grilling or broiling.
Preheat the oven for the Enchiladas Suizas and Manzanos en Crisp.

At serving time:
Broil the Chile Meatballs and serve with the dip and Hot Buttered Rum.
Meanwhile, bake the Enchiladas Suizas and Manzanos en Crisp.
Serve the enchiladas piping hot with the wine, then serve the dessert.

HOT BUTTERED RUM

Christmas tree decorating after skiing, sledding, ice skating, or almost any cold, snowy, robust activity is the perfect time for really good "hot butters." Although this recipe is for one drink, because it should ideally be prepared individually, you can make several at a time by stirring up a batch of the batter (multiply the amounts of ingredients accordingly) and keeping it handy in the refrigerator.

Makes one 8-ounce drink.

1 Tablespoon unsalted butter, softened
1/2 Tablespoon dark brown sugar
1/8 teaspoon ground cinnamon
Few gratings of fresh nutmeg
1/2 teaspoon Grand Marnier
2 whole cloves
2 ounces dark rum
1 cup boiling water
Cinnamon stick
Orange peel, cut in one long strip, optional

In a small bowl combine the butter, brown sugar, cinnamon, nutmeg, and Grand Marnier until well blended. (If you wish to prepare a quantity of the batter, increase the amounts of each of the ingredients proportionally and refrigerate until used.) Place about 1 1/2 Tablespoons of the batter in each mug and add the whole cloves, rum, and boiling water. Stir until well blended. Garnish with a cinnamon stick and strip of orange peel, if desired.

JANET'S CHILE MEATBALLS

Janet Beers Pugh, my childhood friend whom I lured to New Mexico in 1966 and who is now a confirmed New Mexican, developed these for a party. I liked them so much that she generously shared the recipe. They are a snappy variation on Swedish meatballs and, as they can be frozen for at least three months, are an especially convenient appetizer. Vary the dipping sauce if you wish—use your favorite salsa, chile con queso, or even guacamole.

Makes 6 generous servings.

2 large egg yolks or 1 whole large egg
1/2 cup dry bread crumbs
1 cup shredded sharp Cheddar cheese
2 Tablespoons ground pure red chile (use the hotness you prefer—I like New Mexico hot)
1 teaspoon salt
1 pound ground lean beef

Preheat the oven to 350°F (180°C). In a large bowl, if using the yolks, beat together with 1/2 cup water. If using a whole egg, use 1/3 cup water. Add the bread crumbs, cheese, chile, salt, and beef and lightly mix together. Form 1-inch meatballs and place on a jelly roll pan. Bake 10 minutes, then drain well on paper towels and let cool.

These can be prepared ahead and left to await the serving hour, or they can be frozen in rigid containers in layers with wax paper between. To serve, broil over a hibachi in the fireplace on long skewers or under the broiler in your oven. Serve hot and crisp with the following sauce or one of your selection.

CALIENTE DIP

2 hot red pickled cherry peppers, finely chopped
2 whole pickled hot jalapeños, finely chopped
1/2 cup halved and thinly sliced stuffed green olives
1/2 cup thinly sliced pitted black olives
3/4 cup good-quality virgin olive oil

Combine cherry peppers, jalapeños, green olives, black olives, and oil in a saucepan and bring to a simmer. Serve hot as a dip for the meatballs. Even better, serve an additional dip or two—perhaps one mild creamy one and another spicy but cold one.

ENCHILADAS SUIZAS

I developed this adaptation of one of the most popular Southwestern dishes to use green chiles, which are more easily available than the traditionally used tomatillos. Although canned chiles are acceptable, fresh ones or those you have parched and frozen have much better flavor. Always cook the chicken yourself so that you have the wonderfully rich stock to use for creating the sauce.

Makes 6 servings.

THE CHICKEN

3 chicken thighs and legs or 2 chicken breasts
1 large carrot, cut into thirds
1 celery rib, quartered
1 medium Spanish onion, coarsely chopped
1 teaspoon dried thyme, crumbled
1/2 teaspoon salt

THE SAUCE

2 Tablespoons unsalted butter
1/4 cup all-purpose flour
1 cup coarsely shredded Monterey Jack cheese
1 cup coarsely shredded Cheddar cheese
Few sprigs fresh cilantro, coarsely chopped
1/2 cup chopped green chiles (2 to 3 parched and peeled, page 7)

THE CASSEROLE

Vegetable oil
12 corn tortillas
Cooked chicken, removed from the bones and "pulled" or shredded
2 cups coarsely shredded Monterey Jack- Cheddar cheeses
1 cup whipping cream
1/4 cup finely chopped purple Spanish onion

Place the chicken, carrot, celery, onion, thyme, and salt in a large pot; add water to barely cover the tips of the meat and cover. Bring to a boil over medium-high heat, and once reaching a boil, reduce to low heat and simmer until the chicken is tender. The bones should wiggle and the meat should be very tender to the touch of a fork.

Meanwhile, prepare the sauce. Melt the butter, add the flour, and stir together until slightly brown. Then slowly stir in the chicken stock, a little at a time, until a rich, thick sauce develops. Stir in the cilantro and the green chiles. Taste and adjust seasonings.

Heat about an inch of oil and lightly fry the tortillas. Drain well. Then dip each tortilla into the sauce, place a strip of the cooked chicken and a sprinkle of the cheeses in the center, and roll, placing them seam side down in a casserole, preferably an authentic Mexican one.

When all are rolled, distribute the remaining sauce and cheeses evenly over the tortillas. Pour the cream evenly over the entire casserole. Top with a ribbon of the onion. Either freeze for up to 3 months, well covered in moisture-proof packaging, or bake immediately in a 350°F (180°C) oven for 20 minutes. Serve piping hot.

Note: If frozen, bake 30 to 40 minutes or until bubbling hot.

MANZANAS EN CRISP

A year-round favorite with our family, this recipe takes advantage of the fruit of the season. Bake the crisp ahead and warm it in the oven after removing the enchiladas, or bake it along with them. It's a good traveler and keeper, and any leftovers will freeze quite well. The crisp will not suffer if it is frozen whole after baking. Serve with whipped cream or very rich French vanilla ice cream.

Makes 6 servings.

1 1/2 cups light brown sugar
1 1/2 cups all-purpose flour
1/2 teaspoon ground cinnamon
1/4 teaspoon freshly grated nutmeg
3/4 cup unsalted butter
5 medium or 4 large cooking apples, peeled and cut into thick slices (about 4 cups)
2 teaspoons lemon juice

Mix the brown sugar, flour, cinnamon, and nutmeg together in a bowl and cut in the butter with a pastry blender, a food processor, or mixer until it is like coarse meal. Spread the apple slices on the bottom of a 9 x 9-inch buttered baking dish. Sprinkle with the lemon juice, then the crumb mixture. Bake at 350°F (180°C) until the fruit is soft and the crumbs are browned, 35 to 40 minutes. Serve with sweetened whipped cream or French vanilla ice cream.

TRADITIONAL CHRISTMAS EVE SUPPER, NEW MEXICAN STYLE

Champagne
Guacamole with Cherry Tomato Dippers
Green Chile and Chicken Enchilada Casserole
Christmas Salad of Red Sweet Peppers with Belgian Endive and Salsa Vinaigrette
Bizcochitos
Hot New Mexican Chocolate

The holiday season in New Mexico is probably the most colorful in the entire country, its customs a rich mosaic created by centuries of commingling among the three cultures that settled the region. Based on the Pueblo Indian rites subsequently influenced first by the Spanish and later by the Anglos, Christmas celebrations are a brilliant pageant. From the *luminarias*—beautiful lanterns constructed by placing a stubby, long-burning candle in a small paper bag rolled down once or twice and anchored with a layer of sand at its bottom—to the special religious rites—both Indian and Anglo—to the flavorful traditional foods, a Southwestern Christmas is not soon forgotten. The menu for this meal is another in which traditional foods are given some exciting new interpretations. In each dish, Christmas colors happily coincide with the Mexican national colors of red, white, and green, which are always woven into festive menus.

For the guacamole, instead of the predictable tostadas for dunking, I have selected cherry tomatoes and jícama, the crisp, snowy white Mexican root vegetable. For added flavor I suggest a generous squeeze of fresh lime juice with caribe chile and sea salt. The main dish is a light, subtly colored entrée that combines convenience with the traditional savor of enchiladas. Freshly poached chicken is layered with a tomatillo sauce and generously tucked between blankets of softly fried corn tortillas, cheeses, scallions, and both whipping cream and sour cream. The garnish of radish roses and deep green romaine dress it perfectly for this special supper.

The salad has a Southwestern accent in the Salsa Vinaigrette flowing over endive, with slivered red and green bell peppers. Bizcochitos are the most traditional holiday cookies in New Mexico and are always served with hot Mexican chocolate, which is included here in an easier version made with cocoa.

Christmas decorations in New Mexico are always bright. Brilliantly hued table runners created from *ribosas* (scarfs), yarn *ojos de dios* (God's eyes), piñatas, and tinware are some of the most popular decorative items.

MENU PLAN

One day before (or several days ahead):
Make the salsa, if using, for the guacamole and the salsa for the salad.
Bake the bizcochitos.
Prepare the enchilada casserole for baking (the casserole will keep 3 to 4 days in the refrigerator or 3 months in the freezer).
Make the radish roses for garnish.

One hour or some time before:
Prepare the salad ingredients and the dressing and set aside for last-minute combining.
Chill the champagne.
Chill the salad plates and forks.
Prepare the guacamole and cover; cut the jícama into cubes.
Place the bizcochitos on an attractive platter or in a basket.
Heat the oven for the enchilada casserole; warm the plates.
Measure out the ingredients for the Hot New Mexican Chocolate. Warm the tostados, if using.

At serving time:
Bake the enchilada casserole.
Arrange the guacamole on a platter with the cherry tomatoes and jicama; serve with champagne.
Arrange the Christmas Salad and serve with the hot enchilada casserole.
Make the Hot New Mexican Chocolate and serve with the bizcochitos.

—— GUACAMOLE WITH CHERRY TOMATO DIPPERS ——

What could be cheerier or more welcome than guacamole? Cherry tomato dippers coupled with crisp cubes of jícama doused with lime and sprinkled with red squares of caribe chile make for a lovely appetizer—perfect for heralding Christmas or, for that matter, any cherished moments.

Makes 6 servings.

3 ripe Haas avocados
Juice of 1 Mexican lime, divided
1/3 cup finely chopped Spanish onion
1/2 cup cubed red ripe tomato
3 garlic cloves, minced
3/4 teaspoon salt
1 medium to large jalapeño or to taste, minced
1 medium jícama, peeled and cut into cubes
1 teaspoon or more coarse sea or kosher salt
1 Tablespoon caribe or other crushed dried red chile
1 quart cherry tomatoes
12 ounces tostados, warmed or freshly fried, optional
1 cup salsa, your favorite variety, optional

Scoop the avocado flesh from the skins into a shallow bowl. Cut into 1/2-inch squares, using two knives. Add 1 1/2 teaspoons lime juice, the onion, tomato, garlic, salt, and jalapeño. Combine, being careful not to crush the avocado. Taste and adjust the seasonings. Keep tightly covered with plastic wrap until serving time. Arrange the guacamole in the center of a large platter, then circle with a ring of jícama that you have flavored by dousing with part of the lime juice and sprinkling with coarse salt and caribe. Make a larger circle with the cherry tomatoes. Serve, if desired, with tostados and the salsa.

GREEN CHILE AND CHICKEN ENCHILADA CASSEROLE

The fresh, clear spiciness of New Mexico green chiles lacing a creamy tomatillo sauce generously covering chunks of poached chicken makes this an absolutely sumptuous make-ahead casserole. You can prepare it up to three months ahead and freeze, or as much as three days ahead and refrigerate—a blessing during the busy holiday time.

Makes 6 servings.

1 (3- to 4 1/2-pound) roasting chicken
1 quart or more water
3 garlic cloves, divided
1 Spanish onion, cut into thick slices
1 medium carrot, peeled and chopped
1 teaspoon salt
1 quart corn oil
12 corn tortillas
1 (13-ounce) can tomatillos or 1 pound fresh tomatillos boiled in salted water until soft—about
    6 minutes
1/2 cup chopped hot green New Mexico chiles, parched fresh (page 7) or frozen, or use 1
    (4-ounce) can chopped green chiles
1/2 teaspoon salt, optional
1 cup chopped green onions (scallions), including the fresh, tender part of the green tops
1 1/2 cups coarsely shredded Monterey Jack cheese
1 1/2 cups coarsely shredded sharp Cheddar cheese
1 cup whipping cream
1/2 cup sour cream
6 lettuce leaves such as romaine
6 radish roses, prepared in advance

Place the chicken in a 5- to 6-quart heavy stewing pot with a cover. Chop 2 cloves of garlic. Add the water, sliced onion, carrot, chopped garlic, and salt, cover, and bring to a boil over medium-high heat. Once boiling reduce to low heat and cook for 45 minutes or until very tender. Allow to cool in the juices for about another hour. Debone the chicken and remove the skin. Pull the meat into pieces about 1/2 inch wide and not over 2 inches long.

If desired, fry the tortillas—however, to save time and calories this step can be omitted. If frying, heat the oil in a deep-fat fryer or deep frying pan to 375°F (190°C). When hot, quickly slip the tortillas into the hot oil—two or three at a time—holding them with tongs. Drain well on paper towels.

Mince remaining clove of garlic. Prepare the green salsa by placing the tomatillos, chiles, salt, and minced garlic in a food processor or blender and process until puréed.

Using your prettiest and most Christmasy-looking casserole (I particularly like a round or oval one for this), lightly oil the bottom using some of the oil left from tortilla frying. Then begin layering the ingredients. First, place some salsa, then a layer of 3 or 4 tortillas, depending on the size of the casserole. Top with more salsa, then a layer of chicken, a scattering of the green onions, a good sprinkle of both cheeses, and the whipping cream mixed with the sour cream. Evenly divide the sauce and filling ingredients among the layers, ending with the green salsa, in a squiggle around the edges, then the cream mixture, cheeses lightly sprinkled on the salsa, and a pretty toss of onions on top. No chicken should be showing.

If preparing ahead, seal with plastic wrap and refrigerate. To bake, place in a 375°F (190°C) oven and bake until cheeses melt and the dish is hot, about 30 minutes.

To serve, place on heated plates with a garnish of lettuce leaf and a radish rose.

—— CHRISTMAS SALAD OF RED SWEET PEPPERS ——
WITH BELGIAN ENDIVE AND SALSA VINAIGRETTE

This dish is an expression of a favorite salad theme of mine. If Belgian endive is not available, green bell peppers, jicama, or snow-white mushroom slivers can be substituted.

Makes 6 servings.

3 small white heads Belgian endive
2 large red bell peppers
1 small head Boston or red leaf lettuce
2 garlic cloves, minced
1/2 cup virgin olive oil
1/4 cup red wine vinegar
1/3 cup any red salsa

Rinse and cut the endive into halves. Cut off and discard about 1 inch of the heel cuts. Then slice each in half and cut into 1/4-inch-thick slices. Cut red peppers into long, thin slivers. Rinse and pat dry the lettuce leaves. Marinate the garlic at least 30 minutes in the olive oil in a bowl. Combine with the vinegar and the salsa.

To serve, place the lettuce leaves on chilled plates and evenly divide the endive and peppers over them, then drizzle the dressing over all. Or serve buffet style in a lettuce-lined bowl.

Note: The salad and dressing can be prepared hours of even a day ahead. Keep separated until ready to serve.

BIZCOCHITOS

These cookies were originally made to celebrate the victory of Santa Anna's army over Napoleon's army in the battle of Puebla on May 5 in the 1860s (hence the origin of Cinco de Mayo). The Spanish women created this cookie—a shortbread type in the shape of a fleur-de-lis that must be made with lard to be moist and flavorful—to celebrate the end of the French rule. Lacking the cookie cutters, they were made with a small sharp knife into Spanish fans—curling the slender cut ends of each cookie to create a fan shape.

This cookie became the state cookie of New Mexico and are very popular for fiestas, weddings, and any holiday. They are traditionally served following midnight church service on Christmas Eve and the lighting of hundreds of *luminarias* or *farolitas*, and are usually accompanied by Mexican chocolate. Some wonderful old handed-down versions of this recipe call for a pound each of the major ingredients and a dozen yolks—making it easy to remember. I prefer this smaller, more interesting version.

Makes 2 1/2 dozen.

1/2 pound lard
1 cup sugar
1 teaspoon aniseed
1 large egg
2 Tablespoons brandy or sherry
3 cups all-purpose flour (use a high-gluten flour)
1 1/2 teaspoons baking powder
1/2 teaspoon salt
1 1/2 teaspoons ground cinnamon
2 Tablespoons sugar

Using a mixer at high speed, whip the lard to create a very light, airy texture—much like whipped cream. (This is the secret to feather-light cookies.) Add the sugar very slowly and continue beating until well mixed. Add the aniseed, egg, and brandy and continue to beat until fluffy and somewhat frothy. Add the flour, baking powder, and salt all at once and stir on the lowest speed until they are completely incorporated and a smooth dough results. The dough will be somewhat soft.

Tear a 40-inch long piece of waxed paper and place the dough on one end. Fold over the remaining waxed paper and place the dough on a cookie sheet. Using another cookie sheet, press the dough to about 3/8 inch thick. Chill the dough in the freezer until it firms up. Allow at least 30 minutes for the tenderest cookies.

Place the dough on a flat surface, then roll dough between the waxed paper, using a very light stroke with the rolling pin. Since the dough is so short, it is like a rich pie pastry.

The traditional shape is the fleur-de-lis—made to celebrate the defeat of the French. If a cutter is not available, use a sharp knife to cut 2 1/2- to 3-inch rectangles of dough, cutting them at an angle so that the points are elongated. Then 1 to 1 1/2 inches down, make 3/4-inch cuts into the dough on each side of one end only. Or create Spanish fans as described above. Dust with cinnamon combined with sugar in a shallow bowl or on a plate. Bake in a 350°F (180°C) oven until just done, about 10 to 12 minutes. Traditionally they are served white, never browned or even golden.

Note: Most any cookie shape can be used if cutting the fleur-de-lis sounds too difficult. These keep very well stored in a rigid container with wax paper between the layers or for up to 6 months frozen.

— HOT NEW MEXICAN CHOCOLATE —

Mexican hot chocolate is usually made with melted bar chocolate containing sugar, cinnamon, and cloves. This adaptation produces a very similar flavor and a much better texture, as bar chocolate, which does not melt well, always leaves little flecks floating on the surface. Traditionally, this beverage is beaten at the table with a *molinillo*—a specially carved wooden stirrer—just before being poured into heavy earthenware mugs. A molinillo will add a bit of showmanship to your presentation and can be purchased at Mexican specialty stores.

Makes 6 drinks.

1/3 cup cocoa
1 Tablespoon all-purpose flour
1/3 cup sugar
Pinch of salt
3/4 teaspoon ground cinnamon
1/4 teaspoon ground cloves
1 cup water
1 pint half-and-half
1 cup milk
1 1/2 teaspoons Mexican vanilla or pure vanilla extract
1 cup heavy cream, whipped
Freshly grated nutmeg
6 whole cinnamon sticks

Combine the cocoa, flour, sugar, salt, ground cinnamon, and cloves with the water in a heavy 2-quart saucepan. Stir or whisk until very well blended. Heat until just barely beginning to simmer. Gradually add the half-and-half, then the milk, in a very fine stream, stirring all the time. Beat with your molinillo, a whisk, or rotary beater. Heat until hot but do not boil, and keep warm for at least 5 minutes.

Whip the chocolate again just before serving, beating with your molinillo until it is frothy. This is quite fun to do in front of the guests. Serve in large earthenware mugs you have rinsed with hot water. Top with a dollop of whipped cream and a shave of nutmeg, and jab a cinnamon stick into the cream.

NEW MEXICO BUFFET

Hot Spicy Chicken Wings with Creamy Salsa Verde

Santa Fe Lasagna

Lettuce Medley Salad with Julienne of Red Sweet Peppers and Salsa Vinaigrette

Bear Paw Bread

Sweet Butter

Zinfandel

Figs with Port Wine and Mexican Goat Cheese

Coffee

Here is a menu that can be served at any time of the year, for while the combination of foods suggests summer, other than the fresh figs—which can be replaced by any berry, pineapple, or other fresh, somewhat tart fruit—none of its ingredients are seasonal.

About the only familiar dish involved is the Bear Paw Bread, which is extraordinarily good when freshly baked. Try to plan your time to bake the bread shortly before serving time, but if scheduling becomes a problem, French bread or most any peasant hearth-type bread can be substituted, or better yet, reheat a previously frozen loaf of Bear Paw Bread.

The Santa Fe Lasagna is one of my proudest inventions. It is also a flexible dish that can be made when you have the time and set aside in the refrigerator for up to five days and baked just before serving. It also freezes for up to three months.

The appetizer is an increasingly popular treat around the country, and though it requires last-minute frying, it is worth the extra effort. In fact, you will probably not have any trouble recruiting helpers for the frying. The salad and figs are very quickly assembled, rounding out this menu with a simple but elegant grace note.

For decor, aim for a New Mexican accent: clay pottery and baskets for serving, terra cotta tiles or dishes, and earthy russets to browns for the table linens. Cactus or evergreen boughs make a complementary centerpiece, or for an unusual touch, try Southwestern Indian relics.

Menu Plan

Day before (or early in the day or several days in advance):
Prepare the lasagna for baking and refrigerate.
Make the bread dough, planning the risings so that the bread will be baked about 30 minutes before serving dinner—allow at least 4 1/2 hours to be on the safe side. If it has risen to the point it needs to be baked and it's too far ahead of dinner, you can keep it in the refrigerator.
Coat the chicken wings and freeze.

One or two hours before:
Prepare the Creamy Salsa Verde and chill.

Bake the bread.

Heat the oil for the chicken about 20 minutes ahead.

Chill the salad plates and forks.

Prepare the vegetables, Salsa Fresca, and dressing for the salad.

Fill a favorite butter dish and allow the butter to come to room temperature.

Set out the coffeepot.

Arrange the figs on a platter and keep at room temperature. Also set out the cheese on a board or server.

Put the lasagna in the oven just before guests arrive.

At serving time:

Fry the chicken wings and serve with the salsa.

Assemble the salad and serve with the lasagna, Bear Paw Bread, and sweet butter.

Serve the Figs with Port Wine and Mexican Goat Cheese.

Serve coffee.

—— HOT SPICY CHICKEN WINGS ——
WITH CREAMY SALSA VERDE

Based on the famous Buffalo chicken wings, this zippy snack was developed when I was looking for something unusual for an appetizer. I was inspired by Dean Small, director of the delightful array of food shops and eateries in the Heartland Market in the Crown Center Complex in Kansas City, Missouri, when he enthusiastically shared an idea for a similar dish he had created for the market's American Café Restaurant.

Makes 6 servings.

1/2 cup masa harina (if not available, substitute yellow cornmeal)
1 1/2 teaspoons ground cumin
2 Tablespoons ground pure hot New Mexico chile
1/2 teaspoon salt
1/2 cup all-purpose flour
1 cup milk
24 chicken wings
1 quart vegetable oil
Creamy Salsa Verde (page 14)

Combine the masa harina with the cumin, chile, and salt in a shallow bowl. Place the flour and milk in separate bowls. Rinse and pick any pinfeathers off the chicken wings. Blot dry. Dip each wing in the milk, then the flour, the milk again, and then the masa harina mixture. Set on a cookie sheet covered with wax paper. The chicken wings can be frozen at this point for up to 3 months.

If cooking immediately, heat the oil in a deep-fat fryer, preferably with a thermostatic control set at 375°F (190°C). If no thermostat is available, then use a heavy pot and a candy thermometer. While the oil heats, place the wings in the freezer to firm up. (This makes the coating cling better throughout the frying process and makes them more moist inside.) Fry two to three wings at a time, until each is golden, about 3 minutes each, then drain and keep warm in a low oven. Serve warm, with the salsa alongside.

SANTA FE LASAGNA

What dish could find greater favor with diners than one that is the happy marriage of two terrific cuisines? I set about creating a version of that perennial favorite, lasagna, using chorizo, which is sparked with hot New Mexico chiles instead of Italian sausage. A generous amount of the ubiquitous cheeses of the Southwest—Monterey Jack and Cheddar—take the place of mozzarella in this very flavorful entrée.

Makes 6 servings.

1/2 cup vegetable oil
12 corn tortillas
2 cups (about 8 ounces) shredded full-cream yellow Cheddar cheese
2 cups (about 8 ounces) shredded Monterey Jack cheese
6 green onions (scallions), thinly sliced
1 pound chorizo,* removed from its casings and chopped, cooked, and drained
15 ounces ricotta cheese
3 cups half-and-half

Heat the oil in a heavy skillet. Arrange paper towels over paper plates for draining the tortillas. Lightly fry each until soft. Drain well.**

Using some of the oil, lightly oil a 9 x 13-inch baking dish. Place 3 tortillas in the pan, then, using about 1/4 of each, a layer of each of the Cheddar and Monterey Jack, some of the onions, some cooked chorizo, and the ricotta. Repeat until you have four layers. Pour the half-and-half evenly over the dish. (The lasagna can be refrigerated at this point or frozen.) Bake in a 350°F (180°C) oven for 30 minutes or until bubbly.

*If chorizo is difficult to find in your local markets, you can make it at home or alter hot Italian sausage according to the directions included in the Chorizo and Piñon Nut–Stuffed Loin of Pork on page 109.

**Frying the tortillas is optional—you can save time and calories by not frying. To bake, prepare as above and place them on a generously greased baking sheet and bake in a preheated oven at 425°F (220°C) until golden—about 15 to 20 minutes.

LETTUCE MEDLEY SALAD

WITH JULIENNE OF RED SWEET PEPPERS AND SALSA VINAIGRETTE

A crisp, tart salad is a natural accompaniment to the substantial, spicy main dish of this meal. The greens selection can be varied to suit whatever is on hand, but the choices below are especially good.

Makes 6 servings.

2 garlic cloves, minced
2/3 cup virgin olive oil
1 bunch very fresh watercress
1 medium head red leaf lettuce
1 head Boston lettuce
1 medium-size red bell pepper, cut into long, thin strips
1/4 cup Salsa Fresca (page 15)
1/4 cup lime juice
Salt to taste
Freshly cracked pepper to taste

Marinate the garlic in the olive oil for at least 30 minutes. Rinse the greens, tear into largish bite-size pieces, and blot or spin dry. Use about 1 cup of each.

Place the greens in a chilled bowl and top with the pepper strips. Combine the garlic-flavored oil, salsa, and lime juice. I find the zestiness of the salsa dressing perfect without salt and pepper, so taste the salad once tossed, then add salt and freshly ground pepper if you wish and lightly toss again. Serve on chilled salad plates.

BEAR PAW BREAD

This traditional New Mexican Pueblo bread is baked and sold by Indians in front of the Palace of the Governors in Santa Fe, around the plaza in Old Town Albuquerque as well as at little roadside stands and at fairs, fiestas, and rodeos. This bread is sometimes called Isleta Bread as it is the favorite product of the Isleta Pueblo, just south of Albuquerque. It's wonderful freshly baked, oozing with sweet butter and topped with local cactus honeys or jams.

Makes 1 loaf.

1/2 package dry yeast (approximately 1 1/2 teaspoons)
1/4 cup warm water
Pinch of sugar
1/4 teaspoon lard
1/4 teaspoon honey
1/4 teaspoon salt
1/4 cup very warm water
2 1/2 cups all-purpose flour or more (high-gluten bread flour is best)

In a small bowl sprinkle the yeast over the warm water and add the pinch of sugar. Combine the lard, honey, salt, and water in the bottom of a large bowl and stir to dissolve. When cooled to room temperature, combine with the yeast mixture, which should be bubbly by now.

Add the flour, 1 cup at a time. Stir briskly to make a bubbly sponge. Then add flour only until a stiff dough results. Do not add more—if not all of it is used, save it. When the dough is too stiff to continue stirring, turn it out onto a floured board. Knead until smooth and elastic, about 10 minutes or so or until the gluten is well developed. You can tell this by stretching a bit of dough between your fingers. If threads form, gluten is developed.

Place the dough in a clean, oiled bowl, covering it with a damp towel. Then place in a warm place, free from drafts. When the dough has doubled, in about 1 hour, turn it out on the floured board and roll into a flat disk about 8 inches in diameter. Place on a lightly oiled cookie sheet.

Fold over about a fourth of the dough, making certain you lap the top about 2 inches back from the bottom—similar to a stollen. Placing your palm on the folded side of the bread, press it away from you and pull the edges toward you to form a broad U shape.

Using a sharp knife, slash once about 2 inches from each outside edge to form a claw effect on the "paw" shape of the bread. Cover with a damp towel and set aside until doubled.

Meanwhile, preheat the oven to 350°F (180°C) and place a pan of boiling water on the lower shelf. Place the bread on the shelf above and bake for 1 hour, or until it is very slightly brown and sounds hollow when thumped. (This bread is traditionally baked in *hornos*—adobe ovens—using the ashes from piñon wood for heat.)

FRESH FIGS

WITH PORT WINE AND MEXICAN GOAT CHEESE

Although fig trees are popular as a lawn shrub in New Mexico, the best are grown in the mountainous areas of the southern part of the state. I've always savored Cloudcroft figs (Cloudcroft is a resort tucked in the mountains near Ruidoso) as something special, and in this simple dessert their unmatchable sweetness can be enjoyed with a pair of ideal complements.

Makes 6 servings.

36 fresh ripe figs
1 (4-ounce) package Mexican goat cheese, if available
1 (4-ounce) package Montrachet
1 fifth port wine

Rinse the figs and set on pretty crystal or simple clear glass plates or any favorite dessert plates. Do this ahead so the figs are at room temperature. Place the cheeses on a cheese board. To serve, pour the port and give each guest a plate of figs. They are delightful eaten together with the goat cheese.

Note: Some also like to serve a simple water cracker.

OLD EL PASO BORDER DINNER

Frijoles Negros Tostaditas
Chorizo and Piñon Nut–Stuffed Loin of Pork
Tiny Green Beans and New Red Potatoes in Salsa Vinaigrette
Apricot and Sherried Custard Trifle
Cabernet Sauvignon
Coffee

This perfectly adaptable menu—suitable for almost any time or setting—is one to consider when you wish to entertain business or social friends comfortably, yet with flair.

While all the recipes in this menu are original, they show a clear Mexican influence. The tostaditas are similar to nachos, yet are much more Latin in both flavor and appearance. The pork roast features a truly spectacular-looking and tasting treatment for a meat that is all too often prepared indifferently. Any leftovers freeze and reheat well. The salsa-laced garden vegetable salad complements the roast. The finale takes its inspiration from English trifle as well as the traditional New Mexican/Spanish Natillas custard. Select a fine bottle of dry red wine, such as the Cabernet Sauvignon, to place this dinner in the VSOP class.

Subtle pastels such as light yellow, peach, or apricot would be the choice for the table linens. Blue bachelor's buttons, Japanese iris, or lilacs set off by tall white stock, lilies, or whatever is in season would create just the right accent.

MENU PLAN

Four hours before:
Stuff the pork loin, truss it, and place in the oven.
Prepare the Apricot and Sherried Custard Trifle.
After the first hour of pork roasting, coat with the jalapeño jelly, then continue basting every 15 minutes.
Make the Fresh Garden Salsa for the salad; prepare the beans and potatoes and dress with the vinaigrette.
Heat the dinner plates and chill the salad plates and forks.
Prepare the filling ingredients for the tostaditas about 1 hour before guests arrive. Fry the tortillas.
Set out the coffeemaker.

At serving time:
Assemble the Frijoles Negros Tostaditas and serve them warm.
Slice the pork roast and serve with the pan juices in a side dish. Serve the bean and potato salad alongside.
Serve the trifle with coffee.

— FRIJOLES NEGROS TOSTADITAS —

With their black bean topping, these little gems are more Latin American in flavor than Southwestern. Black beans—*frijoles negros*—are increasingly gaining favor as an alternative to the predictable pinto, as their rich, assertive taste is a splendid partner for spicy accompaniments. I always add the Cuban touch of a splash of rum or sherry and a squeeze of fresh lime—an idea used most often in black bean soup.

Makes 8 servings, 32 tostaditas.

1 pint corn oil
8 corn tortillas
1/4 cup bacon drippings or lard
2 large garlic cloves, finely minced
1 large Spanish onion, finely chopped
2 cans (1 pound each) black beans
1 teaspoon salt
1 Tablespoon rum or sherry
1 teaspoon fresh lime juice
1 bunch watercress, rinsed and stems removed
5 radishes, sliced thinly
1/4 cup finely chopped green onions (scallions)
1/2 cup sour cream
1 cup coarsely shredded Monterey Jack cheese

Heat the corn oil in a deep skillet to 375°F (190°C). While oil is heating, line a cookie sheet with several layers of paper towels for draining. Cut each tortilla four times into equal parts, cutting almost to the center. Fry each tortilla until crisp, watching for the bubbles to subside before turning to fry the second side. Drain, tapping each one in the center to separate them into 4 pieces.

In a heavy frying pan, heat the bacon drippings. Add the garlic, and as it begins to turn golden, toss in the onion and cook and stir until it becomes clear. Add the beans and mash with a potato masher or large heavy spoon until they are completely puréed. Season with the salt, rum, and lime juice to taste.

If the beans seem too dry, add a few drops of hot water. They should be about the texture of heavy pudding so they can be spread on the fried tortillas.

To combine, carefully spread a layer of the beans on each tortilla just before serving. Then sprinkle sprigs of watercress over the top of each, a few disks of radish, a toss of scallion rounds, and center each with 1 Tablespoon sour cream topped with 2 Tablespoons shredded cheese.

— CHORIZO AND PIÑON NUT–STUFFED LOIN OF PORK —

Glorious to behold, the red-hued, chile-laden chorizo (Mexican sausage) rolled inside the silken pink white of the pork roast—crusty with a jalapeño jelly glaze—makes for an inimitably elegant entrée.

Makes 6 to 8 servings.

1 (3 1/2- to 4-pound) boneless, butterflied loin of pork
1/4 teaspoon salt
1 pound chorizo*
1/2 cup piñons (pine nuts)
8 ounces Jalapeño Jelly, hot or mild, depending on your taste (recipe follows)

Lay the pork roast out flat, with the inside (side from which bone was removed) facing up. Sprinkle with the salt. Remove the casings from the chorizo and place the sausage meat in a bowl. Mix the piñon nuts evenly into the chorizo. Then lay the chorizo in a long roll on the inside of the roast. (If using Italian sausage or pork sausage, blend in the seasonings first, before adding the nuts.) Bring the two sides together lengthwise. Tie every inch with white cotton twine. Place on a baking pan.

Put in the oven and turn to 350°F (180°C). After the first hour, spread jalapeño jelly on the outside of the roast. Return to the oven and roast and baste every 15 minutes. Continue roasting for 1 1/2 to 2 hours more, or until 170°F (75°C) on a meat thermometer. Reserve the juices and serve on the side.

*If you can't find chorizo, substitute hot Italian sausage and add 1/2 teaspoon ground cumin and 1/2 teaspoon crushed Mexican oregano. If hot Italian sausage is not available, use fresh pork sausage and add an additional 2 to 4 Tablespoons caribe or other crushed dried red chile.

—— HOMEMADE JALAPEÑO JELLY ——

There are many jalapeño jellies on the market, but few are as good as this one—a lovely, richly flavored jelly that captures the freshness of chiles.

Makes 5 (6-ounce) jars.

3 cups ripe red bell peppers
5 jalapeños, finely chopped
1 1/2 cups cider vinegar
6 1/2 cups sugar
6 ounces bottled liquid pectin

Clean jelly jars, then boil in at least 1 inch of water while making the jelly.

Chop by hand or use a food processor or blender to process the peppers into a medium grind. Combine with the vinegar and sugar in a large, heavy saucepan and boil for 30 minutes.

Allow to cool for 10 minutes. Then stir in the pectin and boil for 2 minutes. Check that it is thick enough by doing the sheet test: dip a metal spoon in at right angles to the surface of the jelly and lift it about a foot above the surface. While still at right angles, allow the drops to "sheet" off. If they do not come together and sheet off, continue boiling and test again. Remove from the heat, skim, and allow the jelly to cool. Stir so that the fruit is evenly dispersed, then ladle into sterilized jars. When cool, seal with paraffin.

TINY GREEN BEANS AND NEW RED POTATOES
IN SALSA VINAIGRETTE

What was once the bounty of early spring in the Southwest can now be enjoyed almost all year. Prepared this way, a pair of favorite spring vegetables have a Tex-Mex tang and can accompany a wide variety of Southwestern menus. You can vary the type of salsa here to suit your palate and the other dishes in your meal.

Makes 6 to 8 servings.

8 tiny new red potatoes, well scrubbed and with a 1/2-inch belt of skin removed
1 1/2 pounds fresh small green beans, rinsed and stems removed
1 cup water
1/4 cup white vinegar
1/4 cup virgin olive oil
1/2 cup Fresh Garden Salsa (page 13)
8 fluffy red lettuce leaves, rinsed
8 thin strips of red bell pepper

Place the new potatoes, green beans, and water in a heavy saucepan. Cover and steam about 5 minutes or until the potatoes are just tender, not mushy. Peek once or twice to be sure the water has not evaporated.

Combine the vinegar, oil, and salsa. When the vegetables are done, drain any excess liquid and cover and allow to dry out on the surface—about 5 minutes. Toss with the vinaigrette, and keep tossing every 15 minutes or so until the vegetables have absorbed most of the liquid. After about an hour, serve on the lettuce leaves, garnished with bell pepper strips.

APRICOT AND SHERRIED CUSTARD TRIFLE

Along the border, soft custards combined with fruits are a very popular dessert as they are soothing to the system after a series of intensely spicy dishes. You can vary this basic recipe with different combinations of fruits—currant jam and fresh strawberries are a delicious pair. For calorie counting, omit the cake, double the custard portion, and serve layered with apricot jam, almonds, and stewed apricots.

Makes 8 servings.

2 cups milk
1/3 cup sugar
Pinch of salt
2 Tablespoons all-purpose flour
2 large eggs, separated
1 large egg white
2 teaspoons plus 1/2 cup cream sherry, divided
Several gratings of fresh nutmeg (1/8 teaspoon ground)
1 sponge cake layer, 10 inches in diameter
1/2 cup apricot jam
2 Tablespoons toasted slivered almonds
12 large, extra-fancy dried apricots stewed in 1/2 cup water

Place the milk in a heavy 2-quart saucepan. Stir in the sugar and salt. Place over low heat and cook and stir until the sugar dissolves. Spoon out about 1/2 cup of the warm milk mixture into a small bowl. Carefully sprinkle the flour over the cooled mixture. Stir, and when well blended, add the egg yolks and stir well. Add to the cooled remaining milk mixture. Cook, stirring constantly, until very well blended. Continue to cook until the mixture thickens and coats the back of a spoon. Cool slightly.

Meanwhile, beat the 3 egg whites until very stiff, adding the 2 teaspoons sherry and the nutmeg while beating. Stir the yolk-milk mixture periodically. When cool, fold in the beaten egg whites.

While waiting for the yolk mixture to cool, place the sponge cake on a large serving platter. Sprinkle with the remaining 1/2 cup sherry and allow to marinate until the custard is done. Then spread with the apricot jam.

Place a uniform layer of the slivered almonds on top. Pour the custard over the cake. Garnish with the stewed, cooled apricots, placing 4 in the center and the remaining 8 evenly placed around the edge.

To serve, slice into 8 wedges, being certain to center an apricot on each and to get half of one at the end of each slice.

MICROWAVE MEXICAN FOR BUSY EVENINGS

Spicy Pork Chops, Rancher's Style
Picadillo Rice
Marinated Baby Green Bean Salad
Warm Wheat Tortillas with Fresh Oregano Butter
Lime Ice
Zinfandel

When you find yourself with a tight schedule yet wish to cook for guests, this menu can be cooked and served in thirty minutes if you use a microwave oven, provided the Lime Ice and the Marinated Baby Green Bean Salad have been prepared in advance. If cooking conventionally, allow one hour of preparation time; instructions are given in each of the recipes for cooking either way.

For this time-saving menu, set the table in bright colors with a simple centerpiece of seasonal flowers—peonies are ideal in spring—or a bowl of fruit or vegetables.

You may wish to serve some thin, crisp cookies alongside the Lime Ice.

MENU PLAN

Day before:
Prepare the Lime Ice. (Put in the refrigerator 2 hours before serving.)
Prepare the Marinated Baby Green Bean Salad.

Thirty minutes before:
Prepare the Spicy Pork Chops.
Chill the salad plates and forks.
Warm the dinner plates.
Prepare the Fresh Oregano Butter.
Wrap tortillas in two foil packets of 6 each.
Prepare the Picadillo Rice.
Scoop out servings of Lime Ice, placing them in sherbet glasses, then return them to the refrigerator.

At serving time:
Warm the tortillas.
Arrange the salad on the lettuce leaves.
Serve the Spicy Pork Chops on hot plates with the Picadillo Rice, warm tortillas and Oregano Butter, and the salad.
Serve the Lime Ice.

SPICY PORK CHOPS, RANCHER'S STYLE

This flavorful, quick entrée can be made on top of the range if you don't have a microwave oven. Use previously cooked or frozen Ranchero Sauce if you have some on hand.

Makes 6 servings.

2 Tablespoons vegetable or olive oil
2 cups chopped Spanish onions (2 large)
1 (28-ounce) can whole peeled tomatoes with their juice
2 to 3 large New Mexico green chiles (1/2 cup), parched, peeled, and chopped (page 7) or use
    2 ounces canned chopped green chiles
2 garlic cloves, minced
6 large, well-trimmed, 2-inch-thick loin pork chops (2 to 2 1/2 pounds)

If using the microwave oven, use an 8 x 10-inch Pyrex baking dish and place the oil in the dish, making certain to coat the bottom evenly. A rubber scraper will work fine for this. Add the onion, cover with wax paper, and process on high heat for about 2 minutes, or until the onion begins to sizzle and becomes somewhat clear. If it hasn't after 2 minutes, stir, rotate, and cook another minute. If not using a microwave oven, place the oil in a large deep frying pan that has a tight-fitting cover and heat to medium. Add the onion and sauté until clear, about 5 minutes.

If cooking in the microwave oven, add the tomatoes, green chiles, and garlic. Cover with wax paper and process for 3 minutes, stirring and rotating once. Taste and add salt if desired; also add more peppers if a hotter sauce is desired. If cooking in the frying pan, add the tomatoes, chiles, and garlic and cook for 11 to 15 minutes or until the flavors combine.

For the microwave or the frying pan, place the pork chops evenly across the sauce, spooning about half of it over the tops of the chops. Cover with wax paper for the microwave and process for 15 minutes, turning three or four times, spooning sauce over the top and rotating each time. Continue to cover with the wax paper. If cooking in a skillet, cover and cook over medium-low heat for 40 to 60 minutes, spooning sauce over every 5 minutes or so.

For either method, insert a sharp knife next to the bone to determine doneness. If slightly pink, cook another few minutes until done. Serve piping hot on hot plates with the Picadillo Rice (recipe follows).

PICADILLO RICE

When you've cooked one too many portions of simple white rice, try this delicious Southwestern version of a pilaf. It's quick to assemble, as you add the flavorings after the rice has cooked.

Makes 6 servings.

3 cups water
1 1/2 teaspoons salt
1 1/2 cups rice
2 Tablespoons unsalted butter
1 teaspoon whole coriander seed, crushed
1/3 cup dark raisins
1/3 cup slivered almonds
1/8 teaspoon ground cloves
1/4 teaspoon ground cinnamon

Using a medium saucepan, bring the water to a boil with the salt. Add the rice and butter and stir, then cover and reduce heat. Set a timer for 15 minutes.

Meanwhile, in a small bowl combine the coriander, raisins, almonds, cloves, and cinnamon. When the rice is done, stir in the spice mixture to combine, reserving 2 Tablespoons for a garnish. Cover and set aside to fluff for about 5 minutes or until ready to serve alongside the pork chops. Garnish with the remaining spice mixture.

MARINATED BABY GREEN BEAN SALAD

This simple, fresh, very green salad is perfect for any quick meal. If you have a bit more time, though, prepare a day before you plan to serve and the marinade will have an even richer flavor.

Makes 6 servings.

1 1/2 pounds green beans
2 cups water
1/2 teaspoon salt
1 cup vegetable oil
1/3 cup cider vinegar
1 teaspoon Dijon mustard
1 teaspoon caribe or other crushed dried red chile
2 very thin slices of red Spanish onion
6 large leafy leaves of lettuce

Clean and trim the stem from the green beans. Boil the water with the salt. Add the beans, then steam, covered, for 5 to 8 minutes—only until color deepens and the beans are slightly tender yet still crisp. If cooking in the microwave oven, place in a Pyrex pie plate or baking dish and sprinkle with the salt. Do not add the water. Just cover with plastic wrap and process on high for 2 minutes, rotate a quarter turn, then process another minute. Check for doneness. If not tender enough, process another minute or until done.

Meanwhile, place the oil, vinegar, mustard, and caribe in a wide-mouthed jar and shake well or place in a bowl and whisk until well blended.

Drain the beans and add to the jar or bowl along with the onion slices. Set aside and allow to marinate 2 to 3 hours or even overnight. Shake or stir periodically to distribute the dressing evenly. Serve on the lettuce leaves.

FRESH OREGANO BUTTER

Herb or citrus-zest butters provide a change of pace with wheat tortillas or other Southwestern breads. For freshest flavor prepare this just before serving, but if timing is a problem, it can be made as much as a day ahead.

Makes enough to serve 6 or more.

1/2 cup (1 stick) unsalted butter, softened
1 1/2 teaspoons coarsely chopped fresh Mexican oregano leaves or 3/4 teaspoon dried

Combine the butter with the oregano in a small bowl, then place in a small dish just large enough to hold the butter. Smooth the top and set aside.

LIME ICE

Here is a dessert so refreshing you'll want to prepare it for nearly every meal. I like to make this a few days in advance, then let it mellow two to three hours in the refrigerator before serving. Accompany with thin, crisp cookies alongside, if you wish.

Makes 2 1/2 quarts.

4 3/4 cups water
2 1/4 cups sugar
3 cups freshly squeezed lime juice
1/4 cup freshly squeezed lemon juice
1 Tablespoon grated lime rind

Combine the water and sugar in a 2-quart saucepan. Simmer for 5 minutes to create a simple syrup. Remove from the heat and chill.

Pour the chilled mixture into the canister of your ice cream freezer. Add lime juice, lemon juice, and the lime rind. Mix with a wooden spoon or spatula. Follow the directions for your ice cream maker to create a firm ice. Freeze until 2 to 3 hours before serving, then put in the refrigerator. To serve, form into balls with an ice cream scoop, dipping it into warm water between scoops. I like to serve it in footed sherbet glasses, but wineglasses—especially the tulip or globular types—will also work well.

SUPPER FOR SPRING

Strawberry Margaritas
Tomatillo-Cilantro Cream Soup
Juanita's Special Rio Grande Chicken
Rice and Piñon Salad
Texas Frontier Cake
Pinot Chardonnay
Coffee

Spring signals new beginnings, promising fresh flavors, tempting aromas, and meals as welcome as the new season itself. This supper is a perfect celebration of the long-awaited arrival of spring. What better than a party featuring seasonal foods served up handsomely in an easy-to-prepare-ahead menu?

A light, creamy, green tomatillo soup is followed by a colorful, vegetable-laden chicken dish accompanied by an unusual and delicious rice salad. Ending the meal is a moist, rich Mexican chocolate cake topped by a nut-filled, crunchy frosting—an exciting variation on one of America's favorite desserts.

What makes this menu especially convenient is that a lot of the preparation can be done hours or even a day or two ahead. The rice is best marinated in advance. The vegetables can be readied hours or a day or so before cooking the chicken. Bake the cake up to two days in advance or just hours before serving—it's good either way. The soup takes just moments and has the freshest flavor if prepared just before serving. I've always liked it best at room temperature, though it can be served either chilled or warmed. Decorate the table with spring's bounty of flowers, and complement them with pastel linens and dinnerware.

MENU PLAN

Day or two before (or early in the day):
Bake and frost the Texas Frontier Cake.
Prepare the Rice and Piñon Salad.
Prepare the vegetables for Juanita's Special Rio Grande Chicken.

One hour or some time before:
Cook the Rio Grande Chicken.
Prepare the Salsa Fresca.
Chill the wine.
Chill the salad plates and forks.
Warm the dinner plates.
Set out the ingredients for preparing the Strawberry Margaritas.
Prepare the Tomatillo-Cilantro Cream Soup and chill if desired.
Set out the coffeemaker.

At serving time:
Prepare the Strawberry Margaritas and serve.
Serve the soup.
Arrange the Rice and Piñon Salad and serve with the chicken.
Serve the Texas Frontier Cake with coffee.

——— STRAWBERRY MARGARITAS ———

These luscious, fruity drinks can be made as frosty as you like by adding lots of ice—or they can be made stronger by using less ice. Vary the fruits according to what's available. Apricots and peaches are especially good. I generally don't salt the rims for margaritas based on sweet fruits.

Makes 6 servings.

2 ounces freshly squeezed lime juice
1/2 cup fresh strawberries
1 ounce triple sec
6 ounces tequila, preferably light
2 cups or more ice

Combine the lime juice, strawberries, triple sec, tequila, and ice in a blender and process until well mixed. Taste and add sugar or more triple sec if sweeter drinks are desired.

TOMATILLO-CILANTRO CREAM SOUP

This outstanding soup requires just moments to prepare once you have the stock. Make an extra-rich stock with pieces from the chicken used in the main dish in this menu: Cut off the extra fatty skin at the back and neck cavities and cook together with the giblets, 1 bay leaf, 1/2 teaspoon salt, a generous slice of onion, and 3 black peppercorns. Chicken bouillon paste can be used to create the stock or purchased chicken stock can be used.

Makes 6 servings.

1 (10-ounce) can tomatillos with juice (or cook 3/4 pound fresh tomatillos until soft—about 6 minutes in a bit of salted water)
1 cup freshly made rich chicken stock
1 1/2 cups half-and-half
1 Tablespoon chopped cilantro leaves, plus 6 perfect leaves for garnish
1/4 teaspoon mild red ground chile

Place the tomatillos, chicken stock, half-and-half, and chopped cilantro in a blender jar or food processor. Process on a medium speed until puréed and foamy. Pour into bowls and garnish. Center the cilantro leaves in each bowl and sprinkle with the red chile. Chill, if desired, before serving.

JUANITA'S SPECIAL RIO GRANDE CHICKEN

Select a very young spring fryer, not over two and a half pounds, for this recipe and the freshest, top-quality vegetables. The dish almost prepares itself once the chicken is browned and the vegetables are prepared. Use a large heavy skillet, a Dutch oven, or even a deep cast-iron pot, as long as it has a tight-fitting cover. You can cook this to the almost-done stage and then heat just before serving, a technique I prefer so that I don't have to watch the clock after my guests have arrived.

Makes 6 servings.

2 Tablespoons unsalted butter
1 young frying chicken, about 2 1/2 pounds, cut into serving pieces
3 zucchini, about 1 1/2 inches in diameter and 6 inches long, cut in 3/4-inch slices on the bias
4 ears fresh corn kernels cut off the cob or 2 1/2 cups frozen, defrosted
2 large, fresh red ripe tomatoes (1 pound each), parched, peeled, and cut into wedges
1 cup thin rounds of small white or yellow Spanish onions
3 garlic cloves, minced
1 jalapeño, about 2 1/2 inches long, finely chopped
1/2 teaspoon cumin

Melt the butter over medium heat in a large heavy pot. Add the chicken, skin side down, and turn frequently to brown evenly.

When the chicken is browned, add the vegetables in layers—zucchini, corn, tomatoes, and onions. Sprinkle the garlic, jalapeño, and cumin over the top, cover, and steam, using a medium-high heat to create steam, then reducing heat to just maintain steaming. Check after 30 minutes to be certain all is cooking properly. (If cooking in advance, stop the cooking at this point before the vegetables are completely done.) Then continue to cook for about 30 minutes longer or until vegetables are done.

To serve, place on a platter with the chicken encircled with the vegetables. For added zip and to suit a mixture of palates—from gringos to chile fire-eaters—serve a side dish of salsa (see following recipe). Or add extra chopped jalapeño to the original dish.

SALSA FOR POLLO

1 jalapeño, about 3 inches long, finely chopped
1 small red ripe tomato, chopped
2 slices (1/4 inch thick) red Spanish onion, chopped

Combine jalapeño, tomato, and onion and serve in a small bowl with the chicken.

RICE AND PIÑON SALAD

This recipe came from a terrific idea I developed when looking for a change from the steamed or Mexican rice and tossed salad that so predictably accompany Tex-Mex dinners. Piñons (both the nuts and the tree) are an integral part of northern New Mexico culture—the choice nut for local sweets and confections, a favorite fireplace wood, and the preferred tree for Christmas. However, the trees have recently become increasingly scarce, and as they require centuries to replace, their by-products are not as readily available as they were when I was young. Pine nuts, however, can be purchased as an import, as they are also grown in the Mediterranean (as pignoli) and are used in Italian and Middle Eastern dishes.

Makes 6 servings.

1 cup basmati or long-grain rice
1 3/4 cups water
1 teaspoon salt
1 Tablespoon unsalted butter
6 Tablespoons vegetable or olive oil
2 Tablespoons cider vinegar
1/2 teaspoon Dijon mustard
1/4 cup chopped green bell pepper
1/4 cup sliced pimiento-stuffed olives
1/4 cup piñons (pine nuts)
1 head of red leaf lettuce, rinsed and chilled, or baby mesclun greens
12 to 18 thin slices of red Spanish onion

Combine the rice, water, salt, and butter and bring to a boil. Stir, reduce heat, and cover. Cook 15 minutes over very low heat. Remove cover and fluff with a fork. Set aside while you prepare the dressing.

Combine the oil, vinegar, and mustard in a bowl and wisk to create a smooth dressing, then add bell pepper, olives, and piñons. Stir into rice and chill at least 2 hours before serving. Stir once or twice while marinating.

To serve, place the lettuce leaves on chilled salad plates. Then heap on the rice salad mixture. Top each serving with the red onion rings. If desired, sprinkle on a few extra piñon nuts.

TEXAS FRONTIER CAKE

Once known as funeral cake, this dessert was a favorite in the sparsely settled arid regions of West Texas. In the nineteenth century, early settlers rarely got to a grocery store—sometimes as seldom as once a year. Funeral cake, a very simple recipe with a fabulous flavor, could easily be made from ingredients on hand and stored. It also traveled well as its current name implies—in the West family and friends took (and still do take) large quantities of foods over to the bereaved to help ease the heartache, and this cake was a very popular and delicious offering.

Makes one 9 x 13-inch loaf.

2 cups all-purpose flour
2 cups sugar
1 cup (2 sticks) unsalted butter
1/3 cup cocoa
1 cup water
1/2 cup buttermilk
2 large eggs, slightly beaten
1 teaspoon baking soda
1 teaspoon ground cinnamon or more for a spicier taste
1 teaspoon pure vanilla extract
Chocolate Icing (recipe follows)

Stir together the flour and sugar in a large bowl. Melt the butter with the cocoa and water in a saucepan, bringing to a boil. Pour the hot liquid over the flour mixture and stir well. Add the buttermilk, eggs, baking soda, cinnamon, and vanilla. Beat well and pour into a buttered 9 x 13-inch pan.

Bake 30 minutes at 400°F (200°C) or until cake springs back when touched. Meanwhile, prepare the icing and spread on the cake while it is still hot.

Note: The cake will keep moist, covered with plastic wrap, for several days.

Chocolate Icing

1/2 cup (1 stick) unsalted butter
1/3 cup cocoa
1/3 cup milk
1 pound (1 box) powdered sugar
1 teaspoon pure vanilla extract
1 cup coarsely chopped pecans

Combine the butter, cocoa, and milk in a 2-quart saucepan. Bring to a boil. Remove from the heat and add the powdered sugar. Beat well and stir in the vanilla and nuts. Use for frosting the cake.

GRAND EVENTS

OLD TOWN MERIENDA

Melon Basket with Minted Mexican Fruits
Chile Relleno Casserole
Pan Dulce
Albuquerque Cantaloupe Marmalade
Sweet Butter Balls
Hot New Mexican Chocolate
Spiced Tea
Sugared Sopaipillas
Praline Crown Cake

For a novel and gracious entertainment that makes for a beautiful, even elegant afternoon tea, try a merienda. Originating in Spain and kept alive by Spanish families in New Mexico, meriendas are a wonderfully festive way to host family and friends or even an event like a fund-raiser.

Before the days of the Old Santa Fe Trail, the foods served at a typical merienda were simple and drew from locally available ingredients. An example is Cota Tea, brewed from mint, elderberry flowers, and Mexican oregano—all of which grew wild in the foothills and along the arroyos. Today that tea is still served at meriendas along with Hot Mexican Chocolate, musts for the traditional minded.

This menu for an Old Town Merienda can be served any time from 11:00 a.m. on as either a brunch or tea. It is more substantial than many, as it includes a chile-laden main dish, which you can leave out if you wish to present a strictly afternoon, tea-type merienda. And while many serve only Southwestern or Spanish influenced sweets and pastries, I've added a fresh fruit basket for flavor contrast and color. Oftentimes locally produced specialty wines like chokecherry or wild grape, and occasionally sherry, are served.

The choice of sweet breads was selected to remain true to early customs. Pan Dulce, a treat straight from Old Mexico, is a symbolic sweet bread that is baked in a wide variety of shapes. It is always sold by colorful vendors on Sundays in the plazas of the little villages dotting the Mexican landscape. Sugared Sopaipillas are a specialty of Old Town Albuquerque, where the local culinary historians state they were first served in 1620.

The Praline Crown Cake is a newer recipe I developed with a nod to the custom of making pralines for meriendas. In fact, I've often made the candies and wrapped them in brightly colored tissue to hang from the piñon trees encircling my outdoor patio as a decoration.

Although meriendas are best staged outdoors, they will take well to inside presentation. The appointments I recommend are old Spanish lace or Mexican table linens if available. Or use your best white tablecloth. Decorate with brilliantly colored, oversized Mexican paper flowers or simple, showy garden flowers such as zinnias, dahlias, gladioli, or mums. Use your finest silver service, crystal, or glassware to lend the note of formality that is traditional for these occasions.

Menu Plan

One or two days before:

Prepare the Cantaloupe Marmalade.

Bake the Praline Crown Cake, cool, and spread with topping.

Bake the Pan Dulce and refrigerate if prepared one day before the meal; freeze if more than one.

Make the melon basket and chill overnight.

Make the butter balls using a butterball maker or use a 1/2 teaspoon round measure dipped in ice water, then into warm water. Keep both bowls handy.

Place the finished balls in a single layer on a cookie sheet covered with wax paper, then refrigerate.

Early in the day:

Prepare the fruits for the melon basket and the mint marinade, then marinate 2 hours at room temperature, followed by an adequate chilling period of at least 1 hour.

Combine the dry ingredients for the sopaipillas so that they will be ready for making into a dough 30 minutes before the guests arrive.

Prepare the ingredients for the Chile Relleno Casserole.

One hour before:

Assemble and bake the Chile Relleno Casserole.

Make the Hot New Mexican Chocolate (page 100).

Brew the tea and keep it hot.

Warm the Pan Dulce 10 minutes before serving.

Make the dough for the sopaipillas and let rest. Heat the oil just before the guests arrive.

Just before serving:

Fill the Melon Basket and arrange on a platter.

Place the cake on a footed crystal or glass server.

Set out the Hot New Mexican Chocolate and Spiced Tea.

Cut the Chile Relleno into squares and set the casserole on the table.

Arrange the Pan Dulce in a silver bread basket lined with a lace napkin.

Place the Cantaloupe Marmalade in a glass bowl and arrange the butter balls in a crystal bowl.

Have a previously designated guest help you fry the sopaipillas.

— MELON BASKET WITH MINTED MEXICAN FRUITS —

The beauty of this creation lies in taking the time to create an attractive basket. Just a bit labor intensive, it should ideally be prepared the day before. For large parties—for which meriendas are intended—a big, deep-green watermelon is perfect. If you wish to use smaller containers, twin honeydew baskets cut in sharp zigzags are also attractive. The melons and other fruits will have the fullest flavor if marinated at least 2 hours at room temperature and then chilled, but they should not be held more than 4 hours total.

Makes 14 to 16 servings.

1 large watermelon, 16 to 18 inches long
1 cup water
1 1/2 cups desert or strong-favored blossom honey
Juice of 2 fresh Mexican limes
1 cup fresh mint leaves, well rinsed and mashed
1 medium honeydew
1 large Mexican pineapple, thumping ripe
2 long (8 inches or better) cucumbers
3 papayas
Grape or citrus leaves for garnish, optional

Holding a sharp 12-inch-long chef's knife parallel to the cutting board, cut into the longest side of the watermelon about two-thirds of the way up the melon and one-third of the way into it. Make a similar cut from the other side. Then slice down one-third of the way to meet the lengthwise cuts, creating a 2 1/2-inch-wide handle—being very, very careful not to cut too deep or too far down as ripe watermelon, cut with just too much intensity, can sometimes crack. (You may find, when cutting a pattern, that using a grease marking pencil or a dull pointed knife to score the pattern you wish to follow is a more reassuring approach.) Once you are pleased with your cutting, remove the two pieces of watermelon carefully, rind and all. Trim any ragged cutting areas and cut out the watermelon flesh under the handle. Make 2-inch scallops all the way around the two lengthwise top sides. Leave the handle with straight sides. Chill overnight. Reserve the melon fruit for making melon balls.

Prepare the honey-mint sauce. Heat the water in a small saucepan. When it is simmering, add the honey. As soon as the honey starts to melt, remove from the heat. Add the lime juice and the mashed whole mint leaves, reserving about 6 mint sprigs for garnish. Set aside at room temperature.

About 5 hours or less before the party, make the melon balls and prepare the other fruits. Using the large side of the melon baller, scoop out the watermelon from the basket. Use the smaller side to make honeydew balls. Then cut the pineapple in half, peel, removing the "eyes," and slice into 1-inch-thick slices, removing the woody core. Cut into 1-inch wedges. (Refrigerate the watermelon basket again.)

Peel the cucumbers, then cut them horizontally into thirds. Cut each third in half, then into long, thin sticks—much the same way you probably make carrot sticks.

Peel the papayas, cut in half, and remove the seeds, then cut all the way across each half, creating half-moons. This way each fruit has its own shape, making an interesting array when you present it.

Place all the fruit in a very large bowl, deep enough to allow stirring. Carefully drizzle the honey-mint sauce over the fruit, covering as large an assortment as possible. Allow to set. Then occasionally stir, taking great care not to break up the pieces of fruit. Cover and set at the back of the counter or anywhere out of the way. Once the fruit has set out for 2 hours, chill it until serving time.

To serve, carefully spoon the fruits into the watermelon basket, making certain to save a complete assortment of each for topping it off. Then place on a large silver platter or any other large tray. Tuck the reserved mint sprigs randomly across the top. Garnish the tray with grape leaves, if available, or any broad pretty leaf such as a poplar, orange, or other citrus—even palm fronds. For an added touch, tie a big double bow of a pastel satin ribbon around the melon handle.

—— CHILE RELLENO CASSEROLE ——

Scottsdale socialites first made this dish a hit, and many versions have since evolved. My favorite comes from a terrifically warm, wonderfully accomplished hostess, Patti Stillman, whom I had the good fortune to have in one of my Santa Fe cooking classes a few years back. The last day of the weeklong session is always a party, and Patti was generous enough to share this favorite party recipe. It is simpler than some versions I've had, but it is somehow finer for its simplicity. I recommend it for this menu because it is easy and can be quickly tucked into the oven, and can even be held in a warm oven without losing its quality.

Makes 14 to 16 servings.

4 Tablespoons unsalted butter, divided
2 cups coarsely chopped Spanish onion
10 to 12 New Mexico hot green chiles, parched, peeled, deseeded (page 7), and cut into wide
   strips (about 2 cups)
2 cups coarsely shredded Monterey Jack cheese
2 cups coarsely shredded sharp Cheddar cheese
6 large eggs
1 quart milk
1 teaspoon salt
1 cup all-purpose flour

Use 2 Tablespoons of the butter to coat a large ovenproof casserole (about 10 x 14 inches), preferably a brightly colored earthenware type.

Heat the remaining 2 Tablespoons butter in a sauté pan, add the onion, and cook until it becomes limp. Meanwhile, place the strips of green chiles carefully across the bottom of the casserole and extend them up over the edge to create a crust effect.

Add the Monterey Jack and Cheddar in a flat layer. Beat the eggs, then add the milk and salt, and sprinkle the flour on the surface. Fold to incorporate, then whisk until fluffy and well combined. Pour into the casserole, being careful to create a uniform layer.

Place in a 375°F (190°C) oven for 45 minutes or until a toothpick comes out clean. If necessary, this casserole can be held in a 150°F (65°C) oven until serving time. Open the door for a time to reduce the heat. To serve, cut into squares and serve from the baking dish.

PAN DULCE

On Sundays, fiesta days, or holidays in central Mexico, these carefully shaped sweet breads are available not only in the bakeries but from numerous street vendors enthusiastically selling their wares. Often these pastries are so sweet that, particularly in the villages dotting the mountain valleys south of Mexico City, I can remember as a child being afraid of the droves of bees that were sure to be swarming around them. My Mexican aunt always reassured me that the more bees the better, for they only liked the sweetest, freshest rolls.

Makes 14 to 16 large buns.

THE BUNS

1 cup milk
1/3 cup unsalted butter
1 package active dry yeast
1/4 cup warm water
1/2 cup sugar
1 teaspoon salt
2 large eggs, beaten
5 cups or more all-purpose unbleached high-gluten flour

FILLING/TOPPING

1 cup sugar
1 1/3 cups all-purpose flour
1/2 cup (1 stick) unsalted butter
1 teaspoon ground cinnamon
2 large egg yolks
1 large egg beaten with 2 Tablespoons cream

Heat the milk, add the butter, and cook only until the temperature is hot enough to scald. Cool.
Meanwhile, dissolve the yeast in the warm (about 115°F) water, adding a pinch of sugar. Beat with a fork until it becomes foamy and all the yeast has dissolved.
Add the sugar, salt, and 2 egg yolks to the cooled milk mixture. Use a mixer with a dough hook if available. Add the yeast when it becomes foamy and you are assured it is active. Then add the flour, starting by sprinkling 2 cups over the surface of the mixture. Beat well, incorporating the flour into milk mixture.
Add about 1/2 cup flour at a time and continue beating until a firm, springy dough results. Turn out onto a well-floured board. Knead until smooth and elastic, 5 to 10 minutes.
Place in a buttered mixing bowl. Press the dough down and turn to coat with butter. Cover with a moist cloth and set in a warm, draft-free place to rise. It should double in about 1 1/2 hours. You can tell when it has properly risen when the dough is punched with a finger and a big hole results.

While the dough is rising, prepare the filling/topping. Using a pastry blender or a fork, combine the sugar, flour, and butter to create a coarse texture. Add the cinnamon. Continue to blend until a well-mixed crumbly texture results. Add the egg yolks and stir to blend. Set aside in a cool place.

Divide the dough into 14 or 16 equal pieces. Traditionally an assortment of shapes is made. Favorites of mine are the ears of corn, or *elote*, or the filled horns, called *cuerno*. Some like to make a crisscross marking on the top and sprinkle the topping on it.

To form the ears of corn, roll a piece of dough into a 4 x 8-inch oval, then sprinkle about 3 spoonfuls of filling on it and roll up from one end to the other, placing the seam side down and pulling the ends around the filling at the end of each "ear." When you have created 3 or 4, or as many as you are making, then slash the top of each with a sharp knife, cutting about 1/2 inch apart and only on the very top of each. This is to simulate an ear of corn. Place on a buttered cookie sheet.

The other favorite of mine is the horn, which is like our crescent roll, but filled. To make, roll a piece of dough into the same shaped oval, topping with the filling. Pull the two ends of the oval to the center, creating a triangular shape by folding the sides in. Roll, pushing the dough into a curve. Place seam side down on a cookie sheet.

To make the sticky buns, flatten a ball of dough to about 1/2 inch high and 3 inches across. Either smooth 4 spoonfuls of topping on each or sprinkle on. If smoothed, cut into a crisscross pattern, a diamond shape, or whatever you'd like.

Drizzle the beaten egg/cream mixture onto the horns and corn shapes, and cover the cookie sheets of dough. When doubled, preheat the oven to 375°F (190°C). Bake only until very lightly browned, but hollow sounding—about 15 to 20 minutes. Serve warm. To warm, place in a 350°F (180°C) oven for about 10 minutes. Excessive warming will dry them out and destroy the crunchy texture contrast.

ALBUQUERQUE CANTALOUPE MARMALADE

During the sixties, when I was busy teaching at cooking schools, writing columns, and doing numerous radio and TV shows, many people would share favorite recipes with me. This marmalade came to me from a cook in Albuquerque. After making it, I decided to reserve it in my tested recipe files for just the right moment, which is now.

Makes 7 half-pint jars.

1 medium-size ripe cantaloupe
1 large flawless lemon
1 large navel orange
1 cup crushed or minced pineapple, preferably fresh
Sugar (quantity varies; see directions)

Peel the cantaloupe, remove the seeds, and coarsely process the flesh in a food processor or blender, or chop rather fine. Quarter the lemon and orange. Using great care and a very sharp knife, thinly slice. Hand slicing is far superior here to machine slicing or chopping. Measure the quantity of fruit and add 3/4 cup sugar* for each cup of fruit. Place in a large crock or porcelain-lined heavy pot. Allow to marinate overnight.

Place the fruit in a heavy preserving kettle. Cook, stirring frequently, for 45 minutes or until thick and bubbly. Meanwhile, sterilize the jars and serving container you wish to use by placing them in a large pot with 1 inch of water. Boil, remove from heat, and allow to almost cool.

Skim the marmalade with a metal spoon. Place in sterilized jars and seal with paraffin. (It is not necessary to add the paraffin if you wish to serve within a day or two.) For the merienda, place the cooled marmalade in a pretty glass bowl or even a footed compote.

SUGARED SOPAIPILLAS

These delicious little "sofa pillows" are a must if you wish to carry out an authentic Spanish colonial-inspired merienda. I love them whenever I can get them. Since she was old enough to help, my daughter always fried them for me. She loved to watch them puff up and become instantly hollow in the hot oil, and I was freed to manage other details of the meal. (This, by the way, is a good strategy for entertaining: on the day of your party delegate the task of frying the pillows to a conscientious cook.) They are best eaten when freshly made and are generally served plain, with bowls of fragrant desert blossom honey, as an accompaniment to fiery entrées or sugared, with or without cinnamon, as a dessert.

Makes 4 dozen.

4 cups all-purpose, high-gluten flour
1 teaspoon salt
1 1/2 teaspoons baking powder

1 Tablespoon lard
1/4 cup water
1 package dry yeast (1 scant Tablespoon)
1 1/4 cups milk, scalded and cooled
2 quarts oil
1/2 cup sugar
1 Tablespoon ground cinnamon

Combine the flour, salt, and baking powder in a bowl. Work in the lard using a pastry blender, then your hands, until it is completely and thoroughly blended into the flour mixture.

Meanwhile, heat the water to 115°F, add the yeast, and beat with a fork to activate it. Add to the cooled scalded milk. Then make a hole in the center of the flour mixture and add about two-thirds of the milk mixture. Beat and stir to blend well. Add the rest of the milk mixture if the dough is not too sticky. Mix to combine thoroughly.

Pour out onto a floured board and knead very well until the gluten or protein within the flour will stretch when you pull a small ball apart with your fingers. Threads should extend between your fingers if the dough is well enough kneaded. In cooking schools I have always told the students that they should knead the dough until it becomes clean—does not stick at all to your hands—in addition to passing the gluten test. Place the dough in a clean bowl, cover, and let rest 10 minutes. (I generally leave the kneaded dough right on the board with the bowl over it to save some minutes.)

Heat the oil to 375°F (190°C) in an electric deep-fat fryer. Divide the dough into quarters and cover the portions you are not working with. Place one-quarter on a floured board, using the least amount of flour to prevent sticking and make a smooth uniform disk of dough. Then make what the Spanish in New Mexico call a *repulgar* edging, which is used to edge empanadas and pies of any type. To do this, fold a tiny edge of dough over between your forefinger and your thumb all the way around the dough. This creates a resilient edging that will allow a smooth edge as you roll it out. Roll into a rectangular shape, taking care not to roll the rolling pin over the very edges of the dough, as this creates "ears" that do not puff. Be careful as you roll and cut the dough because, as I always explain to my classes, the dough "is unforgiving" and simply will not work if rerolled—or at any rate, the odds for perfection are greatly reduced. Traditionally, the dough is cut into squares or any desired geometric shape. For this merienda, I recommend 2-inch squares. Repeat the rolling and cutting with the other portions of dough.

For greatest rising, carefully stretch a piece of dough a bit between your hands, being *very careful* not to punch a hole in it. Then slide the dough into the hot fat, keeping the side that had been against the rolling pin up or at the top. As soon as it is in the oil, take long steel tongs and keep the top of the sopaipilla immersed into the fat until it puffs. Turn it, being certain to fry each only until it becomes a very light golden color—not browned.

Drain each on paper towels. Be careful not to fry too many at a time as it will be impossible to watch them and they will not puff. You simply must hold them by the edges into the hot oil until each puffs. The only way around this is to have a much deeper, commercial fryer.

As soon as they are all cooled and still warm, shake them in a brown paper sack with the cinnamon and sugar. Serve in festive cloth-lined baskets.

PRALINE CROWN CAKE

This outstanding moist cake keeps well even days after baking. I particularly like it for brunches or festive affairs because it can be made ahead and serves multitudes, due to its rich, substantial texture.

Makes one 10-inch tube cake.

2 1/4 cups all-purpose flour
1 teaspoon baking soda
1 teaspoon ground cinnamon
1 teaspoon ground allspice
1 teaspoon ground nutmeg
3/4 teaspoon salt
1 cup vegetable oil
1 1/2 cups sugar
3 large eggs
1 teaspoon Mexican vanilla or pure vanilla extract
1/4 cup skim milk
1/2 cup nonfat yogurt
1 cup chopped pecans
1 cup raisins
Praline Topping (recipe follows)

Preheat the oven to 325°F (170°C). Sift together the flour, baking soda, cinnamon, allspice, nutmeg, and salt and set aside. Combine the oil, sugar, eggs, vanilla, milk, and yogurt in the bowl of an electric mixer and beat until thick and lemon colored. This will take about 5 minutes. Sprinkle about a third of the flour mixture on top of the egg mixture and beat on low speed until the ingredients are well mixed. Repeat until all flour mixture has been added. Add the pecans and raisins and fold in.

Pour into a well-buttered 10-inch Bundt pan or tube pan. Bake at 325°F (170°C) for 1 hour or until a toothpick inserted in the center comes out clean. (While the cake is baking, prepare the topping so that as soon as the cake is removed from the pan, you can frost it.) Let stand on a wire rack for 15 minutes or longer before turning out. (A more traditional frontier approach is to cool the cake on a "long neck," a tall glass beer bottle.)

Be very careful when you turn the cake out as it will sometimes start to tear if a nut or a raisin sticks to the top, so do watch it and ease the cake out with some assistance from a narrow rubber or wooden spatula. Then immediately spread the topping on the crown of the cake, letting it drizzle down the sides.

PRALINE TOPPING

1 cup firmly packed light brown sugar
1/2 cup nonfat yogurt
1/3 cup unsalted butter
1 Tablespoon real maple syrup

1 teaspoon baking soda
1/2 cup coarsely chopped pecans

Combine the sugar, yogurt, butter, and maple syrup and bring to a boil, then reduce heat quickly to maintain a low simmer, stirring frequently. Cook until the soft ball stage is reached—234°F (112°C) on a candy thermometer at sea level. Stir in the baking soda and place in a small bowl of an electric mixer. Beat at high speed until creamy, then add the pecans and fold in until well blended. Frost the warm cake.

CHIMI FOR YOUR CHANGO PARTY

Assorted Stuffed Jalapeños

Chimichango Trio with Beef, Pork, and Chicken Fillings

Sour Cream, Hot Red Sauce, Cold Salsa Verde, Chile con Queso, and/or Guacamole Toppings

Tostadas

Natillas with Fresh Pineapple

Sangria

Coffee

Most of your guests at this feast will probably never have heard the story behind the word *chimichango*, so as favorite friends roll their own be sure to tell them about its origins—and show them just how special they are. The word literally means a "bite for my loved one"!

One good occasion for this party is after a sporting event—skiing, boating, or swimming, for example—since, with the exception of the guacamole, there is very little last-minute detail.

Whatever setting you choose, be sure to allow for generous elbow room: with twelve people each trying to roll a chimichango at the same time, things can get a bit crowded. Create a work station with the tortillas wrapped in a slightly moistened linen towel and laid in a basket, surrounded by bowls of fillings, sauces, toppings, and garnishes in a pretty arrangement. Place a small cup of round wooden toothpicks nearby. If possible, use a very large, deep chicken-fryer or electric skillet for frying chimichangos, so more than one can be cooked at the same time. First, give a demonstration of the proper rolling technique to prevent frustration—then take your place at the fryer and let your guests go! (A variation is that you put them all in a 425°F [220°C] oven for 15 to 20 minutes.) If you want to add even more pizzazz, you can create a competition, awarding funny prizes for best efforts.

Mexican mariachi music will really set the tone for the occasion. In the winter, consider having the party in front of the fireplace if your furniture and table arrangement will allow it, and serve the sangria hot instead of over ice. In the summer, have the party on a patio, at poolside, or on a porch. Select a colorful but simple decor. Fiestaware or even brightly hued plastic or heavy, plastic-coated paper plates work well. Bright, simple garden flowers are the choice in the summer, and a rainbow of paper ones work well in the winter to add a gay touch to the table. Since the dishes here are easy to eat, they are fine as lap food, so a sit-down meal service will not have to be arranged.

MENU PLAN

Day before (or early in the day):
Prepare the jalapeños for stuffing.
Make the vegetable stuffing and salsa.
Grate the cheese.
Prepare the sauces, fillings, and garnishes for the chimichangos.
Make the tostadas.

Make the chile con queso, if desired (page 16).
If making guacamole (page 96), chop all ingredients except the avocados.
Make the natillas and peel and cube the pineapple, but do not combine them.
Prepare fruit and syrup for the sangria; combine and chill.

One hour or some time before:
Stuff the jalapeños.
Warm the sauces, fillings, and wheat tortillas for the chimichangos.
Make one batch of sangria and chill the serving glasses, if serving cold.
Set out the coffeepot.

At serving time:
Finish the guacamole, if using, and set out all the fillings, sauces, and garnishes for the chimichangos.
Heat the lard or vegetable oil, or preheat the oven.
Serve the stuffed jalapeños, tostados, toppings, and sangria while guests roll their chimichangos.
Make another batch of sangria and serve with the fried chimichangos.
Arrange the Natillas with Fresh Pineapple and serve with coffee.

— ASSORTED STUFFED JALAPEÑOS —

The sharp, clear flavor of freshly parched jalapeños is unbeatable in this appetizer, and although the chiles are available canned in Mexican specialty shops throughout the country, their flavor suffers in the canning process. While selecting the jalapeños, if you wish for milder ones look for those that are paler in color with broad shoulders at the stem end and a blunt tip. (These pointers apply to the selection of milder chiles of any variety.) If you want to make a much milder version of this dish, marinate the parched and peeled jalapeños overnight or at least an hour in freshly squeezed lime juice or substitute fresh Anaheims or poblanos. While I've included three of my favorites here, the filling variations are nearly endless.

Makes 48 stuffed peppers.

4 dozen fresh blemish-free jalapeños
1 dozen medium shrimp, peeled and deveined
1 cup sour cream
1/4 cup Cold Salsa Verde (page 14)
2 Tablespoons coarsely diced cilantro
1 cup diced tomato
1/4 pound queso (Mexican white cheese) if possible or Monterey Jack or sharp Cheddar
1/2 cup finely diced onion
1 cup thinly sliced red radishes
1/2 cup diced cucumber
1/2 cup cooked yellow corn kernels, preferably fresh
1 teaspoon fresh lime juice
1/4 teaspoon salt
1/2 cup yogurt
3/4 pound chorizo sausage, cooked and crumbled

Parch the jalapeños, following the chile parching instructions on page 7. Place 12 peeled jalapeños on each of four cookie sheets covered with paper towels.

Using a sharp knife, cut each from the stem to the tip, carefully removing the seeds. A small sharp pointed spoon such as a grapefruit spoon works very well for removing seeds. Pop them open using great care not to burst them. The best way to do this is to press both the tip and the stem ends simultaneously.

Prepare the four different fillings. Parboil the shrimp, drain, and cool. Place a spoonful of sour cream in each of 12 peppers. Then insert 1 shrimp in each, placing the tail of the shrimp toward the tip of the pepper. Drizzle a spoonful of salsa over each shrimp. Garnish each with a sprinkle of cilantro and a scattering of diced tomato. Cut the cheese into cubes to fit 12 more peppers. Top each with a few pieces of onion and tomato.

Reserving 1/2 cup of the radish slices, combine the remaining radishes with the cucumber, corn, and 1 Tablespoon of the diced onion. In a small bowl combine the lime juice and salt with the yogurt, then add to the vegetables. Stir together and stuff 12 more jalapeños. Garnish each with the remaining radish slices, arranging them fanlike.

Combine the cooked chorizo with the remaining sour cream and 1/4 cup chopped onion and stuff the last 12 peppers. Garnish with additional onion.

For an informal party, serve all of the stuffed jalapeños attractively arranged in circles on a large tray. Or serve on 12 separate plates, arranging one of each kind on every plate.

CHIMICHANGO TRIO

Since they arrived on the restaurant scene in the early eighties, chimichangos have become one of the top favorites of Southwestern cooking. Border rivalries exist, however, between those who claim credit for inventing this treat. Many seem to agree that these wonderfully crisp, spicy, meat-filled wheat tortillas were created somewhere around Tucson. Confirmed Texans disagree, and insist that a restaurateur in El Paso is responsible for the innovation. No matter. What is fun to know is that the literal meaning of chimichango in Mexico is "a treat for my dearest one"—a *chimi*, or little bit, for my *chango*, which translated literally is "little monkey," an endearing slang term for one's love.

During one of my Santa Fe cooking classes, a favorite student, Patti Stillwell, from Scottsdale, Arizona, developed a terrific presentation for the chimichangos she had prepared, which inspired this party. Lay out the three fillings and let each guest select one or a combination of them. After the chimichangos are fried, the guests can then choose from an assortment of toppings: sour cream, hot red sauce, cold green sauce, or chile con queso.

Makes 12 servings.

BEEF CHIMICHANGO FILLING
3 pounds lean stewing beef
3 medium-size baking potatoes, cut into 1/2-inch squares
9 medium-hot New Mexico green chiles (1 cup), parched, peeled, and chopped (page 7)
2 medium Spanish onions, chopped
3 garlic cloves, minced
1 1/2 teaspoons Mexican oregano
1/2 teaspoon ground cumin
2 1/2 teaspoons salt

Place the beef, potatoes, chiles, onions, garlic, oregano, cumin, and salt in a medium saucepan and barely cover with water. Cover and simmer 1 hour or more, until the beef is very tender when pierced with a fork. Taste and adjust flavoring, if desired. If the mixture is not rather thick, almost dry, remove cover and cook until quite thick.

PORK CHIMICHANGO FILLING
3 pounds cubed boneless pork butt
1 large onion, chopped
3 garlic cloves, minced
2 1/2 teaspoons salt
1 1/2 teaspoons ground cumin
1/4 cup ground pure mild California chile
1/4 cup ground pure hot New Mexico chile

In a medium saucepan with a cover, place the pork butt, onion, garlic, salt, and cumin and barely cover with water. Stew until the pork is very tender—at least 1 hour. Allow to cool slightly, then add the chiles and stir to mix well. Simmer over very low heat until thick.

CHICKEN CHIMICHANGO FILLING

3 chicken breasts, skin on, bone-in
1 medium Spanish onion, chopped
1 1/2 teaspoons salt
4 fresh, mild green chiles (1/2 cup), parched, peeled, and chopped (page 7)
1 cup shredded Monterey Jack cheese
1/4 cup sour cream

Place the chicken breasts in a saucepan with the onion and salt. Add water to barely cover. Stew over low heat until tender—about 30 minutes. Cool, then remove the skin and bones and chop the chicken into large cubes. Add the green chiles, cheese, and sour cream and stir to combine. If dry, add a few drops of chicken stock.

CHIMICHANGO FRYING INSTRUCTIONS

Fillings of your choice
36 wheat tortillas, warmed
2 pounds lard or 2 quarts vegetable oil*

To create a chimichango, place 3 to 4 Tablespoons filling in the center of a wheat tortilla. Fold the top side over the filling, then fold in one side and then the next, envelope fashion; finally fold the bottom up and secure with toothpicks.

Fry in at least 3 inches of very hot lard or enough to bubble up around the sides. Use a large slotted spoon to lower each into the fat to keep it from shattering as it fries. They should get golden on the first side before turning. This should take about 1 1/2 minutes, depending on the temperature of the fat. Turn and brown the second side.

Serve with an array of toppings and sauces, suggesting that each guest add their own preference.

*To bake, prepare as above and place them on a generously greased baking sheet and bake in a preheated oven at 425°F (220°C) until golden—about 15 to 20 minutes.

Note: The hot lard fries these the crispest, leaving a feathery light coating. If you must substitute another shortening, use vegetable oil, but the results will not be the same.

SANGRIA

This spicy, fruity wine concoction is a natural complement for picante foods. Do not be chintzy on your purchase of the wine. Contrary to popular opinion, a poor-quality wine used in sangria yields a poor sangria—I prefer to use a moderately good Spanish Rioja or California Merlot or Cabernet Sauvignon.

Makes 24 servings.

1 cup water
2 cinnamon sticks
1 1/3 cups sugar
2 limes, thinly sliced, rind and all
1 lemon, thinly sliced, rind and all
1 orange, thinly sliced, rind and all
2 bananas, peeled and cut into 2-inch pieces
2 bottles red wine

Boil the water with the cinnamon and sugar. Cook together about 5 minutes. Add the limes, lemon, orange, and banana. Chill when cooled to room temperature.

To serve, place ice in a large pitcher, then add about half of the fruit mixture and 1 bottle of the wine. Serve with some of the fruit in each glass over more ice, adding the wine mixture over all. Make another batch of sangria with the remaining fruit mixture and wine.

NATILLAS WITH FRESH PINEAPPLE

This light, traditional, yet very soothing dessert is just what's called for at the end of a spicy, somewhat filling meal. If at all possible, obtain a very ripe Mexican pineapple, as they tend to be sweeter than other varieties. Do not add the custard to the pineapple until just before serving. For the prettiest presentation, use parfait or sherbet glasses and layer the pineapple with the natillas.

Makes 12 servings.

1 quart milk
3/4 cup sugar
Generous pinch salt
4 large eggs, separated
1/4 cup all-purpose flour
Several generous gratings fresh nutmeg
1 fresh pineapple, peeled and cubed

Scald the milk in a saucepan with the sugar and salt, using medium-low heat. Remove and cool slightly. Add about a half cup of the warm milk to the four egg yolks, then gradually sprinkle on the flour and whisk until well blended. Add this thickening to the warm milk mixture. Place on the heat and cook until thickened, stirring constantly. The mixture should coat the back of a spoon when done. Remove from heat.

Whip the egg whites until stiff peaks form in an electric mixer. Fold them into the custard. Place in a serving bowl and generously grate nutmeg over the top. Set aside until serving time.

To serve, place about three to four pieces of pineapple in the bottom of each sherbet or parfait glass and add a layer of custard, then another layer of pineapple followed by a topping of custard. Grate more nutmeg over the top.

TAMALE ROLL

Guadalajara Beer
Crudités of Fall Vegetables with Special Salsas
Tortilla Stackup
Beef Tamales
Red Chile Sauce
Acapulco Salad
Pecan-Raisin Dessert Tamales
Mexican Coffee

One of my favorite times of year is the fall—when everyone can mix a bit of football-game watching with snacking, sipping, and, for a special occasion, tamale rolling. Tamales are a must for the holidays, and by throwing a "rolling" party you can not only entertain a select group of friends but also have the resources to easily prepare one of the most delicious of all Southwestern foods. Tamales are frankly too tedious to do by oneself, but when guests contribute some of the ingredients and help make the tamales, the work is both fun and rewarding.

Tamales are foods of the ancients, probably developed as a means to stretch out morsels of fillings. They were an especially practical meal in that they were more than likely cooked by being thrown into an open fire. The outside wrap of the tamale varies according to the region. In southern Mexico and Central America, banana leaves are used, while farther north, in Mexico as well as up into Texas and New Mexico, tamales are wrapped in corn husks. Of course, many commercial manufacturers substitute paper and even plastic wraps for cost and convenience—but what a compromise! The flavor and authenticity are both done away with. I have yet to sample an even reasonable facsimile of a real tamale in a store-bought version. So if canned or frozen tamales have turned you off, take heart. I'm sure you'll be very pleasantly surprised with these homemade ones—they are the *best*!

A tamale roll requires the luxury of a long evening or a weekend afternoon and should be presented as a simple kitchen or den party. Use down-home earthenware or pottery—even tin dishes—brightly colored napkins, and a simple centerpiece of vegetables and/or fruits or fall flowers such as chrysanthemums.

Menu Plan

Day before:
Prepare the beef tamale filling and red chile sauce.
Make masa for beef tamales and dessert tamales.
Prepare the Tortilla Stackup and chill.
Prepare the crudités and chill. Prepare salsas.
Chill the beer.

One hour before:

Bake the Tortilla Stackup about 45 minutes before guests are scheduled to arrive to allow time for cutting and garnishing.

Arrange the crudités and place the salsas in decorative bowls.

Soak the corn husks 30 minutes before guests arrive. Set out a large steamer to cook the tamales.

For the beer, set out the lime wedges in a bowl and the coarse salt in another.

Prepare the Acapulco Salad and chill. Make the dressing and reserve. Chill the salad plates.

Set out the coffeepot.

At serving time:

Set out all the ingredients for the beef and dessert tamales.

Serve the crudités and salsas with the beer while guests roll and tie tamales.

Garnish the Tortilla Stackup and serve while the tamales are steaming.

Dress the salad and serve with the beef tamales.

Serve the dessert tamales with coffee.

GUADALAJARA BEER

Years ago I coined the term "poor's man's margarita" for this drink. Tecate beer is usually served this way, as it is one of the few Mexican beers that are sold in cans, but any canned beer can be substituted. As you drink, you get the delightful sensation of the lime/salt taste accenting that of the beer. Wonderful! You will probably want to keep replenishing the lime and salt as you drink the beer.

Lime wedges
Canned beer, preferably Mexican
Coarse salt, such as kosher or sea salt

Ream a wedge of lime generously over the lip of an open can of beer. Sprinkle with salt.

CRUDITÉS OF FALL VEGETABLES
WITH SPECIAL SALSAS

For the crudités, be sure to select a variety of good-quality vegetables. The assortment should contain at least three types of vegetables of different colors and textures. Cut each in a decorative way for added style.

Makes 16 servings.

6 medium carrots, peeled and cut into thin curls with a vegetable peeler
4 turnips, peeled and cut into matchsticks
5 small zucchini, cut into thin rounds with peel on

Soak carrots, turnips, and zucchini in ice water until ready to serve.

SPECIAL SALSAS

For the salsas, I suggest you prepare the Salsa Fresca (page 15) or Colorado (below), depending on the heat preference of your guests—the Colorado is much hotter. Then prepare the Creamy Salsa Verde (page 14) for a mild one.

SALSA COLORADO

A famous restaurant in Santa Fe, New Mexico, gained much of its reputation from this very hot sauce. When they would not divulge the recipe, I decided to figure it out. To my great pleasure, the restaurant confirmed that, with this recipe, I had uncovered their secret.

1 (8-ounce) can stewed tomatoes, chopped (not sauce, nor the Spanish-type stewed tomatoes)
2 teaspoons chile pequin
2 teaspoons freshly squeezed lime juice
2 teaspoons cider vinegar
Generous pinch Mexican oregano
2 garlic cloves, finely minced
1 teaspoon freshly ground cumin
1 teaspoon whole coriander seed, crushed in a mortar and pestle, blender, or grinder

Combine the tomatoes, chile pequin, lime juice, vinegar, oregano, garlic, cumin, and coriander in a glass or pottery bowl and allow to marinate together for at least 30 minutes before serving.

TORTILLA STACKUP

A very easy appetizer whose fillings can be varied, Tortilla Stackup can also be served as a main dish—just cut it in larger portions. For an entrée, you may wish to tuck in stewed meat, such as beef, pork, or chicken, or a whole range of vegetables for a light luncheon dish. Be sure to select only the very freshest wheat tortillas for the best flavor and appearance.

Makes 40 servings.

25 (8-inch) wheat tortillas
1 1/2 pounds Monterey Jack cheese, shredded
1 1/2 pounds full-cream yellow Cheddar cheese, shredded
2 1/2 cups chopped New Mexico green chiles, parched and peeled (page 7)
2 cups thinly sliced green onions (scallions)
3/4 cup (1 1/2 sticks) unsalted butter, melted
1 head iceberg lettuce, finely sliced in chiffonade as for tacos
3 red, ripe tomatoes, chopped into 1/2-inch squares
4 cups sour cream, optional
Salsa, optional (use same as for crudités)

Lightly butter five 8-inch cake pans or use pie pans, soufflé dishes, or casseroles. Then place 1 tortilla in each. Mix Monterey Jack and Cheddar in a bowl, and lightly sprinkle about 1/3 cup of cheese on each tortilla, then 1 generous Tablespoon of the chiles and green onions. Top each with another tortilla and repeat, until there are four layers in each stack. Top each with a fifth tortilla, then brush with the melted butter. These stacks can be prepared several hours or even a day in advance, kept chilled, and then baked just before serving.

Bake uncovered in a 400°F (200°C) oven for 15 minutes or until lightly browned and the cheeses are melted. Cut each, using a very sharp knife, into 8 wedges, pie fashion. Arrange on a large platter, encircling with the lettuce and tomato. Garnish with the sour cream, if desired, or place the cream in a bowl in the center of the platter. Suggest that the guests spoon the sour cream and salsa over each wedge.

BEEF TAMALES

As I was growing up my mother often shared her fond memories of the tamale wagons in the Texas towns where she spent her childhood. Refusing ever to let commercial tamales grace her table, she taught my brother and me as well as other relatives and friends how to make these terrific-tasting homemade ones. When I grew old enough to entertain, I took tamale making one step further, using it as a wonderfully happy excuse for a party.

Assembling tamales can become quite tedious without helpers, so I've always invited at least four couples, preferably eight, to a tamale party. After an evening of sipping and snacking, there is no grand finale like tamales. We always make many dozen and at least two varieties so that the evening's work can be long remembered and savored.

One of life's equities is that although tamales are a lot of work to make, they can be frozen for at least a year without losing any flavor. I freeze them in bags of a dozen each and keep a simple scorecard in the bag so I can easily tell what the remaining inventory is.

For snacking, each medium-size tamale can be placed in a plastic bag and cooked in a microwave oven for about a minute and a half. Check to see that it is heated through, and rotate the tamale a quarter turn if more time is required.

To best enjoy tamales, always serve steaming hot with pots of one or more sauces for spooning over before eating. Be sure to tell gringos or those who have never had the pleasure of the real thing to be careful to remove the husk before saucing and eating.

Makes enough for 10 to 12 dozen tamales.

TAMALE FILLING

3 pounds beef round, cubed
1/4 cup bacon drippings or lard
1/4 cup all-purpose flour
1/2 cup ground mild pure California chile
1/2 cup ground hot pure New Mexico chile
1 quart beef stock, divided
2 teaspoons salt
1/2 teaspoon Mexican oregano
3 garlic cloves, minced

TAMALE MASA

7 cups warm water
12 cups masa harina
3 cups lard
1 1/2 Tablespoons salt
10 to 12 dozen dried corn husks, cleaned and trimmed

Simmer the beef in water to cover for 1 hour or until very tender. Remove from heat and, when cool enough to handle, cut into tiny cubes. (Cutting by hand is by far the best for both texture and appearance.)

In a large pot melt the drippings, add the beef cubes, then stir in the flour. When well mixed and lightly golden, remove from the heat. Stir in the ground chiles. When well combined, add about half the beef stock. Cook and stir until well mixed, then add the salt, oregano, and garlic. If needed, continue adding the beef stock a little at a time. Cook for about 30 minutes or until a very thick and smooth filling has been obtained.

To make the masa, add the warm water to the masa and stir to combine well, then allow to set for 15 or more minutes. The mixture should be the texture of a firm pudding—if too soft, add more masa; if hard and dry, add more water.

When the filling is done, the husks are soaked, and towels have been placed on the rolling table, whip the lard until very fluffy, using the high speed of the electric mixer. Add the salt, then add all the masa with the mixer running on low speed. When all has been well mixed, you are ready to roll tamales. This can be done early in the day.

Soak the corn husks in hot water about 30 minutes before rolling the tamales. Using a rubber scraper, place 2 or more Tablespoons of the masa mixture in a 3 x 4-inch rectangle, centered lengthwise on each husk. The masa should be about 1/4 inch thick. Allow at least a 1 1/2-inch margin on the top, about 1 inch on the sides and more on the bottom.

Place a thin strip of tamale filling down the very center. Hold the sides of the husks up, join them together, and roll to enclose the filling. Fold up the bottom, broader end, and tie using a strip of corn husk, fastening it with a bow, making sure that the broad end is just folded, not crimped. Then either crimp the top together or tie with a strip of corn husk, making a bow. If freezing them, freeze at this point.

When ready to cook, place the tamales upright in a steaming basket, and steam tightly covered for about 45 minutes or until the masa is firm. Check while steaming to be sure there is at least an inch of water at all times to create adequate steam. Tamales are done when they are firm when pressed, but not hard. An inserted knife will come out clean. Do not oversteam as they become hard and are not fluffy and flavorful.

Serve with a generous supply of Red Chile Sauce (page 11; triple the recipe). Serve with a plate for placing husks.

Note: If the tamales are frozen, steam as above, increasing the time to 1 hour and 10 minutes or until done.

ACAPULCO SALAD

Avocados festively accented with oranges, grapes, and jícama and dressed with a tart dressing make an unusual salad that is both beautiful and delicious. Never make it more than 1 hour in advance, although the basic preparation of the fruits can be done ahead. This salad can be halved easily.

Makes 16 servings.

5 large, ripe Haas or Fuertes avocados
1/4 cup freshly squeezed lime juice
2 heads fluffy leaf lettuce
5 seedless oranges, peeled and sliced into thin rounds
2 jícamas, peeled and coarsely shredded
1 large bunch (about 2 cups) seedless white grapes
Acapulco Dressing (recipe follows)

Halve and peel the avocados, then slice them into long, thin wedges. Sprinkle lime juice over all, carefully stirring to coat each piece evenly. Arrange the lettuce leaves on chilled plates or in a large bowl, then alternate wedges of avocado with slices of orange. Surround the edge of the salad with shredded jícama. Sprinkle grapes across the top. Prepare the dressing and drizzle over the salad just before serving.

ACAPULCO DRESSING

2 ripe Haas or Fuertes avocados
2/3 cup freshly squeezed orange juice
1/2 cup fresh lime juice
2 Tablespoons honey
1 teaspoon salt
1/2 teaspoon caribe or other crushed dried red chile

Place the avocado, orange juice, lime juice, honey, salt, and caribe in a blender jar and process until smooth.

PECAN-RAISIN DESSERT TAMALES

These delicately flavored tamales are marvelous served after the robust spicy ones. South of the border, where they are a much more frequent treat, they are considered more appropriate for a snack, either in midafternoon or late at night with hot Mexican chocolate or atole (a cornmeal beverage that has never become very popular north of the border). I keep these on hand for the holidays or for any time we want to celebrate with a festive meal. As with the other types of tamales, these too keep for one year in the freezer. In addition to being steamed, they can also be toasted within the husk on a hot *comal* (cast iron griddle). Just toast and turn until the husks are quite browned. Toasted tamales will be gooey and spongy on the inside instead of more solid as they are when steamed.

Makes 10 to 12 dozen.

1 recipe Tamale Masa (page 148–149)
2 cups sugar (can use half light brown sugar)
1 1/2 Tablespoons ground cinnamon or to taste
2 1/2 cups coarsely chopped pecans
3 cups raisins (half light is most interesting; can be marinated in rum or brandy)
8 to 12 dozen corn husks

While the masa is still in the mixer bowl, add the sugar, cinnamon, and chopped pecans. Spread masa mixture on soaked husks as described for Beef Tamales, sprinkling about 1 1/2 Tablespoons raisins in a strip down the center. Fold and tie with strips of husk. Steam as for Beef Tamales (or freeze in bags of dozens).

Variation: Almost any type of preserves can be substituted for the raisins. Candied fruit can also be used.

PIÑATA PARTY

Seviche

Pinot Chardonnay or other favorite white wine

Cold Cream of Avocado Soup

Olla Bouillabaisse

Jícama Escabeche Salad

Warm Corn Tortillas with Sweet Butter

Beaujolais or other favorite red wine

Peach Ice Cream Pie Cardinale

Mexican Coffee

Brandy

The very first time I savored a Southwestern version of a bouillabaisse was under the starry August skies of Santa Fe. A friend in the pottery importing business had just laid his hands on some wonderful Oaxacan *ollas* (large, fired clay cooking pots) and used the fish stew to christen one of them. I took his wonderful recipe, made the blend of ingredients a little more sophisticated, and added a margarita touch—and the result is the main attraction of a superb outdoor menu.

This party is very easy to put together, but its showy dishes will give the impression that you have slaved over them for hours. Although the meal can be managed in one day, you'll find yourself less pressured if you make the dessert, salad (which must be readied the night before in any case), and the bouillabaisse base a day ahead.

To create a festive party atmosphere, I really do recommend you invest in a piñata, which can be purchased at most Mexican crafts shops. Fill the piñata as you wish, using an assortment of candies, gag gifts, fortune cookies, or whatever will please your guests. Schedule the breaking for the finale of the dinner, a lovely light touch for the end of a party.

Decorate the table with brightly colored Mexican items, a vibrant pink, red, or purple tablecloth, and large fresh flowers. Back it all up with mariachi music or Spanish guitarists—live musicians would really be grand!

MENU PLAN

Day before:
Prepare the Jícama Escabeche Salad.
Make the stock for the bouillabaisse.
Prepare the Peach Ice Cream Pies and freeze.

Early in the Day:
Marinate the fish for the seviche.
Fill the piñata.

Prepare the fish and shellfish for the bouillabaisse and measure out the remaining ingredients.
Prepare the salsa.
Chill the wine.
Rinse and chill the lettuce for the salad.

One hour before:
Finish the seviche and chill.
Prepare the soup and chill.
Wrap the tortillas, ready for warming, 15 minutes before serving.
Chill the salad plates and forks.
Warm the shallow bowls for the bouillabaisse.
Chill the white wine and slightly cool the Beaujolais.
Set out the coffeepot.
Heat the stock for the bouillabaisse.
Arrange the salad on chilled plates.
Warm the tortillas.
Soften the ice cream pies in the refrigerator.

At serving time:
Arrange the seviche in goblets and serve with the white wine.
Serve the soup while you cook the bouillabaisse.
Serve the bouillabaisse, salad, and warm tortillas with the red wine.
Cut the pies into sixths and serve.
Serve coffee and brandy.
Break the piñata.

SEVICHE

Seviche has always been more a specialty of Mexico than New Mexico, which has no seas nearby. Sometimes spelled ceviche, this appetizer of fresh fish or even shellfish is "cooked" by freshly squeezed lime juice—an absolute must here. Although some recipes say lemon is acceptable, to me it is an unacceptable compromise that does not lend the authentic flavor to the dish. My own early affinity for seviche began in the Pacific coastal towns of Mexico, where this recipe originated. Traditionally, fattier fish, such as mackerel or pompano, are preferred, but if these do not appeal to you, you may substitute a lighter fish, such as snapper or sole.

Makes 12 servings.

2 pounds mackerel or pompano, cut into 1-inch squares
1 cup freshly squeezed lime juice (8 to 10 limes)
3 fresh jalapeños, cut into very thin, small strips, removing the seeds and veins (if real hot, consider using less)
1 1/2 teaspoons salt or to taste
2 cups diced fresh red ripe tomato (about 2 large), removing seeds and any watery pulp
1 medium purple Spanish onion, cut into very thin slices and separated into rings
1/2 cup extra-virgin olive oil
1/2 cup coarsely chopped cilantro leaves
12 leaf lettuce cups

Using a china, glass, or stainless steel shallow bowl, place the fish in a single layer, then cover with the lime juice, jalapeños, and salt. Cover and refrigerate for 6 hours, turning once after about 3 hours and spooning the lime juice over all.

In a separate bowl combine the tomato, onion, and cilantro with the drained lime juice. Taste and adjust flavoring. Then pour back over the fish. Gently stir together and refrigerate until ready to serve. Serve in goblets lined with the lettuce cups.

COLD CREAM OF AVOCADO SOUP

This pretty, velvety green soup is a splendid refresher for hot summer nights. Its rich creaminess is best savored in small servings—try it in crystal goblets.

Makes 12 (6-ounce) servings.

4 large ripe, chilled avocados (to equal 4 cups)
2 cups cold, heavy cream
2 cups richly flavored (preferably homemade) chicken stock
1 cup dry white wine, chilled
2 teaspoons salt or to taste
2 Tablespoons jalapeño juice or to taste (from pickled jalapeños)
2 teaspoons ground pure mild red chile

Cut the avocados in half, remove pits, and scoop the flesh into the bowl of an electric blender. Add the cream, chicken stock, and white wine and process until completely puréed. Season with the salt and jalapeño juice. Chill until ready to serve. Serve in goblets, sprinkling the red chile over the top of each.

OLLA BOUILLABAISSE

This Southwestern interpretation of a French classic is wonderfully easy to prepare. Select very fresh fish, even if you have to make substitutions for the suggested ingredients: quality is the key to the fabulous flavor and almost exotic taste of this dish. Firm-fleshed fish, such as the monkfish specified, should be used as the base for this stew; alternatives might be shark, swordfish, or even lobster. For the second fish, select a firm yet milder-flavored variety, such as hake, halibut, or cod. Substitutes for the clams (although I recommend trying to find them) could be shrimp or crab. The south of the border taste is the result of lacing the stew with tequila, triple sec, and freshly squeezed lime juice.

The stock mixture can be prepared hours or even a day before a party. If you have a Mexican olla or big earthenware pot with an interior glaze, use it to cook and serve from. Otherwise, any large casserole or electric buffet server will do. Serve with fresh lime halves to squeeze on top, and for those who can handle it hot, add a side dish of hot salsa as well as crushed dried red caribe chiles.

Makes 12 servings.

STOCK

1/4 cup olive oil
6 cups coarsely chopped Spanish onion (about 2)
2 fresh or dried bay leaves
6 large sprigs fresh thyme or about 2 teaspoons dried
2 Tablespoons minced flat-leaf parsley
8 large tomatoes, parched, peeled, and coarsely chopped
4 teaspoons salt
2 teaspoons caribe or other crushed dried red chile
6 garlic cloves, minced

BOUILLABAISSE

2 pounds monkfish, shark, or swordfish
2 pounds firm-fleshed fish, such as hake or halibut
2 dozen littleneck clams or any 2- to 3-inch clams
2 pounds bay or calico scallops
1/4 cup freshly squeezed lime juice
1 cup pure agave tequila
1/4 cup triple sec
1/4 cup finely minced flat-leaf parsley
1/2 cup coarsely chopped cilantro (optional)
Salsa Fresca (page 15)
6 fresh limes, halved
2 Tablespoons caribe or other crushed dried red chile

Put the olive oil in a very large stewing pot and place over medium heat, then heat until clear. Add the onion, bay leaves, thyme, parsley, tomatoes, salt, caribe, and garlic and stew about 15 minutes, or just long enough to blend the flavors. Then add 6 cups water, stew briefly, and set aside.

Rinse and cut both fish into bite-size pieces, about 1 1/2 inches square. Scrub the clams, place to soak in a bowl of water, and sprinkle cornmeal or oatmeal on top of the clams—this gets rid of the sand in the clams.

Heat the stock to a low simmer, then add the clams and cook 3 to 5 minutes or until they open. Remove and place in a bowl and set nearby. Add the fish and scallops and place the clams on top. Pour on the lime juice, tequila, and the triple sec. Cover and stew for 5 to 7 minutes or until the fish is just done. Remove from heat.

To serve, divide evenly among large shallow bowls, placing 2 clams on the top of each. Garnish with the parsley and cilantro, or serve the cilantro on the side. Serve with side bowls of salsa, lime halves, and caribe.

—— JÍCAMA ESCABECHE SALAD ——

Crisp, crunchy, unusual, and delicious, this salad should be marinated at least a day or more in the refrigerator.

Makes 12 servings.

6 to 8 carrots, sliced into 1/4-inch rounds
2 cups cider vinegar
2 cups water
1 cup vegetable oil
4 medium onions, thinly sliced and separated into rings
12 garlic cloves
2 teaspoons salt
4 teaspoons Mexican oregano
6 to 8 bay leaves
4 to 6 jalapeños (fresh or canned), stemmed and sliced lengthwise into thin strips
4 medium jícamas, peeled, sliced, and cut into 1/2-inch cubes
12 large leaves of red, romaine, or other leafy lettuce

Cook the carrots in a small amount of salted water until slightly tender; drain and cool. Combine the vinegar, water, oil, onions, garlic, and salt. Cook until onions are slightly tender. Add oregano and bay leaves. Bring to a boil, then cool. Add the carrots, jalapeños, and jícamas. Refrigerate at least 24 hours before serving. Keeps for weeks. Serve on lettuce leaves.

Note: Can also be served as an appetizer.

PEACH ICE CREAM PIE CARDINALE

Peach ice cream has always been one of my favorite summer pleasures. We always made it fresh on the farm, and I still prefer to, but I've found that the all-natural premium ice creams so easily available are also excellent and are a perfectly acceptable, time-saving compromise in this recipe. The layers of color are an appealing feature of this dessert: raspberries atop the rich, white vanilla topping and golden peach filling, held in a crisp cookie crust.

Makes 12 servings or two 9-inch pies.

2 cups vanilla wafers, crushed
1/2 cup (1 stick) unsalted butter
1/2 cup light brown sugar
1 teaspoon ground cinnamon
1/2 teaspoon ground nutmeg
2 pints premium-quality fresh peach ice cream
2 pints pure vanilla French ice cream
4 cups fresh red raspberries

Using a food processor or electric blender, process the cookies to yield very fine crumbs. Melt the butter and add it to the crumbs, along with the brown sugar, cinnamon, and nutmeg. Press the crumb mixture into two 9-inch pie pans.

Bake the crusts in a 325°F (170°C) oven until lightly browned, about 10 minutes. Meanwhile, soften the ice cream slightly and gently rinse the raspberries and drain on layers of paper towels to get completely dry.

Cool the crusts. If time is short, you may wish to flash-freeze them to be certain they are well chilled. Then spoon the peach ice cream in a smooth layer into the crusts, using 1 pint for each. Smooth on a layer of the vanilla ice cream, using 1 pint for each. Smooth the top, and freeze until firm.

When solidly frozen, evenly place the raspberries, bottom side up, over the top of each pie. Freeze until ready to serve. To serve, cut each pie into sixths. If very firm, allow to soften in the refrigerator before serving.

TEEN TACO PARTY FOR 12

Frosty Virgin Margaritas

Crisp Corn Taco Shells and Warm Corn Tortillas

Soft Wheat Tortillas

Assorted Fillings
Chilied Beef, Crispy Chicken, and Shredded Ham

Taco Bar
Shredded Lettuce, Chopped Tomatoes, Chopped Onions, Shredded Mixed Monterey Jack
and Cheddar Cheeses, Fresh Garden Salsa, Creamy Salsa Verde, and Caribe Chile

Adobe Bars

Milk

Iced Red Zinger Tea

Here is a party for teenagers that can be held almost anywhere, from a loft to a patio or deck, to a kitchen or dining room—even a picnic or in a barn. What also makes it an ideal menu is that it can be very quickly assembled.

In Mexico, tacos were traditionally treats that busy mothers made for their young children who were underfoot when they were trying to complete a meal. True to their practical origin, they have remained a comfort food and have become popular on both sides of the border. Today tacos are the number one choice among all Mexican entrée items. Thanks to the fast-food enterprises that specialize in tacos and have served millions of them, most Americans expect a taco to be a crisp-fried corn tortilla holding a meat—usually beef—filling, topped with a basic salad mixture of layers of finely shredded lettuce, tomato, and onion, and finished with cheese and salsa. But original Mexican tacos were a soft, freshly baked corn tortilla, traditionally taken right off the hot *comal* or *tapa* and wrapped around whatever filling—meat, beans, or chicken—that happened to be on hand. For another book I wrote, *Tacos, Tortillas, and Tostados* (Irena Chalmers, 1982), I developed twenty-two very different types of filling, including such unusual mixtures as avocado with alfalfa sprouts and flaked fish. The taco is obviously a more versatile food than many people realize, and this menu showcases a few of its many forms. Encourage all guests to "do their own thing." You may wish to give them some suggestions as to the procedure or your favorite ways of combining the fillings and toppings.

For whatever setting you choose, feature lots of oversized paper flowers, which you can make easily if you are so inclined from brilliantly colored, double-faced crepe paper or tissue. I've even made them large enough to stand on broom handles, which are a great decoration at the entry. For these, use the entire width of the paper, which is usually about thirty inches. A profusion of colors and types of flowers, either paper or real, centered on a colorful ribosa (long, fringed scarf) is a great centerpiece. Use pottery, Mexican if possible, to hold the various fillings and sauces, and use colored napkin–lined baskets for the tortillas. Artfully arrange the bowls of filling with the various condiments in circles around them, placing the sauces suggested for each nearest that filling. I generally use a mixture of various brightly colored napkins, rolled up and perkily popping out of large mugs. For this meal, as another appealing feature to teens, there is no need for silverware. Encourage everyone to come in fiesta clothes, and if you wish, provide some inexpensive satin sashes, sombreros, or even make brightly colored ball fringe necklaces.

MENU PLAN

Day before (or early in the day):
Prepare the taco fillings. Freeze the coated chicken and refrigerate the beef and ham.
Fry the corn taco shells (or do this about 1 hour before the party if you have a helper).
Prepare the soft wheat tortillas.
Prepare the Fresh Garden Salsa.
Bake the Adobe Bars.

Two hours before:
Brew the Red Zinger Tea.
Slice the lettuce, chop the tomatoes and onions, and grate the cheeses.
Prepare the Creamy Salsa Verde.
About 1 hour before, heat the oil for the Crispy Chicken taco filling, then fry the chicken pieces until just done—crisp on the outside, still very juicy on the inside. Drain and keep warm in a 300°F (150°C) oven.
Heat the Chilied Beef and Shredded Ham taco fillings.
About 15 minutes before serving, warm the taco shells in a 300°F (150°C) oven or keep warm if just fried, placing a wad of paper towels in each so they won't close as they crisp. Wrap some corn tortillas in foil to warm in packets of 6 each. Also warm the wheat tortillas in foil packets of 6 each.
Warm the dinner plates.
Just before serving, make the Frosty Virgin Margaritas.

At serving time:
Set out all the taco bar items—taco shells, tortillas, fillings, and garnishes.
When you remove the plates and other items from the oven, place the platter of Adobe Bars inside.
Serve the Red Zinger Tea and margaritas in pitchers with a side bowl of ice.

FROSTY VIRGIN MARGARITAS

Though the kick is gone, these drinks still have a fresh, cooling "zap." They can be served either frozen, as indicated, or in pitchers.

Makes 24 servings.

3 (12-ounce) cans frozen limeade, divided
1 (6-ounce) can frozen orange juice concentrate, pulpy variety, divided
1 (6-ounce) can frozen grapefruit juice, divided
32 ounces of ginger ale, divided
2 fresh limes, cut into 24 thin rounds

Put half the limeade, orange juice, grapefruit juice, and ginger ale in a blender. Add some ice cubes and process on high speed; add ice until desired consistency. Serve in large globular goblets with a round of lime as a garnish. Make a second batch with the remaining ingredients.

CRISP CORN TACO SHELLS

Although you can fry taco shells for this party the day before and rewarm them, as I suggest in the menu plan, try to fry them fresh about two hours before serving. Use the two-tongs technique or, easier still, buy taco-frying tongs, which are available in gourmet and department stores. If you must, of course, you can buy the taco shells ready-made. When you make your own, you can offer as many as three colors of corn—yellow, white, and blue—and can fry the tacos three different ways—flat, the traditional U shape, or in the basket or tostado form.

Makes 48 shells.

4 dozen corn tortillas, preferably 1 dozen each yellow, white, and blue (or if serving some tortillas just warmed—fry 24 shells and warm 24 corn tortillas)
2 quarts vegetable oil

Set up a cooking area, allowing a good-sized space for draining the tacos. Place several layers of paper towels under a wire taco rack. If unavailable, make enough small wads of paper towels, about 1 1/2 inches in diameter, for each of the traditional U-shaped tacos you are creating.

Meanwhile, heat the oil to 375°F (190°C) in a deep-fat fryer or in a 5-quart heavy pot, using a candy thermometer to aid in maintaining the temperature, which is critical for good results.

To fry the traditional U shapes, place a tortilla in the basket holder, making sure that the side of the tortilla with the least browned edges is on the outside. Or use 2 tongs to hold either side when frying.

Then immerse in the hot fat until the bubbles slow down, usually about 15 seconds. Fry each until it is crisp, dry, and not shiny looking, which indicates undercooking. Do not overcook, as the flavor and color will not be as good.

As soon as each is fried, remove with tongs and drain—either on the rack or on its side with a wad of paper towels inside, which is important for draining the fat as well as to keep the taco shell from folding together.

If frying them with two tongs, grasp the two opposite sides of the tortilla, making certain that the side of the tortilla with the least browned appearance is on the outside—a tip to make bending easier and breaking less potential. Submerge in hot fat and fry until the bubbles subside and it is crisp, not browned. Drain as above.

To create flat tacos, or tostados, just hold one side of the tortilla with your tongs and fry until crisp. Drain as above, omitting the wads of paper, but topping each with additional paper towels.

To create tostados compuestos, the little baskets, the simplest way is to use either a tostado frying basket or easily create one from an 8-ounce can, such as for tomato sauce.* To fry, place the tortilla on top of the fat and immediately center the can on the tortilla, holding it down with tongs. The edges of the tortilla will flute up around the edges of the can. When the bubbles subside and the tortilla is crisp, remove the fried tortilla from the can using tongs, and place a wad of paper towels on the inside of each. Drain on towels.

*To make the frying mold, punch four equidistant holes in the bottom of the can using a beverage opener. Then turning the can on its side, cut four holes on the side of the can halfway between each of those on the bottom. Wash the can well, removing any labels, and dry thoroughly before using.

SOFT WHEAT TORTILLAS

Wheat tortillas, introduced by the Spanish and popularized in northern Mexico, are today the staple bread of the New Mexicans and other regional descendants of the Spanish. Even more than corn tortillas, they are at their very best when homemade: store-bought are never as fresh or flavorful. Once you acquire the knack of kneading, rolling, and baking them—pointers are included in the following recipe—you'll find you prefer to make your own whenever possible. If you don't have the time to bake tortillas fresh, look for commercial tortillas that are creamy colored, very fresh looking, and not dry and crinkled around the edges. Also, look for tortillas with small brown baking spots—larger spots indicate too-rapid baking. Warm them in packets of foil, placing no more than 6 tortillas in each package. Heat at 350°F (180°C) for 10 to 15 minutes, but no longer or they will dry out.

Makes 18 (12-inch) or 24 (8-inch) tortillas.

8 cups unbleached all-purpose flour
1 Tablespoon salt
1 1/2 Tablespoons baking powder
1 teaspoon sugar
1/2 cup lard
3 cups warm water

Place the flour, salt, baking powder, and sugar in a very large bowl and mix together, then using a pastry blender or your hands, cut in the lard until it is the texture of cornmeal or a handful of the mixture when gripped will hold slightly together and there are no lumps of lard. Make a well in the center, add all the water, and mix well.

Turn the moist dough out onto a floured countertop and knead the dough until it is very smooth and quite firm and springy and will no longer cling to your hands. Cover and let stand in a warm place until a large hole is left in the dough when punched—15 to 30 minutes.

Meanwhile, shortly before the dough is relaxed, heat a seasoned cast iron comal, or griddle, or a cast iron wood- or coal-burning stove lid. Lacking any of these, heat a stainless steel or other heavy griddle that will hold lots of heat and create fast baking.

Divide the dough into balls the size of an egg. Then stretch each, one at a time, holding it up and pulling out the dough. Twist the edges into a small curl over one finger at a time to create an edge that the Spanish-descendant New Mexicans call *repulgar*, which is the same edging used for empanadas and pie pastries (described more fully on page 133).

Roll each tortilla with a small rolling pin called a *bollillo*, the Spanish name for a rolling pin that is only 2 inches in diameter and about 8 inches long. This ensures the best control over the very firm, springy dough. Roll, pressing out from the center and turning so as to create a smooth, evenly round tortilla—it will require lots of downward pressure to roll out. A low (32-inch-high) pastry board or marble is best for rolling them on, as long as it is not too far from where they are to be baked.

To bake, place them one at a time on the heated comal or griddle. Each side is done when it bubbles up and there are dark-brown flecks; then turn to cook the second side. The baked tortilla should have no shiny spots, as they indicate underbaking. When done, place them on a plate covered with a linen towel and keep them stacked, one on another. Serve warm.

CHILIED BEEF TACO FILLING

This is the taco filling most familiar in America. Use very lean beef and fresh pure chiles and spices for richest flavor.

Makes enough for 18 tacos.

1 1/2 pounds very lean ground beef
2 garlic cloves, minced
3 Tablespoons ground pure mild chile
1 Tablespoon ground pure hot chile
1/2 teaspoon Mexican oregano
1/2 teaspoon cumin
1 teaspoon salt

Lightly sauté the ground beef in a large skillet, then add the garlic, mild and hot ground chiles, oregano, cumin, and salt, and cook and stir until well blended and the hamburger has lost its pink color. Drain well by placing all the beef to one side of the skillet and then tilting the pan at a sharp angle with the meat at the top. Pour off the fat, blotting up the balance with a paper towel. Reheat the meat to serve.

CRISPY CHICKEN TACO FILLING

This chicken gains a distinctive flavor from its coating of corn masa, which I flavor with just a dash of chile and herbs. Freezing the coated chicken pieces before deep-frying assures greater breading retention and juiciness. The coated pieces can be frozen for up to three months. They should be fried only until done, thoroughly drained, and served while still hot. (Fry only until golden, and keep warm in a 300°F [150°C] oven which will finish cooking them.) I like to serve these in crisp taco shells, placing the chicken pieces on a bed of lettuce and garnishing them with Creamy Salsa Verde (page 14) and a sprinkle of red tomato squares and caribe.

Makes enough for 18 tacos.

1/2 cup masa harina
1 teaspoon ground cumin
1 Tablespoon ground pure mild chile
1 Tablespoon ground pure hot chile
1 teaspoon salt, divided
1 Tablespoon minced fresh parsley
1 teaspoon Mexican oregano
2 garlic cloves, minced
1/2 cup all-purpose flour

Few grinds of fresh black pepper
3/4 cup milk
1 1/2 pounds boneless chicken breast
1 quart vegetable oil

In a small bowl combine the masa harina with the cumin, pure mild and hot ground chiles, 3/4 teaspoon salt, fresh parsley, oregano, and garlic. Place in a flat, shallow bowl. Place the flour, remaining 1/4 teaspoon salt, and pepper in another bowl and stir together. Place the milk in a third bowl.

Trim the chicken breast of any skin, bone, or membrane and cut into 3-inch-long "fingers" about 3/4 inch in diameter. Spread wax paper on a large cookie sheet. Coat the pieces of chicken by first placing them in the milk, then the flour, then the milk, and finally into the masa mixture. Freeze until firm—at least 4 hours or preferably overnight.

To fry, preheat the oil to 350°F (180°C). Place several pieces of chicken in a frying basket and cook only until the bubbles begin to subside and the pieces are an even golden brown.

Serve with a layer of very thinly sliced lettuce on the bottom of a taco shell, topped by 3 to 4 pieces of the crisply fried chicken, topped by the salsa and garnished with 4 or 5 tomato squares and a sprinkle of caribe chile if desired.

— SHREDDED HAM TACO FILLING —

This filling is not only innovative but is also an excellent accompaniment to the beef and chicken. Although pork is quite common throughout Mexico and the Southwest, it is rarely served smoked as ham. Ham prepared in this fashion is also great in either soft tacos or burritos—for these, try coleslaw and chile con queso as toppers.

Makes enough for 18 tacos.

1 cup chicken bouillon
1 1/4 pounds lean, fully cooked ham, sliced
1/4 cup chopped onion

In a 2-quart saucepan, boil and reduce the chicken stock to 1/2 cup, then add the ham and onion and stir together. Cover and simmer for about 20 minutes. Using two forks pulling against each other, shred the ham. Drain off all juice and keep tightly covered until serving time. If reheating, heat in a covered pan, stirring until uniformly warmed.

TACO BAR

For garnishing the tacos, feature an attractive array of ingredients that everyone can have fun mixing and matching. I've indicated within each of the taco recipes certain combinations that are perhaps the most flavorful or traditional complements, but feel free to try different variations. Teen guests seem to prefer straightforward toppings—nothing terribly unpredictable or exotic—a factor I have kept in mind for the following suggestions.

Makes enough of each for 12 guests.

FINELY SHREDDED LETTUCE FOR TACOS

2 heads iceberg lettuce

Rinse each head thoroughly, removing all coarse outside leaves. Slice in half, cutting down through the core. Cut out and remove the core. Slice very thinly with a very sharp knife. Try to slice so fine that none is thicker than an eighth of an inch. When I teach this, I always say to cut it in an angel-hair shred—leaving the thin slices intact—or to cut so fine that you can almost read a newspaper through it. (This process is called chiffonade in French.) If you have a slicer, you can slice it with a No. 8 blade setting. I do not feel a food processor leaves the slices intact enough.

CHOPPED TOMATOES

3 large red ripe tomatoes

No more than 2 hours before serving, cut each tomato in half through the stem, removing the stem and blossom. Using a very sharp knife, cut into 3/8-inch slices. Then cut each slice into 3/8-inch squares, shaking out excess seeds and juice.

Note: Do not peel, as they will tend to get mushy on the serving table.

CHOPPED ONIONS

1 large Spanish onion

Use a sharp knife and coarsely chop the onion into 1/4-inch squares, trying to keep all of them uniform as the appearance is best that way.

SHREDDED MONTEREY JACK AND CHEDDAR CHEESES

1 1/2 pounds Monterey Jack cheese
1 1/2 pounds dark-yellow full-cream Cheddar cheese

Using a very coarse hand grater, shred the cheeses, taking care not to let very much accumulate in the bowl under the grater. A food processor can be used, but the cheese will not be as coarse or as fluffy. To serve, toss to blend uniformly and place in a bowl.

Fresh Garden Salsa

See the recipe on page 13. Prepare early in the day or the day before for the best marriage of flavors.

Creamy Salsa Verde

See the recipe on page 14. This salsa is best freshly prepared—an hour or so before serving.

Caribe Chile

Put out a small bowl of caribe for guests to sprinkle on the Creamy Salsa Verde.

Coleslaw for Tacos

1 (3-pound) head white cabbage
1/3 cup olive oil
1/3 cup cider vinegar
2 Tablespoons coarsely chopped cilantro or flat-leaf parley
Salt to taste
Freshly ground pepper to taste

Finely shred a half head of white cabbage and place in a large bowl. Add olive oil, cider vinegar, cilantro or parsley, salt, and freshly ground black pepper to taste. Toss together, taste, and adjust flavoring.

ADOBE BARS

Resembling adobe blocks, New Mexico's most traditional home-building material, these cookies are made from a rich combination of layers of butterscotch, chocolate, marshmallow, and pecans. The bars are good travelers so are terrific for picnics. Ice cream goes especially well with them.

Makes 5 dozen.

1 cup (2 sticks) unsalted butter, softened
2 cups white sugar
6 large eggs, 2 whole and 4 separated
3 cups all-purpose flour
2 teaspoons baking powder
1/2 teaspoon salt
2 cups chopped pecans
1 cup semisweet chocolate morsels
2 cups miniature marshmallows
2 cups light brown sugar

Preheat the oven to 350°F (180°C). Beat the butter in a bowl of an electric mixer until it becomes fluffy, then add the white sugar, 2 whole eggs, and 4 egg yolks. Add the flour, 1 cup at a time, along with the baking powder and salt, beating first on low speed until the dry ingredients are incorporated, then on medium speed to combine well.

Butter two 9 x 9-inch baking pans, then smooth half the batter in each, creating a uniform layer. Dividing each between the two pans, evenly sprinkle the pecans, chocolate pieces, and marshmallows over the batter.

In a small bowl of an electric mixer, beat the 4 egg whites until stiff, then sprinkle on the brown sugar a small amount at a time and carefully fold it in until well combined, being sure not to break down the egg whites. Spread over the top of each pan, dividing the meringue evenly.

Place in the preheated oven and bake until an inserted toothpick comes out clean. Cool for about 30 minutes, then carefully cut into rectangular bars. Store until serving time. These can be served cool or slightly warmed.

ICED RED ZINGER TEA

A sparkly ruby-red color, this tea is a very refreshing beverage to serve with the tacos. Create a sangria effect by adding spirals and slices of fruit, as described.

Makes 24 servings.

12 red zinger tea bags or equivalent loose tea (available from Celestial Seasonings and other herbal tea companies)
4 oranges, with the peel cut off into approximately 4-inch spirals
3 lemons, cut into thin rounds
3 limes, cut into small full-length wedges

Two to four hours before serving time, bring 4 1/2 quarts water to a boil, then pour into pitchers. Immediately add the tea bags. When the tea has become a bright red and the flavor is developed, remove the bags and add the orange peel strips and the lemon slices. Allow to set until serving time.

Place ice in the serving glasses, then pour in the tea, adding a spiral of orange peel and a slice of lemon. Garnish each glass with a wedge of lime placed over the rim.

POOLSIDE PARTY

Santa Fe Slings
Alejandrinos
Zucchini Bites in Crisp Blue Cornbread Coating with Salsa Fresco
Barbecued Lamb Kabobs
Summer Vegetable Kabobs
Chile Scampi
Confetti Rice
Mexican Chocolate Ice Cream
Coffee

What I had in mind when developing this menu was a congenial setting on a long, lazy day. Though the meal would be pleasing in most any summertime setting, it's best by a bright-blue pool or a cool lakeside, preferably near a barbecue.

Make the appetizers a group activity by having all the ingredients and the batters handy so that each guest can fry his or her own zucchini and dunk it in the salsa. The barbecuing for the main course is quick—twenty minutes for the vegetables and only ten for the lamb. The shrimp is even quicker and can easily be prepared in an electric skillet outdoors. To complete the meal, what could be more nostalgic than the cranking of an ice cream maker, freezing a perfect dessert for when you're relaxing and enjoying the company of your friends.

Keep the setup simple so that you can entertain with a minimum of preparation. Use buffet service with perhaps a gorgeous array of summertime flowers in the center of the table.

Menu Plan

Day before (or early in the day):
Prepare the marinade and marinate the lamb kabobs.
Parch and peel the jalapeños and refrigerate.
Clean the shrimp and refrigerate.

Three or more hours before:
Prepare the ice cream mixture and start it churning.
Prepare the Salsa Fresca for the appetizers.
Marinate the jalapeños in lime juice.
Prepare the Zucchini Bites and the vegetables for the kabobs.
Prepare the ingredients for the Confetti Rice.
Prepare the batters for both appetizers; stuff the jalapeños.

One hour before:

Prepare the charcoal fire.

Skewer the lamb chunks, set on a jelly roll pan or any large flat pan with a lip, and drizzle with the marinade.

Prepare the wine mixture for the Santa Fe Slings.

Skewer the Vegetable Kabobs and brush with oil.

Prepare the ingredients for the Chile Scampi.

Just before serving, set out a deep-fryer and heat the oil for the appetizers.

Set out the coffeepot.

At serving time:

Set out the Alejandrinos, Zucchini Bites, Salsa Fresca, and their batters. Start to cook the Vegetable Kabobs.

Cook the rice.

Serve the Santa Fe Slings while guests cook their own appetizers.

Cook the Lamb Kabobs and the Chile Scampi.

Arrange the kabobs on a platter and serve with the Scampi and Confetti Rice.

Serve ice cream and coffee.

SANTA FE SLINGS

For a lighter version of this tall, cooling drink, add seltzer water. Of course you can also substitute a different wine.

Makes 12 servings.

6 cups dry red burgundy wine
2 cups orange juice
1/4 cup lemon juice
1 (20-ounce) can crushed pineapple with juice
1/4 cup sugar
1/2 cup dark rum
1 quart seltzer, optional
2 large navel oranges, thinly sliced, rind on

Place the wine, orange juice, lemon juice, pineapple and juice, sugar, and rum in a large pitcher and stir well to combine. Allow to set at least 30 minutes.

Using tall cooler-type glasses, place 3 or 4 ice cubes in each and add the wine mixture, making sure to spoon in some of the pineapple. Splash in the seltzer, if desired, and garnish with an orange slice, cutting a thin cut through the peel so it will drape over the edge of the glass.

ALEJANDRINOS

Here is a very special appetizer from Mexico that, once sampled, will undoubtedly become a frequent feature at your dinner parties. I've adapted the recipe to take the sting out of the jalapeños, marinating them in freshly squeezed lime juice after the seeds and veins have been removed. To guarantee that they'll be as mild as possible, select fresh jalapeños that are large and light in color, with broad shoulders and a blunt tip. (The opposite characteristics in any pepper deliver raw, undiluted heat.) If desired, you can substitute the blue corn batter that is used on the zucchini for the following one based on egg whites.

Makes 24 appetizers.

24 fresh jalapeños, parched and peeled (page 7)
Juice of 1 fresh lime
1/4 pound Monterey Jack cheese, cut into small strips
1 pint cooking oil for pan-frying or 1 quart for deep-frying
3 large eggs, separated
1/2 teaspoon baking powder
3 Tablespoons all-purpose flour
1/4 teaspoon salt
Salsa Fresca (page 15), optional

Using a very sharp small pointed knife, cut each jalapeño in half lengthwise and scrape out the veins and seeds. Marinate in freshly squeezed lime juice in a small shallow bowl for 2 hours at room temperature, turning often and spooning the juice over them. Remove and blot dry, then place a strip of cheese in each and place between two layers of paper towels.

Heat the oil in a deep-fat fryer to 375°F (190°C)—the same used for the Zucchini Bites will work well—or place 1 1/2 inches of oil in a shallow frying pan and heat oil using medium-high heat.

Prepare the batter by beating the egg whites until stiff in the bowl of an electric mixer. In a separate bowl beat the yolks with a whisk, then add the baking powder, flour, and salt. Mix together, adding a few spoonfuls of the egg whites to make a smooth mixture. Fold the yolk mixture into the remaining egg whites. Coat each chile with batter and fry 2 or 3 at a time until golden. Serve with salsa.

ZUCCHINI BITES IN CRISP BLUE CORNBREAD COATING WITH SALSA FRESCA

Make these either a few minutes before serving or, preferably, set a small deep-fryer on the patio table and encourage the guests to cook their own.

Makes 12 servings.

1/2 cup all-purpose flour
1/2 teaspoon baking powder
1/4 teaspoon salt
1/3 cup blue cornmeal
1 large egg, slightly beaten
1/2 cup milk
6 zucchini, about 1 inch in diameter and 5 inches long
1 quart cooking oil
Salsa Fresca (page 15)

Using a shallow bowl, place the flour, baking powder, salt, and cornmeal in it, then add the egg and the milk and mix well. This batter holds and mellows very well, up to 6 hours. Prepare the zucchini by rinsing them, then cutting into 2-inch-long pieces.

To cook, heat the oil to 375°F (190°C). Using long bamboo skewers, pierce each piece of zucchini and dip into the batter, then fry until lightly golden. Drain well. Serve with the picks in them with a bowl of salsa. Enjoy while still warm.

BARBECUED LAMB KABOBS

This is a recipe I've been perfecting since I first began exploring cooking, teaching it, and writing cookbooks. The first time I tried it, in 1960, I loved its succulent flavor, which seems to transcend almost all ethnic boundaries. I was first taught how to make these kabobs by a Lebanese chef from Chicago and have since been given tips on their preparation by various friends, students, and other cooks. Cook the lamb on separate skewers from the vegetables (next recipe), as their cooking times vary. Use either bamboo or metal skewers.

Makes 12 servings.

4 pounds lean lamb, cut from the leg into 2-inch squares
2 cups burgundy wine
1/2 cup chopped onion
2 bay leaves
1 Tablespoon Worcestershire sauce
2 minced garlic cloves
2 Tablespoons soy sauce
1/2 teaspoon dry mustard
6 Tablespoons virgin olive oil
1 teaspoon minced fresh rosemary or 1/2 teaspoon dried
1 teaspoon minced fresh thyme or 1/2 teaspoon dried
1 teaspoon minced fresh basil or 1/2 teaspoon dried
1 teaspoon minced fresh tarragon or 1/2 teaspoon dried
1 teaspoon minced fresh marjoram or 1/2 teaspoon dried

It is easier to have a butcher cut up the meat, but do find a good butcher and be specific, stating that it is for shish kabobs. Have the butcher save the bones and you can boil them in water with herbs and onion and carrot for stock for soups, stews, or even as the base for drinks such as the bull shot.

Combine the wine, onion, bay leaves, Worcestershire, garlic, soy sauce, mustard, oil, rosemary, thyme, basil, tarragon, and marjoram in a large shallow bowl. Mix well, then add the lamb and stir to coat all the meat evenly. Cover and set aside for at least 2 hours, stirring about every half hour as it marinates. If desired, this marinade and lamb can be made up to 3 days ahead, but be sure to stir every half day, and to keep it covered in the refrigerator.

Build a good-sized fire of charcoal briquets, mesquite, or your favorite grilling fuel. Allow to heat until mellow and white tipped (30 to 45 minutes), then distribute the coals. While the coals are heating, prepare the skewers (soak bamboo ones until well soaked if using—at least 30 minutes), placing 2 to 3 lamb chunks on each.

To grill, place the rack about 3 inches above the bed of coals for rare, 4 to 5 inches for medium, and a bit higher for well done. Distribute all the skewers evenly over the grill and cook about 10 minutes, until the cubes of lamb are crisp on the outside and still pink on the inside, or to your desired doneness. Present on a huge platter or chopping block with the lamb kabobs alternating with the vegetables (see following recipe) in a wagon wheel or spoke fashion.

SUMMER VEGETABLE KABOBS

For greatest flavor, color, and control over cooking time, I recommend grilling vegetables in kabobs by themselves rather than alternating them on a skewer with the meat, as is so often done. This way each can be cooked to optimum desired doneness rather than having too crisp vegetables or overdone meat. You can make substitutions for some of the vegetables if necessary.

Makes 12 servings.

4 small yellow summer squash
4 small zucchini
2 small skinny eggplant (often called Japanese eggplant)
1 teaspoon salt
12 small to medium Spanish onions
12 small red ripe tomatoes
24 large mushrooms
1/2 cup good-quality olive oil
1 teaspoon fresh oregano or 1/2 teaspoon dried
1 Tablespoon caribe or other crushed dried red chile

Rinse the vegetables. Cut the summer squash and zucchini into 1-inch-long pieces, making sure to have 12 equal pieces of each. Cut the eggplant into at least 12 cubes, leaving the peel on. Salt the cubes generously and place between two double layers of paper towels. Peel the onions and parboil for about 5 minutes if medium size (not necessary if small). Just rinse the tomatoes. Clean the mushrooms with a moist cloth, removing the stems.

Combine the oil with the oregano and the chile in a small bowl. Skewer the vegetables, alternating types. Put the tomatoes in the very center and a mushroom on each end. When the fire is hot (see previous recipe), brush each with the oil mixture and then grill, turning frequently and brushing with the rest of the oil. Plan on cooking for about 20 minutes to get to the right degree of doneness on a medium fire. These usually take about 10 minutes longer than the lamb shish kabobs. Serve on a large platter, alternating the vegetables with lamb in a wagon wheel or spoke fashion.

CHILE SCAMPI

This spicy, caribe-crusted shrimp dish is delicious with the rice in this menu. On other occasions, it makes a great appetizer.

Makes 12 servings.

3/4 cup extra-virgin olive oil
12 large garlic cloves, coarsely chopped
1 1/2 Tablespoons caribe or other crushed dried red chile
3 pounds large fresh shrimp, peeled, deveined, and well washed
1 1/2 Tablespoons fresh lime juice

In a large heavy sauté pan, heat the olive oil over medium-high heat. Add the garlic, and as it starts to brown, add the caribe and the shrimp at the same time, slightly lowering the heat. Quickly cook and stir. Add the freshly squeezed lime juice, evenly distributing it as the shrimp are cooking. Sauté only until done, about 5 minutes. Serve hot on a heated platter arranged around the edge of the Confetti Rice (recipe follows).

CONFETTI RICE

The bright polka dots of color scattered throughout this flavorful rice create a very pretty center point for the Chile Scampi.

Makes 12 servings.

1/4 cup (1/2 stick) unsalted butter
1 cup diced green bell pepper
1 cup diced red bell pepper
1 cup finely chopped Spanish onion
4 garlic cloves, minced
2 cups basmati rice
1/2 teaspoon ground Mexican oregano
1 teaspoon ground cumin
6 cups rich chicken stock
2 Tablespoons minced fresh parsley

Melt the butter in a large heavy skillet, then add the green and red peppers, onion, garlic, rice, oregano, and cumin. Sauté until the rice looks well glazed and is slightly golden. Add the chicken stock and bring to a boil. Cover and simmer for 15 minutes; do not peek. Remove lid, stir, and set lid ajar to allow to fluff for 5 minutes. Place in the center of a large heated platter, sprinkle with the parsley, and encircle with the Chile Scampi.

MEXICAN CHOCOLATE ICE CREAM

What could be a more appropriate end to the meal than the combination of two of Mexico's favorite and best-known ingredients—chocolate and cinnamon—in a rich, creamy, homemade ice cream?

Makes 1 1/2 quarts.

1/2 cup cold water
2/3 cup sugar, divided
2 cinnamon sticks, 3 inches long
12 ounces dark sweet chocolate, broken into pieces
1/4 cup (1/2 stick) unsalted butter, cut into pieces
3 cups whipping cream
6 large egg yolks

Combine the water, 1/3 cup sugar, and cinnamon sticks in a small heavy saucepan and bring to a boil. Cook for 1 minute over medium heat. Remove and discard cinnamon sticks. Add the chocolate and butter. Let stand several minutes until melted. Stir until mixture is smooth.

Add the chocolate mixture to the cream, which is handiest if placed in a large bowl with a pouring lip. Beat the yolks until thick and lemon colored. Add 1/3 cup sugar and beat until well blended. Combine with the cream and chocolate. Cool. Transfer to an ice cream maker and follow the manufacturer's directions.

FOURTH OF JULY FIREWORKS PATIO PARTY

Assorted Mexican Pizzitas

Summer Vegetable Crudités with Olive-Anchovy Salsa

Grilled Peppered Chicken with Lime

Cold Pasta Salad with Jícama, Walnuts, and Mango

Flaming Mexican Bananas

Assorted Cold Mexican Beers

Crisp White Wine such as Pinot Chardonnay

Mexican Coffee

Though family traditions vary widely, almost everyone enjoys a Fourth of July barbecue. For this unconventional menu I've developed a happy array of easy-on-the-cook foods that are conveniently served—just right for a patio or deck setting. If it rains, these dishes will still do you proud indoors, but try to be an umbrella barbecue chef where the chicken is concerned, for it is much blessed by grilling.

Strictly Southwestern inspired, the starters are an assortment of pretty little pizzitas. Three toppings are offered to grace the tops of these crisply fried whole corn tortillas so that everybody can choose their favorite: chorizo rests atop a bed of refried pintos sprinkled with mixed Monterey Jack and Cheddar, guacamole serves as a happy bed for a brace of shrimp, and Chilied Beef Taco Filling is covered with cheeses, tomato, and onion. A second appetizer, a New Orleans-inspired salsa featuring olives and anchovies, serves as a dunk for summer vegetables. The northern New Mexican-style chicken is wonderful, sparked with the flavors of Chimayo caribe chiles and basted with a mixture of freshly squeezed lime juice, virgin olive oil, onion, and garlic—tinged with Mexican oregano. Barbecued over mesquite or any other hard wood, it is both succulent and light.

The cold pasta salad is a spanking-new takeoff on an Italian standard but incorporating the flavors of Mexico—sheer bliss results. The crunch of the jícama and walnuts complements the soft pasta, and the pungency of the mango nicely accents it. Serve iced crisp white wine such as Pinot Grigio or Sauvignon Blanc as the beverage.

As a finale, what could be more dramatic than flaming bananas? Straight from Spain, the sparkling flavors set the tone for the fireworks ahead. Mexican coffee is recommended alongside.

Create a red, white, and blue color scheme, beginning with an appropriately colored gingham tablecloth—even yard goods will do. If your table is not easily covered because of its size, you can use a long runner instead. Use bright red or blue oversized napkins, folded in fan shapes and placed in goblets. Center the table with a lavish bouquet of white daisies mixed with blue iris. Use red, white, and blue lacquered or plastic throwaway dishes, and you're set.

Menu Plan

Day before (or early in the day):

Prepare the filling ingredients except the guacamole for the pizzitas. Prepare the salsas to accompany these.

Prepare the Olive-Anchovy Salsa and the crudités; tightly cover and refrigerate.

Prepare the Cold Pasta Salad and refrigerate.

Chill the beer and wine.

Two hours before:

Prepare the chicken baste and coat the chicken as directed.

Fry the tortillas for the pizzitas and keep warm.

Make the guacamole.

Start the fire in the grill.

Prepare the pizzitas.

Chill the salad plates. Rinse the greens and pat dry.

Set out the coffeepot.

Set out the ingredients for preparing the bananas on a tray.

At serving time:

Grill the Peppered Chicken while you serve the pizzitas and vegetable crudités.

Arrange the Cold Pasta Salad on the lettuce leaves and serve with the chicken.

Cook and flame the bananas in front of the guests and serve with ice cream.

ASSORTED MEXICAN PIZZITAS

Use at least three combinations of toppings for these lovely little Southwestern pizzas—anything that you would fill a taco with. Three of my own favorites follow—chorizo-bean, avocado-shrimp, and chilied beef. If you are serving around the barbecue, you may wish to let your guests assemble their own pizzitas and then just set them on a baking sheet on the grill to melt the cheeses.

Makes 36 pizzitas.

1 quart vegetable oil
3 dozen corn tortillas
1 (16-ounce) can refried beans
1 pound chorizo sausage, fried, crumbled, and drained
1 1/2 pounds coarsely shredded Monterey Jack cheese
1 1/2 pounds coarsely shredded full-cream yellow Cheddar cheese
3 large red, ripe tomatoes, chopped into 1/4-inch squares
1 large Spanish onion, finely chopped
1 recipe guacamole (page 96)
36 medium shrimp, shelled, deveined, and cooked
1 recipe Chilied Beef Taco Filling (page 164)
1 small head iceberg lettuce, finely shredded
1 cup each two or three salsas (see pages 13–15)

Heat the vegetable oil in a deep-fat fryer to 375°F (190°C) or use a candy thermometer in a deep pot to maintain the proper heat, which is necessary for crisp, not greasy or overly browned tostados. Using tongs, lower one tortilla at a time into the hot oil to be sure they don't curl as you fry them. Keep the tostados warm, once fried, in a 250°F (130°C) oven. (Or you can bake them in a preheated 425°F [220°C] oven using a baking sheet pan and a smaller sheet pan set on top of the tortillas for the first 5 minutes, then removing to enhance browning and crisping. Bake until crisp—about 7 or more minutes. This saves about 50 calories on average of retained fat.)

For the chorizo-bean pizzitas, place 12 tostados on a baking sheet and spread a layer of the beans on each tostado, then generously sprinkle on the meat—about 1/4 cup—then a sprinkle of the Monterey Jack and Cheddar, followed by a garnish of some tomato squares and a bit of onion. Heat 8 to 10 minutes in a 400°F (200°C) oven or for 30 seconds each on a glass, paper, or pottery plate in a microwave oven or on the grill.

To assemble the avocado-shrimp pizzitas, place a billow of guacamole on the center of each of 12 tostados, encircling it with 3 shrimp each. Scatter on a few squares of tomato for garnish and tuck lettuce around the edges.

To assemble the beef pizzitas, place a layer of the chilied beef on the bottom, topped with the cheeses, tomato, and onion. Heat at 400°F (200°C) as for the chorizo-bean ones.

Serve the pizzitas on a huge platter garnished with the lettuce. Set out bowls of the salsas and remaining tomatoes and onions for the guests to garnish and flavor their own.

— SUMMER VEGETABLE CRUDITÉS —
WITH OLIVE-ANCHOVY SALSA

Patterned after New Orleans olive relish, this is a delightful, light, change-of-pace dipping sauce for summer vegetables. Select the smallest sizes of vegetables for the crudités for the prettiest serving arrangement.

Makes 12 servings.

1 cup chopped red ripe tomato
1 cup finely chopped Spanish onion
1 cup sliced pimiento-stuffed olives
2 Tablespoons chopped flat anchovy fillets (about 8)
1 cup finely chopped jalapeños, juice added
3 zucchini
3 yellow summer squash
1 bunch carrots
1 bunch scallions
1 bunch radishes, cleaned and made into roses
1 pound tiny green beans, parboiled 3 minutes and drained

Combine the tomato, onion, olives, anchovies, and jalapeños. Rinse the zucchini, squash, carrots, and scallions. If need be, cut into varying shapes, such as rounds for the zucchini, strips for the carrots, etc. If they are small enough to leave whole do so, just buy more. To serve, place a bowl of the salsa in the center of a cloth- or napkin-lined basket, then encircle it with the vegetables.

GRILLED PEPPERED CHICKEN WITH LIME

Light, easy, and luscious, this is a favorite basic recipe I use very often. The flavorful grilling baste works wonders on shrimp, any variety of firm, white-fleshed fish, veal, or even pork chops. The marriage of tastes and the resulting juiciness of the meat are the reward for preparing the baste and applying it ahead of time. I have found that about one hour of countertop marination will do the trick.

Makes 12 servings.

3 (2- to 2 1/2-pound) frying chickens, quartered
Juice of 3 limes
1 cup virgin olive oil
1 large Spanish onion, finely chopped
3 large garlic cloves, minced
1/4 cup caribe or other crushed dried red chile
1 1/2 teaspoons salt
1 teaspoon Mexican oregano

Rinse the chickens and remove any pinfeathers and excess skin and fat. Place in a large glass baking dish.

In a bowl mix together the lime juice, oil, onion, garlic, caribe, salt, and oregano and apply generously to both sides of each chicken quarter. Loosely cover and set aside for 1 hour.

After 15 minutes, build the fire in the grill. If using mesquite wood chips or any other type of aromatic enhancer, soak them at this time for applying when you distribute the coals. When the coals are whitish gray, scatter them evenly in a circle large enough to cook all the chicken. Place the grill about 5 inches above the bed of coals and allow to heat thoroughly.

Distribute the chicken pieces on the grill, skin side down. Watch the grilling carefully; if there are any flareups, extinguish them with a water mister. Keeping a large piece of aluminum foil handy also is a good idea as it can help to control a blaze. Turn the chicken pieces frequently for the most flavorful and juicy result.

The chicken is done when the leg and thigh pieces can easily be bent at the joint. This should take about 45 minutes. Remove and keep warm. (This chicken is even good cold, should any pieces survive.)

COLD PASTA SALAD
WITH JÍCAMA, WALNUTS, AND MANGO

Serve this beautiful salad to add a Mexican flair with pretty, complementary colors and textures. If jícama is hard to find, you can substitute radishes, selecting round red ones and slicing them very thinly with the peel left on; oranges, plums, or nectarines can substitute for the mango. You might find this salad wonderful enough to experiment with other combinations.

Makes 12 servings.

1 Tablespoon salt
2 Tablespoons vegetable oil
6 quarts water
1 pound pasta shells
2 jícama, peeled and cut into thin matchsticks (2 cups)
1/2 cup thinly sliced red Spanish onion, separated into rings
1 Mexican mango, peeled and cut into half-moon slices
1 cup English walnut halves
2/3 cup walnut oil
1/3 cup red raspberry vinegar or any good wine vinegar
Salt to taste
24 leaves of fresh leaf lettuce

Put the salt and oil in the water and bring to a boil, then add the pasta shells. Boil about 5 minutes or according to package directions. Take care not to overcook. Drain and rinse well with cold water.

Meanwhile, prepare the vegetables and fruit, then combine with the cooled pasta. Whisk the walnut oil and vinegar in a small bowl to combine well. Lightly salt the salad, then add the dressing and gently toss together. Allow to marinate at room temperature, stirring occasionally, for 2 hours, then refrigerate, preferably overnight. Serve centered on a fluff of freshly picked leaf lettuce on chilled plates, or if eating buffet-style, place alongside the chicken.

FLAMING MEXICAN BANANAS

Savored for centuries in Spain, this dessert was introduced to the Southwest via Mexico, and may have borrowed a bit from New Orleans.

Makes 12 servings.

1 cup (2 sticks) unsalted butter
12 firm ripe bananas, peeled and strings removed
1 cup light brown sugar
1 long continuous strip of orange peel
1/2 teaspoon ground cinnamon
Several gratings of fresh nutmeg (about 1/4 teaspoon)
1/2 cup light rum
1/2 cup white sugar
1/2 cup dark rum, warmed
12 scoops of very rich vanilla ice cream (about 2 pints)

Melt the butter in a large chafing dish, electric skillet, or large skillet that can set on the grill, such as a cast iron one. Place the bananas in the butter, taking great care not to break them. Sprinkle on the brown sugar. Add the orange peel, cinnamon, and nutmeg.

Cook over low heat, gently rolling the bananas as they cook to caramelize them slightly. Add the light rum after about 5 minutes cooking time. When the bananas have become light golden and glazed, sprinkle with the white sugar and pour over the slightly warmed dark rum. Ignite, keeping a lid or some foil handy to dampen the flame if it gets out of control.

To serve, place the scoops of ice cream in large shallow dessert dishes and place a banana alongside each, topping it with sauce.

TEXAS BARBECUE FOR 50

Confederate Bourbon Punch

Keg of Beer

Nachos Rancheros

Texas Caviar

Barbecued Beef Brisket

Barbecued Drumsticks

Ranch-Style Pinto Beans

Nine-Day Coleslaw

Sourdough Biscuits

or

Lonestar Soda Biscuits

Deep-Dish Apple Pie

Dad's Homemade Ice Cream

Cowboy Coffee

Somehow barbecuing and grilling have become bigger than ever. One thing is certain: they are a real bundle of fun, and not terribly hard on the host and/or hostess. A little planning, such as I have outlined here, will allow you to join in all the good times with your guests and not work too much.

The menu for this barbecue feast recalls traditional big-family get-togethers, and appropriately, the recipes are all family favorites. Several are three generations old, gleaned from actual Texas chuckwagon cooks my grandfather got to know. From the "knock your socks off" Confederate Bourbon Punch straight through the barbecued beef, ranch-style beans, and the wonderful sourdough biscuits to my grandmother's favorite back-porch slaw—all topped off with homemade apple pie with Dad's Homemade Ice Cream—this is Texas cooking at its best.

This is really an outdoors party, and can be staged anywhere from a backyard to a pasture. Since we lived on a farm and later a ranch, we nearly always pit-barbecued, and while I prefer this method for the Barbecued Beef Brisket, it can just as easily be cooked indoors. Two ovens will be a big help, though clever scheduling will allow you to get by with one. If you are using a city setting, drag in some bales of hay and decorate with rope, halters, saddles, bridles—even beat-up old boots and cowboy hats. If you do not have access to any of these, contact your local beer distributor; it generally has huge, wonderful posters that help set the scene. For the fun of it, ask everyone to come in western dress. Use bandannas for napkins and gingham cloths for the tables. Play hoe-down, western, or bluegrass music, or better yet, get a fiddler or two.

MENU PLAN

One week (or several days before):
Roast the Barbecued Beef Brisket.
Prepare the barbecue sauce for the chicken.
Prepare the coleslaw.
Freeze ice molds for the punch, placing thinly sliced rounds of orange, peel and all, and maraschino cherries in the molds (see instructions, page 203). Make sure the molds will fit into the serving container.
Grate the cheeses for the nachos, fry the tostados, and prepare the pico de gallo.
Prepare the Sourdough Starter.

Day before:
Prepare the Texas Caviar.
Prepare the Frijoles Supremos for the nachos.
Shred the beef brisket.
Combine the starter, water, and flour for the biscuits.
Prepare the pies for baking.

Early in the day:
Barbecue the chicken legs and hold in a Styrofoam or other insulated container for last-minute reheating.
Make the ice cream.
Prepare the Sourdough Biscuit dough and let rise.
Cook the beans.
Prepare all the ingredients for the beef brisket sauce.

Two or more hours before:
Marinate the fajitas and assemble the Nachos Rancheros for baking.
Simmer the beef brisket in the sauce.
Bake the pies.
Shape and bake the Sourdough Biscuits.
Tap the beer keg and bleed off the top foam.

One hour before:
Make the guacamole for the nachos.
Grill the fajitas for the nachos.
Prepare the punch.
Set out everything for making boiled coffee.
Bake the nachos just before serving.

At serving time:

Set out the Texas Caviar with crackers and endive.

Arrange the nachos platters and serve hot.

Reheat the Barbecued Drumsticks and serve with the Barbecued Beef Brisket, Ranch-Style Pinto Beans, Coleslaw, and Sourdough Biscuits.

Serve the pie with ice cream and coffee.

—— CONFEDERATE BOURBON PUNCH ——

An heirloom from the heady yet painful postwar celebrations, this punch supposedly served as a strong reminder that the southern spirit still remained rugged and determinedly independent. You can play with the fruit and liquor combinations, but don't tamper with the bourbon—the punch won't be authentically Texan if you do. We always liked to serve this from five-gallon cream cans, but lacking one of those, try to find a very large punch bowl, pot, or even a large trash can that has been thoroughly cleaned.

Makes 100 servings.

20 black tea bags
2 1/2 quarts boiling water
10 cups sugar
1 gallon ice water
5 (12-ounce) cans frozen orange juice concentrate
5 (12-ounce) cans frozen lemonade concentrate
Ice molds prepared with maraschino cherries and thinly sliced rounds of orange, peel and all (prepared following instructions on page 203)
2 liters good-quality bourbon

Steep the tea in the boiling water. Leave the bags in long enough to create good strong tea, about 10 minutes. Add the sugar, stirring until it dissolves. Add the tea mixture to the ice water, then add the orange juice and lemonade and stir until well mixed. Add the ice molds, then add the bourbon and serve over ice.

NACHOS RANCHEROS

Almost every Tex-Mex menu—and even Old Mexican ones—features some version of nachos. They are an old standby for good reason: the flavor and texture contrasts are irresistible. New combinations are springing up all over, yet are always based on the original—a crisply fried, quartered tortilla topped with a melt of Monterey Jack cheese and a circle of jalapeño. Some of the popular new additions include a nestle of richly flavored frijoles refritos, or a topping of freshly prepared salsa, guacamole, chile, chorizo, fajitas, or carnitas. I have developed a special Texas-size version for this barbecue that I know you'll like.

Makes 50 servings.

5 dozen corn tortillas
2 quarts vegetable oil
3 cups coarsely shredded Monterey Jack cheese
3 cups coarsely shredded full-cream sharp golden Cheddar cheese
1 (12-ounce) jar pickled jalapeños, cut into thin rounds (1 1/2 cups)
1 double recipe Frijoles Supremos*
1 double recipe Fajitas (page 39), cut into thin strips about 1 inch long
1 cup very thinly sliced green onions (scallions)
1 double recipe guacamole (page 96)
1 double recipe pico de dallo (page 40)

Using a very sharp knife, cut each tortilla into quarters pinwheel fashion, not cutting completely through to the center. Meanwhile, heat the oil to 375°F (190°C). Using tongs or a frying basket, lower the tortillas into the hot oil and fry each until golden and crisp. Drain well. Then tap the center of each to break it into four parts. (Or, if desired, they can be baked as noted under Pizzitas, page 180.)

Using two very large platters or even baking sheets, place a layer of tostadas on each. Mix the Monterey Jack and Cheddar, and generously sprinkle 4 cups of cheese over the tostadas. Sprinkle with the jalapeño slices. Warm in a 350°F (180°C) oven until the cheese just melts. Remove from oven.

Two inches in from the edge of each platter, spoon an edging of frijoles around the circumference. Top with a thin ribbon of the remaining 2 cups cheese, but do not cover the frijoles. At the outside edge, arrange a ring of the fajitas strips.

Scatter the green onions randomly over the frijoles and the cheese-crusted tostadas. Return to the oven only long enough to melt the cheese topping on the beans.

In the center of the platters, mound three generous scoops of guacamole on each, leaving a bit of the cheese-crusted tostadas showing between each. Drizzle some pico de gallo over each mound of guacamole, reserving the balance to serve in a small bowl alongside.

Serve bubbling hot, urging the guests to pull the cheese-crusted tostadas apart with gusto and to dip or spoon the other toppings on top.

*For Frijoles Supremos, prepare the beans the same way as the Frijoles Negros (page 108), substituting 4 one-pound cans refried pinto beans for the black beans. Omit the rum and lime juice. (If refried beans are not available, substitute pinto beans and mash them.)

TEXAS CAVIAR

Sometimes called caponata, this marinated eggplant mixture is a delightful light appetizer. When guests learn it's called caviar they immediately start guessing just what it's made of—and few are ever right.

I like to spread this on crisp whole wheat crackers or the petals of Belgian endive. It can also be served as part of an antipasto, at the center of a plate of romaine lettuce, or as a side dish with roast beef or lamb.

Makes 50 servings.

5 medium-size eggplants
1 Tablespoon salt
1 Tablespoon caribe or other crushed dried red chile
3/4 cup extra-virgin olive oil
3/4 cup freshly squeezed lemon juice
1 cup thinly sliced green onions (scallions), including some of the green
1/2 cup chopped flat-leaf parsley
5 garlic cloves, minced
1 cup capers
1 1/2 teaspoons Mexican oregano, ground or crushed
3 boxes assorted whole wheat crackers
10 heads Belgian endive, optional

Bake whole unpeeled eggplants in a very hot oven until the skins blister uniformly. Allow to cool slightly, then remove and discard peel. Place the eggplant pulp in a food processor and pulse on and off until of a smooth consistency, but with a few small chunks remaining. If you do not have a food processor, chop and mash until fairly smooth.

Add the salt, caribe, oil, lemon juice, onion, parsley, garlic, capers, and oregano and mix well. Chill at least 4 hours or until it is cold and the flavors are well blended. Serve with baskets of crackers and a plate of endive, if desired, separated into individual leaves.

BARBECUED BEEF BRISKET

For a traditional big Texas bash, entire steers would be smoked carefully and slowly in an enormous pit dug right out near where the party was to be. My grandfather was always the pit master for our family affairs and started preparations three or more days before the celebration, first by butchering the steer, then by grooming the pit, which was never filled in between parties. He lined the bottom with fire brick (do be careful, by the way, if you decide to build your own pit: I've seen explosions occur when water-bearing rock such as limestone was used as a lining, and explosions don't do wonderful things to barbecuing meat), laid over it a substantial amount of hardwood logs, and covered the pit with sturdy fencing held up about eight inches above the fire. A margin of space was allowed so that more logs could be thrown down and pushed under the fencing, which held the steer. The fire had to be frequently tended, so shifts were set up to make sure the coals were kept alive.

Assuming that you probably wouldn't want to take your barbecuing quite this seriously, I've developed a fabulous-tasting barbecued brisket that can be done in your oven.

Makes 50 servings.

25 pounds beef brisket
1 1/2 cups liquid hickory smoke
12 onions, chopped medium-fine
1 1/2 cups cider vinegar
1 1/2 cups firmly packed dark brown sugar
3/4 cup strong, spicy dark mustard
2/3 cup dark molasses
1 1/2 teaspoons cayenne pepper
Several drops of liquid hot pepper sauce to taste
1 1/4 cups Worcestershire sauce
1 1/2 quarts ketchup
3 cups commercial chili sauce (tomato based)
3 lemons, thinly sliced in complete rounds, skin and all, removing the ends and the seeds
1/3 cup salt or to taste
1 Tablespoon freshly ground black pepper

Place the meat, fat side up, on a trivet or baking rack in a large roaster. Place the liquid smoke in the bottom of the pan, rubbing the outside of the meat with a little of the smoke. Cover and roast at 325°F (170°C) for 6 hours or until very tender. Turn after 3 hours. For the last hour, remove the lid to allow the roast to brown. Test for tenderness—it should almost fall apart. Remove from the oven and allow to cool. Seal in a plastic, stainless steel, or glass container and refrigerate overnight. Place the pan juices and fat in a separate container.

The next day trim away any excess fat. Then shred the beef by pulling it with two meat forks and your hands. Separate it into short shreds—if any are over 3 inches, slice with a knife. Lift off the hardened fat from the pan juices and place it back in the roasting pan. (Use only a generous cupful, discarding the rest of the fat but reserving the juices.) Melt the fat, placing the roaster on a burner. Add the chopped onion and cook and stir until the onion becomes limp. Then add the vinegar, brown sugar, mustard, molasses, cayenne pepper, hot sauce, Worcestershire, ketchup, chili sauce, lemons, salt, and black pepper. Simmer 30 minutes.

Add the beef to the sauce, stirring as you add it. Simmer uncovered very slowly, either on the surface or place it back in a 325°F (170°C) oven. Stir frequently. Add the reserved pan juices as it cooks down, being careful not to get it too soupy. Once all the pan juices have been added, add water to keep the meat moist. Simmer at least 1 hour before serving. This meat actually improves with setting at low heat, making it a great buffet party dish.

Serve as is, or with soft buns or cornbread for making sandwiches.

BARBECUED DRUMSTICKS

Chicken barbecues are another favorite throughout the South for big get-togethers. The sauces are similar (only lighter, a bit tarter, and often hotter) to those used on beef. Legs seem to take to barbecuing best as they are easily cooked and are a bit neater to eat. However, entire chickens can be barbecued—use six or seven whole birds for this recipe if you wish to substitute.

Makes 50 servings.

3 cups ketchup
3 cups cider vinegar
3 cups water
3/4 cup firmly packed light brown sugar
1 1/2 cups yellow mustard, ballpark variety
1 1/2 cup (3 sticks) unsalted butter
2 Tablespoons salt or to taste
6 garlic cloves, minced
1 Tablespoon cayenne pepper
3/4 cup Worcestershire sauce
50 chicken legs, drumstick and thigh attached

Combine ketchup, vinegar, water, brown sugar, mustard, butter, salt, cloves, cayenne pepper, and Worcestershire in a saucepan and cook together, uncovered, until somewhat thickened, about 30 minutes.

Prepare a large charcoal briquet fire, allowing it to develop a white ash. Position the grill 5 inches above the briquets. Place the chicken legs on the hot rack, skin side down. When seared, turn each and grill the other side until light golden.

Remove the chicken to large 9 x 12-inch loaf pans or other large high-sided pans and drizzle some of the sauce over the tops. Turn and add more sauce to the other side, using only about half of it. Cover the grill rack with heavyweight aluminum foil. Poke several holes in the foil to allow the smoky heat to come through.

Place the chicken legs on the foil, scraping out any excess sauce from the loaf pans onto the top of the chicken. Grill the first side until it sets up, then turn, drizzle with more sauce if necessary, and grill the second.

Continue saucing and turning until all the pieces are done. This should take about 1 hour. To test for doneness, wiggle the joint, and if it moves easily, it is done. Or insert a sharp knife into the thigh on the underside, all the way to the bone. If done, the juice will be clear. Serve hot with any remaining sauce.

RANCH-STYLE PINTO BEANS

Deep in the heart of Texas—or, for that matter, anywhere out West—beans are a mainstay. Perhaps out of necessity they are simply prepared—plain boiled beans have always been served with ranchers' food. Easterners bake beans; westerners, if dyed-in-the-wool, just don't. The hearty, nutlike flavor of pintos takes well to this simple preparation, and the recipe has only one critical requirement: you must search out some real smoked country ham hocks. They do make a difference in the flavor. I have found that they are becoming increasingly available throughout the country, especially in butcher shops.

Makes 50 servings.

5 pounds dry pinto beans
5 pounds country ham hocks
3 Spanish onions, chopped
5 garlic cloves, minced
5 large carrots, peeled and finely chopped
5 large celery ribs, finely chopped

Thoroughly rinse and sort through the beans, discarding any off-color ones. Place in a large heavy cooking pot, adding water to about 4 inches above the beans. Bring to a rapid boil. Turn off the heat and set aside, covered. (This method cuts the cooking time in half.)

Prepare the ham hocks, trimming off excess fat, but leaving the rind on as that is the smokiest part.

After the beans have soaked for 1 hour, add the onions, garlic, carrots, celery, and ham hocks, return to the heat, and cook until beans are just tender, 1 1/2 to 2 hours. Stir occasionally, and watch to be sure there is enough water at all times. Add boiling water as needed.

Taste and add salt if needed. Serve as is. These beans freeze very well and can be used for very flavorful refritos.

NINE-DAY COLESLAW

Here is another recipe passed down in our family from the Texas ranching days. My Swedish grandmother used to make it in a large crock, set a plate on it, and leave it in a corner of the back porch or the cellar. It earns its name honestly—due to the pickling process of the dressing, it really will last nine days without refrigeration, though it never manages to remain uneaten for that long in our house.

Makes 50 servings.

3 (3-pound) heads white cabbage
3 medium-size green bell peppers, diced
6 medium Spanish onions, finely chopped
3 Tablespoons salt
3 cups vegetable oil
3 cups white vinegar
3 1/2 cups sugar
1/3 cup celery seeds
1 1/2 teaspoons freshly ground black pepper

Shred the cabbage, chopping it into very small, thin pieces. Place in a large crockery bowl, adding the green peppers and onions, then sprinkle with the salt and toss through the cabbage and vegetables.

Place the oil, vinegar, sugar, and celery seeds in a saucepan and bring to a boil. Simmer, stirring to dissolve the sugar, then pour immediately over the cabbage, peppers, and onions. Sprinkle on the freshly ground black pepper and stir to combine well. Set aside for at least 2 hours at room temperature. If making ahead, you may wish to refrigerate, but it truly is not necessary.

SOURDOUGH BISCUITS

One of the musts in any barbecue—that is, if you can lay your hands on some good, yeast-based sourdough starter—is sourdough biscuits. They are flaky and delicious and simply the best base there is to build a barbecue sandwich.

You can make your own starter if you have the time and the patience. My great-aunt Emma always prepared starters for our family, and even for neighbors if they neglected to keep theirs fed. As a child, I loved to watch her fuss over the procedures. She carefully pointed out the pitfalls: temperature—her tip was to place the starter on the warming shelf of her huge wood-burning range; the type of flour—she was adamant that one should always use good-quality all-purpose unbleached flour; and humidity—never begin a starter when it's rainy and damp. Her overall recipe involved using a bit of potato water (from cooking potatoes), a pinch of sugar, water, and flour, placing the mixture in an open gauze-covered crock and setting it aside for a couple of days. One's nose will then tell the story. The new starter should smell somewhat sour and yeast-like, but not sharp or overly pungent or foul. It should be light gray in color, and the surface should be bubbly. The very best procedure is to get a start from someone or even to buy the sourdough starter powder available at specialty stores and follow the package directions. If you do wish to create your own, I recommend the following proportions:

SOURDOUGH STARTER

2 cups lukewarm water, previously boiled 5 minutes
1/2 cup potato water, from cooking boiled potatoes
5 cups all-purpose flour
1 teaspoon sugar

Place the water in a good-size crock, at least a gallon capacity to allow for draft and expansion. Add the flour and sugar and beat with a wooden spoon. *(Never use metal utensils or pans when dealing with live sourdough starter as a metallic taste will quickly result.)*

Cover with cheesecloth or any loosely woven piece of clean cloth that will allow air to come in yet will protect the surface. Set aside in a warm, draft-free place. Leave for a day, then beat again with a wooden spoon. If tiny bubbles come to the surface, the starter is in the process of developing. If not, wait another day anyway just to see if luck will be on your side.

On the second day, remove the cloth. Smell and look to see if little bubbles are rising to the surface. If the starter has the odor and appearance mentioned above—go for it! If not, and time and perhaps your patience are running short, use commercial sourdough starter or make the Lonestar Soda Biscuits instead.

SOURDOUGH BISCUITS

Makes 60 medium-size biscuits.

1/2 cup sourdough starter
8 cups all-purpose flour, divided

2 teaspoons baking soda
2 teaspoons salt
2 Tablespoons sugar
1/2 cup melted bacon drippings or melted lard, cooled to room temperature
1/2 cup (1 stick) unsalted butter, melted

In a gallon or larger crock, feed 1/2 cup starter with 4 cups pure water and 5 cups flour. Beat with a wooden spoon until well combined. The mixture will appear somewhat lumpy and will be watery. (The lumps disappear as they ferment.) Cover with a plate and set in a cupboard overnight.

Early the next day, add the baking soda, salt, sugar, bacon drippings, and 1 cup of the flour. Beat well, using a mixer with a dough hook, if available.

Continue adding the flour, beating after each addition until too stiff to beat. Then turn out onto a floured board and knead the dough until it is smooth and satiny. Lightly oil the dough with vegetable oil. Place in a bowl and cover with plastic wrap or a moist cloth. Set in a warm place, free from drafts.

When the dough has doubled in bulk, punch down. Allow to stand for 15 minutes. Then begin forming the biscuits. Roll out about one quarter of the dough at a time on a lightly floured breadboard. Cut with a 2 1/2- to 3-inch cutter or an inverted drinking glass that has been dusted in flour before cutting each biscuit.

Coat 4 baking sheets with the butter. Rub each biscuit top in the butter and then turn over on a buttery place on the pan. Crowd the biscuits together; they should be touching each other but not pressing each other.

Bake in a preheated 375°F (190°C) oven for 20 minutes or until lightly golden. Allow to cool 10 minutes in the pan before removing to cooling racks.

LONESTAR SODA BISCUITS

If you can't get the starter for the sourdough biscuits, try these, a recipe handed down from an old trail cook who knew my Swedish grandfather during his years in Texas at the turn of the century. At that time they were always baked over an open campfire in a heavy cast-iron Dutch oven. They are very crisp on the outside and soft as heaven within!

Makes 60 medium-size biscuits.

9 cups all-purpose unsifted flour
4 teaspoons baking soda
4 teaspoons salt
1 1/2 cups lard, cut into pea-size bits, plus 2 pounds additional lard for frying
1 quart buttermilk

In a large bowl, preferably crockery, combine the flour, baking soda, and salt, making sure they are well mixed. Add the lard bits and work with a pastry blender or your hands until the mixture resembles coarse meal. Make a well in the middle of the flour mixture, then pour in the buttermilk. Stir carefully, with a folding motion, so as to moisten all the flour and create a smooth dough without overworking it.

In a heavy Dutch oven or deep-sided frying pan, heat 1/2 pound of the lard to a temperature of 375°F (190°C).

Meanwhile, begin shaping the biscuits. Working over a bread board, lightly flour your hands and pull off egg-size pieces of dough and shape into balls. Shape and fry only a quarter of the dough at a time.

With a slotted spoon handy, drop two or three balls of dough into the hot lard, turning them to coat the outsides evenly. Continue to add balls of dough until the bottom of the pot is covered and all have been coated with hot lard. Cover and fry for about 4 minutes, then turn them and fry the other side for another 4 minutes or longer—until they are golden brown and puffy on both sides. Drain well on paper towels. Keep warm until serving time. Repeat three more times, adding 1/2 pound lard and heating it to 375°F (190°C) each time before frying. Continue until all have been fried.

Note: In addition to being great with the barbecue, they can be served with warm apple butter and unsalted butter oozing all over them.

DEEP-DISH APPLE PIE

Apple pie, a favorite on almost everyone's lists of comfort foods, features in this version a lacing of raisins, lemon zest, and sour cream. Made in large 9 x 13-inch baking pans, the lattice-crusted beauties just have to be complemented by a rich lather of Dad's Homemade Ice Cream.

Makes 50 servings.

4 recipes pastry (recipe follows)
3 3/4 cups fragrant blossom honey
2 1/2 cups sour cream
1 cup all-purpose flour
1 1/4 teaspoons salt
2 teaspoons ground nutmeg
2 teaspoons ground cinnamon
2 1/2 Tablespoons finely grated yellow lemon rind
7 1/2 quarts tart cooking apples, peeled and thinly sliced
2 1/2 cups golden raisins
1/2 cup heavy cream
2 large egg yolks
1/2 cup sugar

Prepare the pastry and line three 9 x 13-inch baking pans with it. Reserve remaining pastry.

Combine the honey, sour cream, flour, salt, nutmeg, cinnamon, and lemon rind in a very large bowl. Stir to combine, then add the apples and raisins. Gently fold the apples into the sour cream mixture so as not to break the pieces.

Divide among the three pastry-lined pans. Then roll out remaining pastry, and using a scalloped cutting edge if available, or a sharp knife, cut into 3/4-inch-wide strips. Weave the strips into a lattice topping.

In a bowl whip the cream and egg yolks together, then brush over the top of the crusts. Sprinkle with sugar and a very light sprinkle of the cinnamon and nutmeg.

Bake on the bottom shelf of a 450°F oven for 15 minutes, then reduce the heat to 350°F (180°C) and bake until done, 30 minutes or more. The crusts should be golden and the apples soft.

Do not cut until the pies have cooled at least an hour. You may cut each into 20 pieces by making 3 cuts on the 9-inch side and 4 cuts on the long side. Or you can just spoon it out. Serve warm with homemade vanilla ice cream.

MY FAVORITE PASTRY

We only had two recipes for pastry in our family: a complex, French-inspired version, and this one, a simple, very flaky, and very delicious alternative.

Makes enough pastry for two 9-inch crusts.

1 1/2 cups all-purpose flour
3/4 teaspoon salt
1/2 cup lard
1/3 cup ice water

Combine the flour with the salt in a bowl, then mix in the lard with two knives or a pastry blender, mixing until it reaches a fine, mealy texture. Keep the bowl and the shortening cold. Pour in a few drops of ice water at a time, mixing all the time. Pat the pastry together, combining all that will hold together. Add only enough water to create a dough that will hold together.

When well combined, put half the dough in the refrigerator and roll out the rest into the first pie crust. Place this crust in the pie tin and add the filling. Only then roll out the top crust.

—— DAD'S HOMEMADE ICE CREAM ——

Homemade ice cream was like a religion when we lived on the farm all during my teen years. We made it year-round on Sunday afternoons, in a multitude of variations. Somehow, though, we always came back to this recipe. Dad experimented constantly with just how much heavy cream to milk made for the greatest flavor and texture. This is the final result.

Makes 2 gallons.

2 rennet tablets
2 Tablespoons cold water
3 quarts whole milk
3 pints heavy cream
3 cups sugar
2 1/2 Tablespoons pure vanilla extract, Mexican if possible
6 large eggs, beaten until quite fluffy
1 teaspoon salt

Crush and dissolve the rennet tablets in the cold water. Mix the milk, cream, and sugar together in a large heavy pan and warm to 110°F. The temperature is critical; it will feel just comfortably warm, similar to the temperature of a baby's bottle.

Remove from the heat. Then quickly stir in the vanilla, eggs, and salt, including the rennet mixture. Pour at once into the freezer can of your ice cream freezer while the mixture is still liquid. Do not disturb for about 10 minutes or until the mixture thickens. Then freeze according to the manufacturer's instructions.

After the ice cream becomes firm, remove the dasher, pack the ice cream down within the can, cover, and repack the freezer with 4 parts ice to 1 part rock salt. Then cover with a heavy cloth and allow to ripen for 2 to 3 hours.

COWBOY COFFEE

Out on the range, plain, honest food prevails—even when it comes to coffee. Actually, there are only a few tips to keep in mind to brew really excellent campfire coffee, all of which are given below. It helps to have a giant-sized, old-fashioned porcelain pot, of course, but any large stewing pot will do.

Makes 75 cups.

19 cups medium-ground coffee
Few grains of salt
2 quarts cold water
Extra cold water or 1 beaten large egg white, optional

Mix the coffee with the salt and cold water. Meanwhile, boil 8 quarts water over a campfire or in the kitchen. Remove from the heat and add the cold water–coffee mixture. Replace on the fire, then bring just up to a boil and immediately remove—watch carefully for the first small bubbles, as the coffee should not really boil. Allow to steep for 5 minutes.

If the coffee doesn't look clear, stir in a small amount of cold water or a beaten egg white. Serve.

FIESTA

Margarita Punch

Beef Flautas

Chicken Envueltos

Carnitas de Puerco

Assorted Garnishes of Guacamole, Sour Cream, Salsa Fresca,
Creamy Salsa Verde, and Salsa Colorado

Sombrero Salad

Sangria, optional

Las Cruces Pralines

Aunt Virginia's Buñuelos

Just the thought of the word *fiesta* recalls the excitement of a celebration: the brilliant colors; spicy, flavorful foods; potent, fruity drinks; and the ever-present background of happy, spirited mariachi music. Originally, fiestas were Spanish festivities surrounding a religious holiday or feasts in honor of a saint. Today a fiesta can take place any time you want to throw a large party with a Mexican theme.

I've created a menu that will be a great pleasure for the host and/or hostess to prepare and a memorable meal for the guests. All the foods can be easily served and eaten in a stand-up party setting, and all are both directly descended from Mexican origins and traditional party foods from the Southwest.

The whole theme of a fiesta lends itself best to an outdoor patio setting, but the party can definitely be staged in any large room or combination of rooms. Decorate with huge vases of brightly colored paper flowers or assorted garden flowers. If entertaining outdoors, I like to tie paper flowers and yarn *ojos de dios* (God's eyes) to some trees, and do a sugarplum tree arrangement—tying pralines to the tips of branches.

MENU PLAN

Two or more days before:
Prepare the pralines.
Prepare the buñuelos.
Prepare the carnitas.
Poach the chicken breast for the envueltos. Cut into matchsticks.
Prepare ice rings for the Margarita Punch.

Day before:
Prepare the beef taco filling for the flautas.
Prepare the fruit syrup base for sangria (page 142), if making.
Prepare the salsas for the flautas, envueltos, and carnitas.

Early in the day:
Rinse the salad greens and make dressing.
Shred lettuce for the plate garnishes.
Arrange a platter of buñuelos. Tie pralines on a tree or place in a basket.
Chop ingredients except avocado for the guacamole, ready for last-minute preparation.

Two hours before:
Chill the salad plates and forks.
Roll the flautas and fry just before serving.
Roll the envueltos and keep warm.
Place the carnitas in ovenproof pans for heating.
Make the guacamole.

At serving time:
Garnish the platters of flautas and envueltos.
Warm the tostados and carnitas.
Set out all the salsas, guacamole, and other garnishes.
Toss the salad and arrange in the sombrero.
Make the Margarita Punch and the sangria (page 142), if serving.

MARGARITA PUNCH

Although the very best margaritas are always made of fresh, pure ingredients, for massive extravaganzas they are a bit hard to pull off unless you have a real bar crew to help. Through experience, I developed this formula, which is quite acceptable and much preferable to bottled mixes or bar mixes. If you must be a purist, the recipe for real margaritas is on page 82.

Makes 48 four-ounce drinks.

3 quarts all-natural agave silver tequila
3 (12-ounce) cans frozen limeade (made from real limes)
Ice cubes
2 fresh limes, thinly sliced for ice rings*

Using an electric blender, process the margaritas in proportions of 1 1/2 parts tequila to 1 part frozen limeade with an equal volume of ice cubes. Process until slushy and serve in a punch bowl with an ice ring.

*Create two or more ice rings by freezing a thin layer of water in ring molds. When firm, lay out a circle of thinly sliced lime. Add just enough water to cover the lime slices and freeze until firm. Then fill balance of the mold with water and freeze until hard. To use, warm the mold briefly in warm water, just enough to remove the ice mold, and place in the punch bowl before adding the Margarita Punch.

BEEF FLAUTAS

Flautas are aptly named, translating literally as "flutes." They are formed by rolling a corn tortilla around a filling that can consist of anything you would use to fill a taco. (Beef is the most popular filling, but chicken and pork are also used.) The flutes are then deep-fried until crisp. Sometimes these are called taquitas and are rolled into a round shape.

Makes 36 servings.

36 corn tortillas
2 quarts cooking oil
4 1/2 cups Beef Taco Filling (page 164)
6 cups finely shredded iceberg lettuce, about 2 heads
1 double recipe guacamole, made from 4 avocados (page 96)
2 cups sour cream
Freshly made salsas (pages 13–15)

Select the freshest possible corn tortillas, never using frozen. Wrap in four packets of foil and warm in a 300°F (150°C) oven until soft and pliable, 10 to 15 minutes.

Meanwhile, heat the oil in an electric deep-fat fryer or electric skillet to 375°F (190°C). Place one warm tortilla at a time on a flat work surface, then spoon a 3/4-inch strip of filling down the center of each, using about 3 spoonfuls of beef filling. Roll one side over the filling, and continue to roll, cigar style. (These round-shaped ones are called taquitas.) For a touch of Mexico, wrap slightly on the bias to create a lily-like shape with one end smaller than the other.

Roll all the flautas first, unless you have a partner, in which case one can roll while the other fries. Then fry each in the hot fat until crisp and golden. Drain well. Serve on a large platter garnished with the lettuce and topped with the guacamole and sour cream. Let your guests add their salsa of choice.

CHICKEN ENVUELTOS

Envuelto, which means envelope in Spanish, is another apt name for an appetizer—in this case, delicious filled and rolled tortillas that are similar to soft tacos. Other fillings can be substituted, but chicken has always been my favorite.

Makes 36 servings.

3 pounds boneless, skinless chicken breast
1 1/2 quarts well-seasoned chicken stock
1 Tablespoon jalapeño juice
Salt to taste, optional
36 corn tortillas, preferably blue corn
3 Tablespoons coarsely chopped fresh cilantro
12 jalapeños, fresh or pickled, deseeded and cut into very thin strips
6 cups finely shredded iceberg lettuce, about 2 heads
3 red ripe tomatoes, cut into 1/2-inch cubes
Salsas of choice (pages 13–15)

Place the chicken in the stock with jalapeño juice. Cover and cook until done, 20 to 30 minutes. Allow to cool in the broth, then cut into 2-inch matchsticks. Reserve the stock for future use. Taste the chicken and add salt if needed. Wrap the tortillas in several foil packets and warm them in a 300°F (150°C) oven for 10 to 15 minutes.

Mix the cilantro with the chicken. Then divide the filling evenly among the warmed tortillas, creating a 1-inch-wide strip of filling down the entire center of the tortilla. Top each with 3 strips of jalapeño. Roll and place seam side down on an ovenproof platter. Keep warm until ready to serve, then garnish with the lettuce around the entire perimeter of the platter. Sprinkle with the tomato cubes and serve with side dishes of salsas.

CARNITAS DE PUERCO

For a long time popular vendor snacks throughout the little villages and cities of Central Mexico, carnitas occasionally have made their way onto restaurant menus in the Southwest. They deserve greater acclaim, as their flavor is nearly unsurpassed. For family and smaller dinner parties, I like to use meaty, country-style spareribs in this recipe, but for a stand-up party they are a bit tough to handle. Follow the cooking directions carefully so the pork does not fall apart: some fat left on the strips of meat is critical. I prefer carnitas dipped generously in salsa fresca, and eaten either plain or rolled into a third of a warmed wheat tortilla. For those who like more elaborate garnishes, serve guacamole and/or sour cream.

Makes 36 servings.

9 pounds pork shoulder
12 garlic cloves, minced
2 1/2 Tablespoons salt
2 Tablespoons ground pure hot New Mexico chile
12 (10-inch) wheat tortillas
Salsa Fresca (page 15)

Trim the skin off the pork and trim away all the bones. (The bones can be cooked with the pork strips for a treat for the cook. In this case you do not have to trim them out.) Cut the pork into strips about 2 inches long, 1 inch wide, and 1/2 inch thick. Take care to leave the fat in the pieces as it is necessary for flavor.

Place the meat in one layer in one or more large heavy skillets; take care not to overlap any of the pieces. Sprinkle with the minced garlic, salt, and chile. Add water to come just to the top of the meat but not cover it.

Bring to a boil, then reduce heat to maintain a gentle simmer. Do not cover. Watch the meat; you do not want it to overcook as it will fall apart. As the water begins to evaporate, stir the pieces of meat, rotating each piece so it will brown on all sides in its own juices. (At this point it is a good idea to remove a piece or two and make a cut to be sure they are done. If not done, add more water and continue to simmer only until well done.) This cooking process caramelizes the browned crust overall and is what creates the very special flavor. Once you are stirring the meat, you may need to raise the heat to enhance the browning process.

Serve warm in a large heavy earthenware bowl with a bowl of toothpicks. Cut the warmed wheat tortillas in thirds, and keep them warm in a terra-cotta warmer or wrapped in a cloth-lined basket. Place Salsa Fresca and any other desired garnish nearby.

SOMBRERO SALAD

Crisp, crunchy watercress with its very own pepperiness, combined with the rich, bacon-like taste of arugula and tangily laced with a freshly prepared, New Mexico–inspired vinaigrette makes for a wonderful salad—especially when accented with bright-red, vine-ripened, just-picked beefsteak tomato wedges. Try to find a huge Mexican sombrero to serve the salad bowl in.

Makes 24 servings.

9 Tablespoons extra-virgin olive oil
3 large garlic cloves, minced
1 1/2 teaspoons caribe or other crushed dried red chile
6 Tablespoons red wine vinegar
3 large beefsteak or similar vine-ripened tomatoes, about 4 inches across, or 6 smaller ones
6 cups well-rinsed arugula leaves
6 cups well-rinsed watercress
2 pounds warm corn tostadas
1 cup oil-cured black olives

Chill the well-drained greens. Combine the oil, garlic, caribe, and vinegar in a bowl and let sit about an hour at room temperature. Cut the tomatoes in half vertically, removing the stem and blossom ends. Then cut into 1/2-inch-thick wedges.

To serve, combine the tomato wedges with a little of the dressing, and toss the arugula and watercress with the remainder until well mixed. Place a pinwheel arrangement of tomato wedges in the center of the greens.

If a huge Mexican straw sombrero is available, bash in the crown and place the salad bowl in it. Encircle the brim with warmed tostadas. Add an edging of tostadas to the salad. Sprinkle the salad with black olives.

LAS CRUCES PRALINES

In New Mexico, nearly every Mexican restaurant has pralines at the checkout counter. Did you ever wonder why? A major reason is that the rich sweetness is very calming to a singed palate—a common condition in New Mexico where all natives pride themselves on how hot they can make and eat their own chile-laden specialties. Outside Las Cruces is one of the most beautiful pecan farms, where the crops are grown in three levels. The pecan trees are encircled with strawberry beds to provide a second crop from the soil, and the farm has a whole gaggle of geese to keep the strawberries weed-free. The pecans grown in this rich, river-bottom soil are some of the largest I have ever seen. Large, meaty pecans make the very best pralines. This recipe is foolproof if you work fast when you start to dip the candies out.

Makes 48 medium-size pralines, 36 large.

1/4 cup (1/2 stick) unsalted butter, plus extra for preparing saucepan
1 cup firmly packed light brown sugar
2 cups white sugar
3 Tablespoons light corn syrup
1/4 teaspoon salt
1 cup half-and-half
1 teaspoon Mexican vanilla or maple flavoring
2 cups large, fresh pecan halves

Butter the entire inside of a heavy 3-quart saucepan. Add the sugars, syrup, salt, half-and-half, and butter and cook very slowly over medium-low heat until the mixture reaches the medium firm ball stage or 246°F (118°C) on a candy thermometer. To test in cold water, add a few drops of the candy to about 2 inches of cold water. It should quickly pull together in a ball that does not fall apart. Then remove from heat.

Let the candy cool somewhat, away from drafts. Cover 4 large baking sheets with heavy wax paper. When the surface of the candy is warm, not hot, add the vanilla and beat a few strokes to combine it, then add the pecans and beat until it becomes creamy and loses its gloss.

Quickly spoon out, using two large metal serving spoons, scraping one inside the other to form the pralines. If the candy does not spread as you portion it out, return to a low heat, add a few drops of half-and-half, and beat until it loosens somewhat. Let the pralines cool on the baking sheets.

For a fiesta touch, wrap each praline when it has cooled in brightly colored fuchsia, purple, and orange tissue paper and tie with contrasting yarn or straw strings. Tie them onto a pine or cedar tree if outdoors, or a large branch in a bucket that could be used as a centerpiece for the serving table.

—— AUNT VIRGINIA'S BUÑUELOS ——

My Mexican aunt, originally from Monterrey but well traveled and schooled in the entire country's specialties, taught me many, many wonderful dishes. She had a flair for creating excitement in the kitchen and a love for elegant dining. These simple yet delicate-looking cookies were always given to my cousins and myself to prepare. Although a bit time-consuming, they are fascinating to make, and I've always found that children get great pleasure from helping with them, as they do with sopaipillas.

Aunt Virginia's buñuelos differ quite a bit from those found in northern New Mexico, which are sopaipillas served in a caramelized syrup with nuts and raisins, and are far removed from the type featured on many Mexican restaurant menus, which are often nothing more than a deep-fried wheat tortilla. These are most similar to Swedish rosette cookies.

Makes 6 to 8 dozen.

2 quarts oil
2 large eggs, divided
4 cups water, divided
5 cups all-purpose flour, divided
1 teaspoon salt, divided
2 cups powdered sugar
Rosette irons

Heat the oil in an electric deep-fat fryer, frying pan, or wok. If not using an electric thermostatically controlled appliance, use a candy thermometer to maintain 375°F (190°C). Put 1 of the eggs, 2 cups of the water, 2 1/2 cups of the flour, and half the salt in a blender and process until the mixture looks like heavy cream, scraping down the sides of the blender jar to prevent any lumps. Place the batter in a shallow bowl.

To fry the cookies, heat the rosette iron in the oil, then dip the iron two-thirds of the way into the batter, and return it to the hot oil. Cook until the sides of the cookie begin to pull away from the iron and are very lightly browned. The cookie should easily slip off the iron; sometimes you need to pull it off, however, using very gentle pressure and a fork.

Shake the cookies in a brown paper bag with 1 cup of the powdered sugar. Keep sugaring them as you fry them as the sugar sticks best if applied soon after they are fried.

Make another batch of batter, using the remining egg, water, and flour and fry the remaining cookies.

Note: These keep very well in an airtight container for several days at room temperature. They also freeze very well if stored in rigid containers layered between wax paper. An alternative coating is cinnamon sugar made from 1 cup sugar and 1/4 cup ground cinnamon.

CHIMAYO WEDDING PARTY

Chorizo Empanaditas

Miniature Blue Corn Tamales with Chicken and Green Chile Filling

Salsas with Freshly Fried Tostadas

Caribe Chile Enchilada Casseroles

Coleslaw de Jardin

Wedding Cake

Wedding Punch

Coffee

Traditional New Mexican weddings were among the impressive and beautiful celebrations in colonial days, with the carefully preserved Old Spanish customs closely followed.

Even the period before the marriage was regulated by many food-centered customs. Parents were responsible for their children's betrothal, which began with a letter *de pedimento* written by the village scribe, asking for the girl's hand in marriage. This masterpiece of flowery language was then presented to the girl's parents from the boy's parents and godparents. Propriety required that any response be delayed. When an appropriate time had passed, then another scribe-composed letter was sent.

Following the girl's acceptance, her relatives were invited to the betrothal feast, called the *prendorio*, which often was the first time the bridal pair actually met. After the boy gave his bride-to-be a ring, the guests assembled for an elaborate reception. Foods normally served were bizcochitos (anise-flavored cookies), puches (egg wafers), marquesotes (sponge cake), suspiros (sighs), and other pastries. Sometimes main dishes were served, sometimes not.

After this meeting, the bridegroom formally became part of his bride's family. The parents of the groom were subsequently required to provide the *donas*, or trousseau, which consisted generally of trunks full of fine fabrics, jewelry, mantillas, rebozas, shawls, shoes, hosiery, laces, fine linen for undergarments, silks, satins, and many other items. The bridegroom even furnished the wedding dress. The bride had to bring a dowry. Many times this was substantial, consisting of property, livestock, and household goods.

The preparations for the nuptial feast itself were intense. The bridegroom's father, who was responsible for providing the food, started days before with butchering, barbecuing, and harvesting. The bride's mother prepared the chile dishes, baked goods, and all the other foods.

On the wedding day, the bridal pair kneeled before their relatives to receive their blessing before going to the church, which was already surrounded by musicians playing joyful tunes. Following the ceremony, the bridal party returned to the bride's home, where the wedding sponsors turned the couple over to their parents by reciting long verses (*versos de entrega*), and a feast similar to that which follows was served. Today, families in northern New Mexico, especially around the town of Chimayo, still maintain some of these fine festive ways, particularly when it comes to the feasts following the weddings. I have developed a menu approximating one of these feasts, but be warned that preparations for this major party must start a few days ahead. This meal is, in fact, a fine one for celebrating most any joyous occasion—a wedding is not a prerequisite. Generally the food is served buffet style on a fresh flower—bedecked table, preceded by children, waiters, or waitresses carrying around trays of the empanaditas, miniature tamales, and tostadas with salsas.

An outdoor setting is grand for this; otherwise, a very large living/dining room or hall is required. For a wedding theme, use laces to grace the tables and arrange bouquets of pastel pink and white flowers. Create runners of stephanotis nestled with pink rosebuds tied with narrow pink satin bows. A Mexican theme could be substituted if this menu is not being served as a wedding party, using decorations of colorful linens, flowers, sombreros, etc.

Menu Plan

Two or more days before:
Prepare the Chorizo Empanaditas for baking.
Roll the tamales and refrigerate.
Prepare the enchilada casseroles for baking and refrigerate.
Freeze the ice molds.

One day before:
Bake the Wedding Cake layers.
Prepare the salsas.
Prepare the tostadas.
Prepare the coleslaw.

Early in the day:
Frost the Wedding Cake, but don't decorate with smilax and rosebuds until just before the party.
Set the buffet tables, having one for the main dishes and one for the cake and coffee.

Two or more hours before:
Steam the tamales and keep warm.
Garnish the coleslaw.
Warm the tostadas.
Place the salsas in serving bowls and keep chilled.

One hour before:
Bake the empanaditas.
Bake the enchilada casseroles.
Get the coffee ready to make.
Add fresh flowers to the cake.
Make the first batch of punch and place an ice mold in it.

At serving time:
Have children or waiters pass hors d'oeuvres while readying the main buffet table.
Set enchilada casseroles and coleslaw on main buffet table, cake and coffee on the dessert table.

CHORIZO EMPANADITAS

Empanadas are found in all Spanish-settled countries, and while they vary somewhat in interpretation, their general form remains the same: a filled, fried, or baked turnover. Their cousins, found around the world, are Cornish pasties, piroshki, wontons, knishes, and even our American turnovers or fried pies. Empanadas can be filled with savory or sweet fillings. Although savory fillings are generally placed in a yeast-leavened dough and the sweet fillings in a pastry, this recipe is an exception. I developed these Chorizo Empanaditas for a patio party many years ago in Albuquerque, and they have been a very well-received hors d'oeuvre ever since.

Makes 150 empanaditas.

THE PASTRY

12 cups all-purpose flour
7 cups lard
4 large eggs
1/4 cup dark apple cider vinegar
2 1/2 Tablespoons salt
1 1/4 cups ice water

THE FILLING

3 pounds fried, crumbled, and drained chorizo sausage
3/4 cup chopped medium-hot New Mexico green chiles that have been parched and peeled
   (page 7)
3 pounds crumbled queso fresco, Mexican goat cheese, or white Cheddar, shredded
1 cup finely chopped Spanish onion

To make the pastry, first blend the flour with the lard in an electric mixer, using the lowest speed, until well mixed. Beat the eggs, vinegar, salt, and water together and add all at once to the flour mixture. Mix until blended, continuing to use the low speed. Set aside while you combine the filling ingredients. Mix together the chorizo, chiles, cheese, and onion. Taste and adjust seasonings.

Roll about a sixth of the dough at a time to a thickness of 1/8 inch. Cut into rounds with a 4-inch cutter. To prepare the empanaditas, place a spoonful of the filling to one side of the center, then fold over and crimp the edges. Make the traditional Spanish fluted edging, called the repulgar, by pinching a small amount of dough at a time, starting from one edge of the fold, and then overlapping each pinch between the thumb and the forefinger. Or press the outside edge with floured fork tines.

Bake on cookie sheets in a preheated 400°F (200°C) oven for about 15 minutes or until lightly golden. Serve warm on platters or trays. You may wish to serve these with a dish of salsa for guests to dip their own.

MINIATURE BLUE CORN TAMALES
WITH CHICKEN AND GREEN CHILE FILLING

Blue corn is one of the most cherished delicacies of northern New Mexico. Part of the heritage of the Pueblo Indians, who are still the chief cultivators, it has a nutlike flavor due to its deeper pigmentation, piñon roasting, and lava-wheel grinding. If you can't obtain it, substitute white or yellow corn masa.

For this party, the tamales are made small—two-bite size. Use real corn husks and tie each with a corn husk string, as detailed in the tamale recipe on page 149. Any other tamale recipe can also be made miniature—making them a great appetizer to have on hand since they can be frozen for a year.

Makes 15 to 18 dozen miniature tamales.

2 chickens, cooked, boned, and shredded (page 93)
2 cups sour cream
4 cups coarsely shredded Monterey Jack cheese
Salt, optional
1 recipe Tamale Masa (recipes 148–149)
15 to 18 dozen dried corn husks
12 New Mexico hot green chiles, parched, peeled (page 7), and sliced into thin strips

In a large bowl combine the chicken with the sour cream and cheese. Season with salt, if desired. Prepare the masa (substituting blue masa for the yellow), following the instructions with the recipe. Soak the husks.

Following the rolling instructions on page 149, make the tamales about a third smaller, using a patch of masa on the husk 2 1/2 x 2 inches. Place a strip or two of the green chile down the center of each, then spoon on the chicken filling and roll and tie as detailed, tying the top or more pointed end of husk with a bow and tie the bottom or wider end loosely to allow the grease to escape as they are steamed upright.

The tamales can be frozen at this point or set aside in the refrigerator for up to 3 days. Steam as described in the tamale recipe. These are very juicy and flavorful and do not need a sauce.

SALSAS WITH FRESHLY FRIED TOSTADAS

Freshly prepared salsas will always top the commercially prepared ones in every respect. For this traditional menu, I suggest you prepare the hot Salsa Colorado (page 146) and the mild Salsa Verde (page 14). The same holds true for tostadas. Freshly fried ones that are still warm are tremendous, especially if you can find top-quality tortillas, carefully made from ground pure masa harina. If possible, include a combination of white, blue, and yellow tostadas for this party. See the instructions on page 162.

CARIBE CHILE ENCHILADA CASSEROLES

Caribe chile almost spells Chimayo, so much so that in New Mexico it is generally labeled Chimayo chile rather than the more generic caribe. As far as it can be determined from history, the term *caribe* (which means crushed northern New Mexico chiles grown in the Chimayo area) originated in the Caribbean, where they were most probably the first cultivated chiles. Developed by the Caribe Indians, the chiles were valued by the Spanish from the time of Christopher Columbus since they took the seeds with them, generously sharing them wherever they settled.

Caribes are smaller than the other New Mexico chiles, and owing to both the variety and the very high-altitude northern growing conditions, they have a hot but somewhat sweet flavor. Maroon in color, rather than red or orange red, they yield a wonderful, very piquant sauce in this recipe. If you are serving guests who have an unseasoned palate, I suggest you substitute ground pure California mild chiles for part or even all of the caribe.

Makes 50 servings.

2 1/4 cups caribe or other crushed dried red chile
9 cups water
1 1/4 cups lard
1 1/4 cups all-purpose flour
11 1/4 cups beef bouillon
1/4 cup minced fresh garlic
1 teaspoon crushed Mexican oregano
1 teaspoon ground cumin
2 Tablespoons salt (add gradually—amount depends on the saltiness of the bouillon used)
1 quart vegetable oil
100 corn tortillas, blue, yellow, or white
4 1/2 cups coarsely shredded Monterey Jack cheese
4 1/2 cups coarsely shredded full-cream Cheddar cheese
9 large Spanish onions, chopped
9 pounds beef chuck, roasted slowly, cooled, then shredded
6 to 8 leaves romaine, coarsely torn
1 medium red ripe tomato, chopped into 1/2-inch cubes
4 cups sour cream

Place the caribe in a large shallow baking pan in a thin layer and roast in a 300°F (150°C) oven for 10 minutes or until the color darkens. Watch very carefully as the chile burns easily. Put these roasted flakes in a large cooking pot, then add the water. Cover and simmer for 30 minutes. Strain through a metal sieve, rubbing the chile skins with the back of a large wooden spoon to get the maximum pulp. Reserve the pulp.

Melt the lard in a large pot, then add the flour and cook and stir until it is lightly browned. Reduce the heat and gradually add all of the bouillon. Add the chile pulp and the garlic, oregano, and cumin. Simmer together about 30 minutes to allow the flavors to develop. Taste and add salt as needed.

Meanwhile, heat the oil to 375°F (190°C) and lightly fry the tortillas. Drain each well between layers of paper towels.

Butter 4 large, preferably Mexican pottery, casseroles. Layer the ingredients, starting with a thin layer of sauce, followed by tortillas, more sauce, cheeses, onion, and beef. Make each casserole four tortilla layers deep, ending with a topping of sauce, cheeses, and onion.

The casseroles can be made up to two days in advance and refrigerated. If making in advance, do not add the final topping of sauce. Reserve for adding to the top of the casserole just before baking.

Bake in a 375°F (190°C) oven for 30 minutes or until bubbly and cheeses are melted. Serve garnished with lettuce and tomato, tucking it into the corner of each casserole.

Garnish the center of each casserole with a mound of sour cream. Wait to add it until just before taking each casserole to the serving table, otherwise it will melt somewhat and not be as attractive.

─────── COLESLAW DE JARDÍN ───────

This salad was selected for both its convenience and its virtue as a good flavor counterpoint. Prepare several hours or a day ahead. The cabbage should be crisp, yet well flavored.

Makes 50 servings.

8 large heads cabbage, preferably 4 purple and 4 white, about 18 pounds total, thinly shredded
8 large bell peppers, chopped, reserving 6 thin slices of the full round of pepper for garnish
8 bunches green onions (scallions), thinly sliced (4 cups)
8 large carrots, coarsely grated
3 Tablespoons kosher or coarse salt
2 1/4 cups cider vinegar
1/2 cup sugar
2 Tablespoons caribe or other crushed dried red chile
2 cups corn oil
1 head romaine lettuce for garnish

Place the cabbage, chopped bell peppers, green onions, and carrots in a large bowl or crock. Sprinkle with salt and stir to mix. Combine the vinegar, sugar, caribe, and oil in a small bowl and drizzle over the mixture. Toss well. Taste and adjust flavor. Store at room temperature at least 2 hours before placing in the refrigerator. Stir periodically. Serve in a large bowl, encircling the edge with romaine lettuce leaves stashed into the slaw. Create a ring of the pepper rings in the center.

WEDDING CAKE

In northern New Mexico, a sponge-type cake is the traditional choice for weddings. I find it rather too simple for a special occasion, so instead have taken the liberty here of sharing my mother's favorite white cake, which has graced many wedding receptions, birthdays, and anniversaries. It's very moist and flavorful, and I hope you'll like it as much as our family does.

Makes 50 servings.

2 cups (4 sticks) unsalted butter, softened, plus extra to butter pans
12 cups sifted all-purpose flour
3 Tablespoons baking powder
1 teaspoon salt
6 cups sugar
2 cups milk
2 cups water
1 teaspoon almond extract
1 Tablespoon pure vanilla extract
12 large egg whites, beaten until stiff

Preheat the oven to 375°F (190°C). Butter layer cake pans and line with wax paper. I suggest you use a very large pan for the base—a 16-inch round one—then a 12-inch, 8-inch, and very small 4-inch one. This is the equivalent of eight 9-inch layers.

Sift flour once, measure, then add baking powder and salt and sift together three times. Using an electric mixer, beat the butter until fluffy. Gradually sprinkle on the sugar while beating at a low speed. Cream together until light and fluffy. Add the flour alternately with the milk and water, a small amount at a time. Beat after each addition, using medium-low speed.

Add the almond and vanilla extracts, then switch to the lowest speed and begin folding in the meringue. Pour the batter into the prepared pans. Bake in the preheated oven for 20 to 30 minutes or until a toothpick comes out clean. Let cool in the pans before turning out, then fill and frost as follows.

WEDDING CAKE FROSTING AND FILLING

6 cups sugar
2 teaspoons light corn syrup
2 2/3 cups boiling water
8 large egg whites, beaten until stiff
1 Tablespoon plus 1 teaspoon pure vanilla extract
2 cups raisins, chopped
2 cups pecans, coarsely chopped
24 white figs, chopped
Smilax
16 tiny pink rosebuds, each tied with a bow of narrow pink satin ribbon

Combine the sugar, corn syrup, and water in a saucepan. Bring quickly to a boil, stirring only until the sugar is dissolved. Boil rapidly, without stirring, until a small amount of syrup forms a soft ball when dropped in cold water or the syrup reaches 240°F (115°C) on a candy thermometer.

Pour syrup in a fine stream over the beaten egg whites, beating constantly on high speed with an electric mixer. Continue to beat until very firm peaks form and will hold in place when dropped on a piece of wax paper—10 to 15 minutes. Fold in the vanilla.

Mix the filling in a separate bowl: place the raisins, pecans, and figs, then add some of the frosting, a large spoonful at a time, just until it is of a spreading consistency. Reserve balance of frosting for the top and sides of the cake.

Place the bottom cake layer on a large tray, mirror, or foil-covered board. Smooth on a layer of filling, add the next cake layer, repeating until the filling is between each layer. Frost the top and sides, creating swirls with the frosting.

Decorate with smilax arranged in little nosegay swirls around each layer and on top. Center each nosegay with a pink rosebud, arranging four alternately spaced nosegays around the rim of each layer and four rosebuds on the top.

WEDDING PUNCH

This pastel-pink punch is an excellent one for large parties of any type. I recommend it for weddings—even if it lacks a clear New Mexican orientation.

Makes 100 4-ounce servings.

2 to 4 ice molds
1 bunch stephanotis
1 bunch lily of the valley
4 fifths of dry white wine, chilled
1 pint Grand Marnier
1 cup grenadine syrup
8 bottles brut champagne, either pink or white
4 (28-ounce) bottles seltzer or soda water
2 pints strawberries

Prepare the ice molds in round ring molds a day or more in advance. Freeze about a 1/2-inch layer of water in each mold. Then place stephanotis twigs in a garland all the way around the mold. Intersperse lily of the valley. Add just enough water to barely cover the arrangement and carefully place in the freezer so as not to disrupt your design. Freeze firm, then add water to the top of the mold and freeze solid. I recommend that you make at least two of these—more if a party of long duration is planned, which is the custom in Chimayo. There, wedding dances customarily last all night.

Combine one-quarter of the ingredients at a time in a large punch bowl. Pour 1 bottle of white wine, 1/2 cup of Grand Marnier, and 1/4 cup grenadine syrup into the bowl. Stir together, then carefully pour 2 bottles of the champagne and 1 bottle of the seltzer down the side of the bowl, stirring gently when all is added. Put an ice mold in the bowl. Continue to make batches of punch as needed.

INDEX